TIME TO LEARN

TIME TO LEARN

How a New School Schedule is Making Smarter Kids, Happier Parents, and Safer Neighborhoods

Christopher Gabrieli
Warren Goldstein

JOSSEY-BASS
A Wiley Imprint
www.josseybass.com

Published by Jossey-Bass
A Wiley Imprint
989 Market Street, San Francisco, CA 94103-1741—www.josseybass.com

Grateful acknowledgement is made for permission to reprint the following:

Text excerpts from the article entitled "Saved By The (Later) Bell," by Lisa Prevost, from The Boston Globe, April 29, 2007 edition, reprinted by permission of PARS International Corp.

Text excerpts from the article entitled "Tough Choices in Education," by David P. Driscoll, from The Boston Globe, February 28, 2007 edition, reprinted by permission of the author.

Names and other identifying information of students and parents have been changed.

Readers should be aware that Internet Web sites offered as citations and/or sources for further information may have changed or disappeared between the time this was written and when it is read.

Limit of Liability/Disclaimer of Warranty: While the publisher and author have used their best efforts in preparing this book, they make no representations or warranties with respect to the accuracy or completeness of the contents of this book and specifically disclaim any implied warranties of merchantability or fitness for a particular purpose. No warranty may be created or extended by sales representatives or written sales materials. The advice and strategies contained herein may not be suitable for your situation. You should consult with a professional where appropriate. Neither the publisher nor author shall be liable for any loss of profit or any other commercial damages, including but not limited to special, incidental, consequential, or other damages.

Jossey-Bass books and products are available through most bookstores. To contact Jossey-Bass directly call our Customer Care Department within the U.S. at 800-956-7739, outside the U.S. at 317-572-3986, or fax 317-572-4002.

Jossey-Bass also publishes its books in a variety of electronic formats. Some content that appears in print may not be available in electronic books.

Library of Congress Cataloging-in-Publication Data has been applied for.

ISBN: 978-0-470-25808-8

Printed in the United States of America

FIRST EDITION
HB Printing 10 9 8 7 6 5 4 3 2 1

CONTENTS

We dedicate this book to the extraordinary people—teachers, principals, and leaders—who are making the new school day a reality, and showing what schools and children can really achieve.

PREFACE

It turns out we didn't have to know each other well at all before deciding to write this book together. It did, however, help a lot that we'd already arrived, independently, at its central idea: that the 2:30 school dismissal bell makes no sense at all, and that kids and teachers, parents and neighborhoods would all benefit immensely from an expanded school day.

We come from different worlds. Chris Gabrieli has been an entrepreneur and venture capitalist, a candidate for statewide office in Massachusetts, and an education reformer. Warren Goldstein has been a nonprofit executive, writer, and college history professor for the past twenty years. Our paths crossed only once—in a voting booth–and the less said about that the better.

But one of the real pleasures of talking through the project that became *Time to Learn* was gradually discovering just how much we actually had in common. As we discussed our thoughts about public education, we found ourselves returning over and over to the importance of our own education and especially that of our children. The son of immigrants, Gabrieli went to Harvard—an experience that profoundly changed the course of his life. Though the great-grandson of immigrants, Goldstein was only the second person in his family to earn a B.A.; that it was at Yale was a piece of good luck that's followed him around ever since. It also got him started on the path of helping a generation's worth of college students to get their own degrees.

But our children turned out to be most important to our discussions—and to this book—not least because we have eight of them between us, but mainly because we've each (along with our spouses) spent immense amounts of time trying to make sure that they had high-quality academic instruction, engaging teachers, a challenging range of extracurricular activities, music lessons, athletic opportunities, and attention paid to their emotional, social, and spiritual development. We have struggled with the bewildering, overlapping, and conflicting demands of our kids' school and out-of-school schedules, our own professional obligations, and our worries that modern life offers far too many destructive temptations for children whose time isn't well organized. In fact, one of our children wrote in his college application essay that he only began playing the sport that is his life's passion—Ultimate Frisbee—at the insistence of his mother, who feared he was "starting to hang out with a bad crowd." All true. At one point Gabrieli realized he and his family were juggling no less than twenty-five distinct extracurricular activities for their five children.

Like all parents, we want what's best for our kids, and we've often mourned the fact that there's just not nearly enough of it in our schools. We have paid close attention to whether our children have been gaining the core academic skills and knowledge they need, and where they have not, we have switched schools or added outside help. As working parents we have raged against the inefficiency and foolishness of dismissing school at 2:30 in the afternoon. And we have spent evenings too numerous to count first tussling with our kids over doing homework, and then discovering that we couldn't even help them with their assignments. So when we see an expanded school day, with time for both academic rigor and a well-rounded education, in which kids run to their enrichment classes in robotics or martial arts or cooking, and in which their teachers help them get homework done before leaving school, and in which teachers talk about their students with caring, knowledge, and passion, we see the kind of education we have coveted for our own children.

Gabrieli came to the education public-policy arena more than a decade ago, but became intensely involved in time and learning when Mayor Thomas Menino appointed him chairman of Boston's Task Force on After-School Time in 1999. He then organized and chaired the After-School for All Partnership, which raised $25 million for after-school programs in the city. He discovered, however, that even though after-school programs were making an enormous difference in children's lives, philanthropy alone could not meet the needs of children. With Jennifer Davis, he co-founded Massachusetts 2020, an education think tank and advocacy platform for after-school issues, and eventually became convinced that expanded time inside schools would be an even more far-reaching solution to the problem faced by most schools and parents. As a result, he worked with the state legislature, successfully crafting the idea, and then securing funding for the first statewide rollout of the "new school day," launched in September 2006 in ten Massachusetts public schools. Today, he works with a team at Massachusetts 2020 on the Massachusetts effort and with another team on the national agenda via the National Center on Time and Learning (NCTL).

Aside from raising his kids and teaching his students for the past two decades, Goldstein has been thinking and writing about education issues for a long time. He has also worked as a consultant to the Long Island Community Foundation for fifteen years, and in that capacity has helped provide grant support to a wide variety of organizations seeking to improve after-school programs, early childhood education, and public education itself. He was delighted to join with Gabrieli to intervene directly in the debate over how best to transform our schools for the better.

We wrote *Time to Learn* because we think it's just the right time for a practical, large-scale transformation in American public education. We think it's "time to learn" from the available evidence—and we give you a ton of it in what follows—that our children need more "time to learn" all of what they need to succeed and thrive in the twenty-first century. No one knows exactly how long the standard school schedule has clocked in at about six-and-a-half hours a day, or how it got to be that way, but just about everyone knows it's not giving kids or teachers enough time to produce high school graduates well prepared for higher education, for the workplace of our newly global economy, or for citizenship in our democracy.

Fortunately, there's also a good bit of evidence out there that with more time, intelligently used, kids do learn more—in some cases a whole lot more—and do get *smarter,* as we put it in the subtitle. But expanding the school day turns out to be one of those linchpin reforms that, once put in place, produces a slew of additional benefits. It gives students involvement in the artistic, cultural, and athletic activities that have been seeping out of the conventional school day. It really does make parents happier—because their children thrive and because it mostly gets rid of the perplexing, often maddening, always anxiety-producing gap between the school dismissal bell and the time most parents get home from work. After all, what group of working parents would ever have given their approval to a school day ending in the early afternoon?

As police know all too well, that twilight zone in the late afternoon when the majority of young people are unsupervised holds great risks for them and for their neighborhoods. Many of us cling to the fantasy that our children are mostly engaged in wholesome play, "just being children," or doing their homework. TV advertisers, junk-food manufacturers, video game developers, online marketers, drug dealers, and gang recruiters know better. So parents, children, and whole neighborhoods are better off when students are engaged and supervised longer and better.

We wrote *Time to Learn* for everyone who cares about public education: for teachers, for parents, for principals and superintendents; for members of school boards; for local, state, and federal legislators and their staffs; for mayors and county executives and governors and their staffs; for employers and community-based organizations and cultural institutions; for grantmakers and state departments of education; and for taxpayers concerned about how best to improve their local public education, as well as improve the safety of their neighborhoods. And since you're holding this book right now, you care something about public education—so we wrote it for you! And we produced it in time to dovetail with the 2008 presidential election—we like to think big!

This appears to be a book about a new educational policy—and it's surely that. But at a deeper level it's really a book about change—about a change that's happened; a change that's under way; a change that, with your help, could transform American public education.

ACKNOWLEDGMENTS

In researching and writing this book we have accumulated many debts, far too many to acknowledge properly in this limited space. We would both like to thank our literary agent Wendy Strothman, who introduced us on a hunch we might be able to write a book together, helped us shape the project, and found it a home at Jossey-Bass. Our editor Lesley Iura has given us just the right mix of criticism and encouragement—and perhaps most impressive, kept us to our initial deadline. We have been grateful for the copyediting of Hilary Powers, who deftly untangled our prose while helping us refine the arguments in this book.

We also want to acknowledge with gratitude the wonderful assistance of Crystal Bish, who (as special assistant to Gabrieli) has worked long and late hours to hunt down dozens of pieces of information and keep us from making errors, served as additional eyes and ears on school visits, contributed extensive research on many of the topics in this book, and alerted us to the wonderfully apt term "opportunity gap."

We both want to express our gratitude to the staff of the NCTL and Massachusetts 2020 for paving the way in this field and then for educating us about issues, for giving us critical readings of earlier versions of the manuscript, and for keeping us from making mistakes too numerous to mention. Jennifer Davis in particular deserves thanks and praise; for almost a decade she has been Gabrieli's essential partner and co-founder in all of this work. David Farbman has consistently and cheerfully given us the benefit of his deep knowledge of this and other education issues. Helenann Civian, Ben Lummis, Jeff Paquette, Claire Kaplan, Beth Herbert, Blair Brown, Emily Raine, Ann McCall, Joe Ganley, and the others that make up this team helped us directly and helped us by making the Massachusetts Expanded Learning Time (ELT)

Initiative work. Valuable colleagues helping to take our work nationwide via the NCTL include Leigh Hopkins, Celine Coggins, Tracy Spicer, and Jill Norton. Linda Desatnick keeps juggling all the balls that would otherwise fall to earth. This is a much better book because of them. Of course, as much as we'd prefer to blame them, we take responsibility for any remaining errors.

This book is inspired first and foremost by our experiences in Massachusetts. The ELT Initiative is the result of many people with different roles working together. We have dedicated this book to the teachers, principals, and leaders who have made it happen at new day schools across the nation.

We must thank specifically the legislative leadership in Massachusetts, especially the first to make it possible—co-chairs of the Education Committee, Senator Robert Antonioni and Representative Patricia Haddad—and Governor Deval Patrick for embracing and advancing the vision; Commissioner David Driscoll and then Commissioner Jeffrey Nellhaus and their great ELT team of Lise Zeig, Sarah McLaughlin, and Karen Vigue, and the Massachusetts Board of Education for their support under consecutive chairmen, first Chris Anderson and then Paul Reville. We realize how much daring commitment it took for the first districts to step forward and recognize the leadership of superintendents Joan Connolly, Nick Fischer, Jim Caradonio, Tom Fowler-Finn and Tom Payzant. Finally, state teachers' union leadership, in particular Anne Wass and Paul Toner of the Massachusetts Teachers Association, and Kathy Kelley, Tom Gosnell, and Ed Doherty of the American Federation of Teachers-Massachusetts have stepped forward and made it all possible.

We also gratefully acknowledge the funders who have supported Massachusetts 2020 and the NCTL: first the Nellie Mae Education Foundation and Nick Donahue and Lynne D'Ambrose—they were first and have always advised as well as supported; the Eli & Edythe Broad Foundation, who changed the game for us; and numerous generous supporters including the Barr Foundation, the Yawkey Foundation, the Boston Foundation, the Amelia Peabody Foundation, the Hewlett Foundation, the Balfour Foundation, and the Bank of America Foundation.

Warren Goldstein would like to thank Interim Provost Joseph Voelker and Interim Arts and Sciences Dean Harry Workman of the University of Hartford for making it possible for him to give this book the time it needed. Thanks also to Jim Fraser of the Steinhardt School of Culture, Education, and Human Development at New York University, who gave us a very thoughtful and helpful reading of an early version of the project.

The late Norman Mailer once observed that writing books is the closest men get to experiencing the pain of childbirth. Goldstein offers his deepest thanks to Donna Schaper, who has tolerated her husband's labor on this book with exceptional generosity and good cheer. When he began working with Gabrieli, it never occurred to him that this boundlessly energetic conversationalist on everything from state and national politics to the vagaries of the Boston Red Sox pitching staff would also turn out to be a dauntingly astute reader, editor, and writer—and end up a good friend. What good luck!

Gabrieli expresses his deep appreciation and love to his wife, Hilary, whose extraordinary moral compass, family devotion, and shared commitment to public service inspire, and whose already expanded day and week took on more load to help him focus on the book—as far as Gabrieli knows, John, Abigail, Polly, Lilla, and Nick are still alive and well! He also thanks his brother, John, for his advice, support, and help—not just on this. And to Nader Dareshori—the man with the plan that this book could happen. And finally to Goldstein—what a partner, colleague, and mensch.

Boston and New York   CHRISTOPHER GABRIELI AND WARREN GOLDSTEIN
February 2008

ABOUT THE AUTHORS

Christopher Gabrieli is an entrepreneur in the business, public policy, and nonprofit arenas. He is the co-founder and chairman of Massachusetts 2020 and the co-founder and co-chairman of the National Center on Time and Learning. Massachusetts 2020 leads the first statewide effort in America to introduce the new school day. The National Center on Time and Learning works to research how schools expand time to strengthen learning; supports public policy at the local, state, and federal level; and provides technical assistance to schools, districts, and states seeking to expand time for learning.

Chris began his career as the co-founder of GMIS, a pioneering health care software company that became the leader in its field. Subsequently, he spent fifteen years as a general partner of Bessemer Venture Partners, a leading early-stage venture capital firm, where he helped create, finance, and build dozens of biotechnology and healthcare companies. He remains a senior partner at Bessemer and is also a partner of the Ironwood Equity Fund.

In addition, Chris serves on numerous civic and university boards. In 2002, he won the Democratic primary for Lieutenant Governor and he came in second in the Democratic primary for governor of Massachusetts in 2006.

Chris and his wife Hilary live in Boston with their five children.

Warren Goldstein is professor of history and chair of the History Department at the University of Hartford, where he was the 2006 recipient of the James E. and Frances W. Bent Award for Scholarly Creativity. Author most recently of *William Sloane Coffin, Jr.: A Holy Impatience,* Goldstein has received fellowships from the John D. and Catherine T. MacArthur Foundation, the National

Endowment for the Humanities, and the Louisville Institute. His essays about history, education, religion, politics, and sports have appeared in the *Chronicle of Higher Education,* the *New York Times,* the *Washington Post,* the *Nation, Christian Century, Commonweal,* the *Times Literary Supplement, Tikkun,* the *Yale Alumni Magazine,* and numerous other newspapers. The father of three grown children, he lives in New York City with his wife, the Rev. Donna Schaper, and blogs at www.TrueBlueBlogger.org.

TIME TO LEARN

INTRODUCTION
The Promise of a New School Day

We're learning more than we usually do from teachers. And it keeps me out of trouble.
—MARKUS WATSON, 8TH GRADER

Last year we would hurry to get something done, and this year we can take our time and do it right. We have a lot more time for reading, math, and science, and you get more time at recess and gym.
—ANDREW GIBSON, 6TH GRADER

I used to sit with her and go problem by problem on her math homework. Not anymore—I ask her if she needs help, and she says, "No, no. I got it."
—DAWN OLIVER, PARENT

All experience hath shewn, that mankind are more disposed to suffer, while evils are sufferable, than to right themselves by abolishing the forms to which they are accustomed.
—U.S. DECLARATION OF INDEPENDENCE

TIME TO LEARN IS ABOUT a new, expanded school schedule that we call the "new school day": a proven, practical, achievable reform that is already transforming American public schools for the better.

We've written *Time to Learn* because this transformation isn't happening nearly fast enough. In this country, too many of us—even those deeply involved in education—settle for a stagnant, often mediocre educational status quo, mostly because we believe that large-scale change in a huge, bureaucratic system is all but impossible, and that the public schools are the best anyone can hope for. We are, as Thomas Jefferson saw so well, more "disposed to suffer" than to embrace change, even in the face of mounting tangible evidence that an expanded school schedule helps teachers and schools make smarter kids, happier parents, and safer neighborhoods. In this book we aren't seeking to abolish all the forms you're used to; we're asking you to consider the evidence that expanding and redesigning the public school day can dramatically improve what schools are providing to children, to families, and to American society.

Already, more than a thousand schools in the country have broken loose from the forms of the past and adopted the new school day—by which we mean they've added significant learning time—at least one or two hours—to the school day. Some are experimental public schools whose founders began with the premise that they needed more time to teach children what they needed to learn. Some are "turnaround schools" in urban districts, using more time to help to reverse years of low performance. The newest wave consists of standard public schools choosing to expand and redesign the school day to both strengthen core academics and ensure a well-rounded education.

In *Time to Learn*, we argue not from educational theory or abstract logic but from a combination of common sense, our own experience, hard data, and personal observation of existing school practice that the new school day works. That's why this book is about a change that's already happened, is in the process of happening, and needs to happen on a large scale for the American dream to continue to be a reality in the twenty-first century.

Since we believe the school schedule needs a thoroughgoing overhaul, we must be prepared to show why there's something wrong with the education it's providing at present. We want to be very clear here. This book is not about assigning personal or institutional blame for the problems of our public school system. We know too many deeply committed, talented, creative, and hard-working teachers, principals, and leaders in education— which is why we've dedicated this book to them. *Time to Learn* describes a huge step we can take toward fixing these problems. Before we discuss solutions, however, we need to give you a look at what's wrong.

Public Education Is in a Rut

In fact, public school education is spinning its wheels in three distinct ruts. First, it has been stagnant for at least a generation, showing no real progress. Second, it cannot seem to abolish or even significantly narrow the "achievement gap," the painfully well-documented disparity in academic performance between poor students, especially those of color, and more affluent students. And finally, we, parents and citizens alike, are mired in a mix of complacency and resignation regarding the expectations we hold for our public school system. Why, in other words, do so many of us believe it's enough for our children to graduate from high school with minimum passing skills? Have we really considered whether schools are fully preparing our children for higher education or for the work world of the twenty-first century? Why does it seem utopian or unrealistic to expect schools to help children reach their full academic potential and have a truly well-rounded education?

Stagnation

First, what do we mean by *stagnant?* Just this: after decades of extraordinary educational progress in the last century, advances that fueled American prosperity and distributed its benefits more widely than ever before in our history, we are, educationally speaking, dead in the water. The high school graduation rate doubled between 1920, when only four in ten Americans graduated from high school, and 1976, when about eight in ten did so. Since then, we've made no progress. Once the acknowledged world leader, the United States now ranks behind the Czech Republic, Norway, Canada, the Slovak Republic, Sweden, Japan, and South Korea. Likewise, the college graduation rate grew from about 10 percent in 1950 to about 27 percent in 1996, and then stalled.

Few Americans realize that, in a highly competitive job market increasingly demanding postsecondary education, only a quarter of students entering an American high school will earn a bachelor's degree within the next fifteen years. In other words, almost three-fourths of *every* group of ninth graders still won't have any kind of college degree at age thirty. While the United States is tied (with Canada) for the lead among developed countries in the percentage of older adults (aged thirty-five to sixty-four) with an associate's degree or higher, we are tied for seventh in the percentage of younger adults (aged twenty-five to thirty-four) who've gained the same degrees—behind Canada, Japan, South Korea, Sweden, Belgium, and Ireland.

Since 1983, when the blue-ribbon report *A Nation at Risk* warned that "the educational foundations of our society are presently being eroded by a rising tide of mediocrity," we have witnessed a huge increase in public spending and a steady parade of educational reform ideas—including state academic standards, smaller class sizes, phonics versus whole language, computers in the classroom, charter schools, school-based management, "small learning communities," and high-stakes testing. And yet, doubling real educational spending from 1975 to 2002 has yielded paltry results. For example, on the long-term National Assessment of Educational Progress, known both as the NAEP and more widely as "the nation's report card," seventeen-year-olds' reading scores remained completely flat from 1971 to 2004, while their math scores only increased 2.6 percent between 1978 and 1992, and then stayed flat until 2004.

That's one reason the accountability movement of the past decade has attracted so much support from policymakers. And it's why we now live in an educational universe governed by the No Child Left Behind Act (NCLB). In this new world, schools are responsible for "adequate yearly progress" in which their students are expected to increase their scores on state-administered standardized tests to the point that 100 percent of students in grades 3 through 8 become "proficient" in mathematics and reading by the year 2014. Schools that consistently fail to show steady improvement may be taken over by states and reorganized. As Superintendent Joan Connolly of Malden, Massachusetts put it at a school board meeting devoted to consideration of the new school day, "I have a lot of worries . . . that keep me up in the night." The 2014 deadline, "is not that far away," she continued, while "the amount of movement we need to make each year is getting steeper, as the trajectory by which we're measured gets steeper." She went on: "I'm also worried because teachers constantly tell me that they don't have enough time to do all that they're required to do. . . . I worry about not enough of us in the Malden school community feeling the urgency with which we must change. . . . I worry that everyone doesn't fully understand the intense scrutiny we're under in the era of high-stakes testing and accountability."

Whatever one thinks of NCLB, and a good deal of ink has been spilled about its pros and cons, it is undeniably a response to the universally acknowledged, often shocking failure of public schools to fully educate our children. Increasingly, education professionals believe that it's time to rethink the entire system. As Massachusetts' outgoing commissioner of education wrote early in 2007, in a *Boston Globe* op-ed,

> After more than four decades as an educator, there is one question I just cannot answer: Why has so little changed in public education? We've made schools handicapped accessible, wired them for the Internet, lowered class sizes, and made school lunches more nutritious. Some communities have full-day kindergarten, many students are reading and writing earlier and better than ever, high schools offer advanced placement courses by the dozen, and vocational-technical schools have expanded to include everything from biotechnology to robotics.

> On the surface there have been plenty of improvements, but when you dig deeper it's clear that little of substance has changed in public education since the days of Horace Mann. . . . The average class day is still just six hours long, leaving children on the street midafternoon . . . in a nation that is lagging far behind internationally. We have entered what can only be described as a crisis in American public education, and we seem to be sleeping through it.

Since the end of World War II, most American children have attended school for approximately six and a half hours per day. Most dismissal bells ring around 2:30 PM, some as early as 1:30.

That's why, despite the widespread impression that children spend much of their time in school, the truth is they go to school for only about 20 percent of their waking hours. That's right—about one-fifth of their waking hours. Basically unquestioned for decades, these numbers help explain why American families are so poorly served by their own public schools.

While schools haven't changed fundamentally since World War II, the world has, often in stunning ways. Computers, the Internet, the end of the Soviet bloc, the rise of China and India, and the massive migrations of people and jobs have transformed the global networks of trade, communications, and manufacturing—with profound consequences for American society. The Bureau of Labor Statistics forecasts that 60 percent of jobs now being created require at least some postsecondary education and training, and researchers project that a bachelor's degree confers a $1 million lifetime earnings advantage over a high school degree. Our K–12 schools met our needs better when access to the middle class was broadly available through blue-collar jobs that didn't demand higher education.

Society has also undergone profound transformations. Consider that in 1960, for example, 30 percent of women participated in the workforce; now 70 percent do. The old school day depended on mothers or grandmothers or neighbors being home for children when school got out. In most working families they aren't, and haven't been for decades, while the number of single-parent families has skyrocketed—an estimated 60 percent of today's children will spend at least some of their childhood in a single-parent home. Record numbers of children spend record amounts of time unsupervised. Parents themselves admit that at least a third of children in grades 6 through 8 are in "self-care"—they look after themselves.

THE ACHIEVEMENT GAP

Most disturbingly, urban public schools (accounting for 30 percent of the total number of students) simply do not manage to educate their prime constituency of low-income students, who are falling further and further behind their more affluent suburban counterparts, reinforcing a stubborn fact of educational life.

Nationally, according to Columbia University Teachers College, "by the end of fourth grade, African-American, Latino, and poor students of all races are two years behind their wealthier, predominantly white peers in reading and math. By eighth grade, they have slipped three years behind, and by twelfth grade, four years behind. By the end of high school, black and Hispanic students' reading and mathematics skills are roughly the same as those of white students in the eighth grade." This is happening at a time when American demographics are changing extremely rapidly: the percentage of minority children has surged, nearly doubling from 1972 to 2005, chiefly driven by growth in our Latino population. Nationally, children of color make up 42 percent of the school-age population and the percentage continues to grow. In fact, in the western states, they are now the majority. The immigration boom has led to a doubling over the last twenty-five years of students who speak a language other than English at home. All these changes considerably increase the need for us to grapple with, reduce, and ultimately eliminate the achievement gap.

To see how severe the issue is today, take Newark, New Jersey, which spends more than $20,000 per student per year, among the very highest allocation in the nation. In 2004–05, just 37 percent of Newark graduates—a total of 752 students from thirteen high schools—passed the High School Proficiency Exam, which New Jersey's own Commissioner of Education described as a "middle-school-level test."

After decades of urban revitalization, no city in the country is even close to drawing middle-class suburbanites back into its public schools. When is the last time you heard a parent say, "You know, we're thinking about moving back into the city to get better schools for our kids"? For the last quarter century urban districts have been losing parents who dream about having the money to get into suburban school districts—not vice versa.

COMPLACENCY

Given this stagnant and mediocre system, the question we need to ask—all of us: parents, teachers, principals, school board members, public officials—is, Why do we *continue* to pledge allegiance to a six-and-a-half-hour day that is short-changing millions of our children? Polling data offers some clues to this puzzle. More than 60 percent of Americans (as measured by a Phi Delta Kappa/Gallup poll) give the entire school system grades of C, D, or F. On the other hand, when it comes to their own community schools, or the schools their children attend, the grades improve markedly. Roughly half the respondents give their community schools an A or B, and 70 percent give the school their oldest child attends an A or B. We seem, in other words, to be convinced that the system as a whole is mediocre, while at the very same time we believe that the schools closest to us are just fine. Both cannot be true. We appear to have taken up residence in a town like Garrison Keillor's fictional Lake Woebegone, but one where all the *schools* are above average.

Are parents in suburban middle- and upper-middle-income communities wrong to be satisfied with their schools? The problem is that being on the winning side of the achievement gap doesn't necessarily mean that middle-income students are getting all they need in school. In fact, their parents have every reason to fear that their neighborhood schools don't give their children the skills needed to succeed in our rapidly changing, technologically advanced, postindustrial global economy. They also have good reason to worry that the national emphasis on high-stakes testing in core academic subjects has squeezed music and the arts, experiential and creative learning, even recess, out of the middle-class school day as well. Their children may be passing English, math, and science courses, but few achieve what most employers or college admissions officers consider genuine proficiency in these subjects.

While higher education has increasingly become a necessity for employment success, admission to college has become more competitive and federal scholarship aid buys less than it used to. Once students arrive at college, their struggle is far from over. College teachers have been charting the decline of freshman reading and writing skills for decades. If you doubt this, ask any professor you know, and be prepared for a long lecture! Less anecdotally, many public colleges and universities find themselves forced to provide academic remediation to nearly one-third of first-year students—because too many high school graduates, even in such apparently high-performing states as Massachusetts, are seriously underprepared for college-level work.

Today's schoolchildren will work as adults in a truly global-ized economy and society. And yet, most first-year college students find themselves terrified by their required basic math course. More and more jobs require technological competence, but in math achievement, American students rank twenty-fifth among advanced countries; not only behind their counterparts from India, China, and Japan but also behind Finland, Canada, Australia, the Slovak and Czech Republics, Ireland, Poland, and Hungary.

Out of a visceral sense of this inadequacy, combined with resignation about the possibility of change in the schools, many middle-class and upper-middle-class families use enormous amounts of time, emotional energy, tuition money, and gasoline shuttling their children among a dizzying array of activities, from math and SAT tutoring to lessons in art, music, drama, and dance, or to traveling competitive sports programs. While some parents argue that the current school schedule, at least in afflu-ent suburban districts, is working, the truth is that it only works because millions of parents are now providing their own version of a new school day, sometimes burning out their own children— and themselves—in the process. Otherwise, newspapers and mag-azines wouldn't be featuring so many articles on "overbooked children" and their frazzled families.

We know that risks and temptations for children have never been greater, ranging from such traditional threats as smoking, alcohol, drugs, fast cars, and petty crime to more modern ones: violent video games, HIV/AIDS, and Internet predators. We also know that half of all high school students are sexually active, but we pay less attention to the fact that many teen pregnancies get started between 3 and 6 PM. Why, then, don't we pay more atten-tion to the reality that by locking school doors all afternoon, most communities shut down their largest public buildings, push-ing students into cars, the street, their homes, and whatever pub-lic places will have them? The current school schedule provides recruits for teen gangs, whose activity has reached epidemic pro-portions in suburban as well as urban school districts, from Los Angeles to Long Island. Less dramatically but no less tellingly, how many adults, especially seniors, enjoy walking into a business when the entrance is surrounded by a large group of loitering teenagers?

Families and the nonprofit sector have struggled to fill the gap between school dismissal and the evening, by and large without success. Despite media reports suggesting that most children are fully occupied, even overscheduled, after school, the reality is that fewer than half of all students report any after-school activities at all. Perhaps even more striking, nine in ten children participate in no formal daily after-school program, a number that includes *94 percent of middle-schoolers.* Especially in low-income communities, television stands in for adults. Four in ten African American fourth graders watch six or more hours of television a day. Day in and day out, working parents know and juggle the painful challenges posed by the current school schedule.

Here's the secret about our current school schedule, which seems to be a largely unquestioned fact of life: it has *no* positive supporters, only negative ones: those who worry that change is difficult, expensive, or inconvenient. *No one* defends the six-and-a-half-hour day on teaching or learning or social grounds. People do argue that the current schedule costs less than any change would bring, but we must point out that the current system also incurs (but does not recognize) the short-term cost of after-school and day care programs, extra tuition for enrichment and lessons, and the immense burden of the juvenile justice system. In the long term, of course, workers who don't leave school with adequate skills will themselves pay in lost income and benefits, while the entire economy, tax base, and society pay in lost growth, dynamism, and creativity. We start, therefore, from the premise—based on overwhelming and depressing evidence—that the current school schedule, which we call the "old school day," has proved itself an enormously expensive, astonishingly inconvenient, outdated educational policy that came into being almost by accident, the mediocre results of which we see every day. It's run its course.

TIME TO LEARN: CORE IDEAS OF THE NEW SCHOOL DAY

In this book we tell the story of a new school day, a new schedule already in place in more than a thousand public schools that offers a genuine solution to our educational crisis. A powerful, realistic, attainable transformation of American public education, the new school day reinvigorates children's lives, dramatically improving academic success while narrowing the achievement gap, broadening and deepening what children learn, helping teachers become more effective, bringing greatly needed relief to parents, and making kids and neighborhoods safer by reducing juvenile crime, drug and alcohol abuse, teen pregnancy, car accidents, and mindless television watching and video-game playing. These are large claims. If we didn't have the evidence, we wouldn't be making them.

RESULTS

Instead of narrowing the school curriculum to focus on reading and math, the new school day opens up the range of subjects students study and get exposure to. In new day schools, students explore music and the arts, a remarkable variety of enrichment activities, as well as a range of programs in social and emotional learning. All these activities contribute mightily to helping children receive a truly well-rounded education. There's good evidence that the new school day improves the overall school learning climate by raising attendance and by reducing disciplinary referrals and what are blandly called "serious incidents."

The new school day also produces that most elusive of academic results: striking improvements in test scores. We have lots more examples in the rest of *Time to Learn,* but for the moment, here's a brief taste.

In Massachusetts, after just one year of the Expanded Learning Time Initiative, which added 30 percent (about two hours) to a redesigned school day in ten urban elementary and middle schools, the ELT schools not only improved their own performance; they improved faster than the rest of the state. The average *proficiency rate*—that is, the percentage of students scoring Proficient or Advanced on the statewide test known as the Massachusetts Comprehensive Assessment System—compared to the schools' performance for the four previous years, jumped 44 percent in math, 19 percent in science, and 39 percent in English language arts.

Measured against statewide averages, the ten ELT schools began to make progress in the single most difficult task in public education these days: closing the achievement gap. In math they narrowed the gap modestly, by just 2.4 percent. In science they shaved it by nearly 15 percent. In English language arts, they took a huge bite out of the gap, narrowing it by more than 35 percent!

Another group of schools we talk about in this book are public charter schools belonging to the well-known Knowledge Is Power Program, or KIPP network: fifty-seven elementary, middle, and high schools serving fourteen thousand overwhelmingly low-income (80 percent) African American and Latino (90 percent) students in seventeen states (and the District of Columbia), with concentrations in Houston, Texas, Newark, New Jersey, and Washington, D.C. KIPP schools all use 60 percent more time than the standard school schedule, going from 7:30 AM to 5 PM and involving some Saturday classes and several weeks during the summer. By every measure—national, statewide, and local—KIPP students not only improve themselves, they also outperform the great majority of their peers. Take KIPP D.C. Key Academy, in which 88 percent of eighth-grade students tested Proficient or above in math in 2006, more than three times the rate of D.C. eighth-graders as a whole (which was 27 percent); and 81 percent scored at least Proficient in reading, two and a half times the district total (32 percent). That same year 90 percent of KIPP Houston High School tenth graders passed the Texas statewide math exam, as compared to 49 percent of other Houston tenth graders. KIPP Ujima Village Academy in Baltimore was the highest-performing public school serving middle grades in the city in 2006; its seventh and eighth graders achieved the highest math scores in the state of Maryland.

These extraordinary results could be repeated for city after city, but let's leave KIPP for the moment with this astonishing statistic. Nearly four-fifths of students who complete KIPP's eighth grade (the network consists mostly of middle schools) have entered college; nationally, the proportion for low-income students is less than one in five.

THE CORE IDEA

Our core idea is so simple and obvious we made it the title of this book: children need enough *time to learn*—to build the skills and develop the knowledge and well-roundedness required to work and thrive in the twenty-first century.

Of course time alone isn't enough.

Nothing considered by itself is enough to turn schools around—not the most gifted teachers, most inspiring principals, newest buildings, or most up-to-date equipment. Time, however, is an indispensable foundation for new levels of student achievement and educational success. And, like any precious resource, it can be wasted. Simply tacking extra time poorly spent onto the current school schedule, for example, doesn't get the job done.

How the New School Day Is Different

In effective new day schools, teachers and principals talk constantly about how to make best use of time. They wrestle with finding the best ways to apply more time in core academic subjects, to help teachers incorporate more individualized instruction and project-based learning into their classes, and to balance added core academic time with more time for engaging enrichment in arts, music, drama, sports, and other essential aspects of a well-rounded education. They discuss and debate how to use data to inform their initial redesign plan for expanded time and then how to modify their approaches based on subsequent data. They work to balance added time for students with added time for teachers to work and plan together and to benefit from professional development. They blend more time for current teachers with the addition of time and services from outside individuals and community-based organizations. They use time as a tool to support other innovations and reforms.

When well used, added time bestows many blessings. Principals don't have to choose between math and social studies, between reading practice and science, or between core academics and arts, music, drama, or sports. Because the school day isn't so rushed, they're having fewer disciplinary problems and seeing fewer special education referrals. Kids are getting more opportunities and more choices for enrichment than ever before. And the kids' test scores are going up.

We think the evidence is clear—from teachers themselves as well as from test scores—that the new school day allows teachers to become far more effective in the classroom. A genuinely new school schedule uses significantly more time—ideally about two hours a day—to redesign the entire school schedule. Principals and teachers spend a good bit of up-front time planning how to use these new hours to deepen, enrich, and customize their program so students can

- Master core academic subjects
- Practice new skills
- Receive individualized instruction and tutoring
- Get exposure to a broad array of topics
- Experience the arts, music, drama, and sports

In this book we take you inside new day classrooms to show how children are using the new schedule to ask questions and to learn actively through projects, experiments, and hands-on use of newly gained skills. Children occasionally grumble about the new schedule at first, but the evidence is that they soon come to accept it. Some, surprisingly enough, downright love it. "The teachers answer my questions," kids of all ages say over and over. How poignant! What else should school be about, if not answering kids' questions? In one school that had begun the expanded schedule, the district had a funding crunch and reverted to the old schedule. Kids demonstrated in favor of keeping the new school day at the School Board meeting! One said he had friends who dropped out because they couldn't keep up any more—they didn't get their questions answered. How can anyone be satisfied with a school schedule that prevents teachers from answering their students' questions?

We listen to teachers in new day schools who love the extra time, which means they can allow classroom discussions to flow more freely and still provide small group and individual teaching for students based on skill level. An expanded school schedule engages students more fully, and children learn better in a more stimulating environment. By reducing the pressure on the system to cram math and reading and science into too few hours, the new school day opens up the schedule for subjects that students enjoy and teachers like to teach. Asked about the impact of Massachusetts' new school day on student academic performance, fully 70 percent of the teachers in new day schools said it was better (23 percent saw "no impact" and a tiny minority, 7 percent, thought it was worse).

Why It Works

Teachers and principals have found that the new school day makes possible a series of fundamental changes.

First, students and teachers get more time on task. Students who fall behind get the time to catch up. Instead of experiencing the classroom as a place for failure and boredom, kids have success. Students who are already keeping up have a chance to explore more. In science, longer classes allow students to carry out experiments from beginning to end in a single session. No instructional technique benefits from a rushed school day.

"More time on task really makes a difference for our students," says Dr. Jean Teal, principal of Miami Edison High School. "Kids can really get that intensive instruction they need, where their weaknesses lie. It gives more opportunity to work with students. Teachers can develop their lessons and have kids engage for longer periods of time, using all these best practices we've put into place with our students." As one social studies teacher mourned after her school canceled the new school day for budget reasons, "The amount of material I could get through was amazing. You could introduce a concept, introduce primary sources to study it, have kids explore it in a group, and then come back and discuss the subject more in detail."

Students get more opportunities for experiential learning and enrichment activities. Arts, music, drama, and recess—most of which have been reduced or eliminated in recent years on behalf of so-called core academic subjects—return to the classroom. At the Timilty Middle School in Boston, for instance, all students submit a project to the citywide science fair. At the Matthew J. Kuss School in Fall River, Massachusetts, according to the *Boston Globe*, "The once hit-or-miss drama program now regularly puts on major productions. . . . The troupe last fall staged a production of *Macbeth*, with the performers in professionally made costumes."

Teachers gain a greater ability to work with diverse skill levels at the same time. Longer periods enable teachers to divide the class into groups, and to make room for individual and small-group tutoring—and more students stay more engaged, rather than drifting off into inattention and eventual disciplinary problems and failure. Students and adults get to interact more and develop stronger relationships—one of the crucial foundations of student achievement.

Schools restore academic subjects that had been scaled back or even dropped due to the emphasis on core instruction and high-stakes testing in reading, writing, and math. Students are able to study crucial academic subjects such as science, history, social studies, and foreign languages. Finally, teachers have time to work with each other in planning how they teach their students, time that almost never exists in the current school schedule. From Miami to Boston, Houston to Newport News, principals and teachers talked to us about the importance of teachers' getting more (and more targeted) professional development—training to be more effective—as well as much more grade-level and subject-area planning time. These crucial new hours allow teachers to assess their students' progress and their own techniques, and to zero in on kids who need extra help.

MAKING KIDS SMARTER

The real test of the new school day is that it's already working, and in some cases working wonders, for hundreds of thousands of students in schools that have already adopted it:

- In public charter schools
- In elite private schools
- In affluent suburbs where parents create a new day by purchasing after-school activities
- In the thirty-nine-school School Improvement Zone in the poorest big city in the country—Miami
- In Massachusetts, where the Expanded Learning Time Initiative is rapidly growing

Still, even successful experiments only rarely sweep through the nation's school districts on their own. We've written this book to give the new school schedule an additional boost.

Charter Schools

Charter schools, new public schools across the country that have been granted the autonomy to act independently of many district and union rules and regulations, have widely adopted an expanded schedule. Eager to conquer the achievement gap, crusading educational pioneers founded many of these charter schools. By their own reckoning, they simply cannot get the job done without considerably more time.

Take, for example, the well-known KIPP schools—fifty-seven nonprofit public charter elementary, middle, and high schools across the country. Founded by two young Teach for America teachers in Houston in a legendary all-night session, KIPP schools all depend on a regular school day of 7:30–5:00, regular Saturday school, and three weeks during the summer: 60 percent more learning time than most public schools. They have had extraordinary academic success with a population almost universally consisting of poor urban students of color, almost all of whom enter KIPP schools with skills well below their grade level.

KIPP co-founder Mike Feinberg puts it this way. "We are painfully aware that after the first day with our kids in fifth grade, we have less than eight years on the clock to get them ready for college, which is why we have a sense of urgency, why we need them to come early and stay late." Living in Texas, he uses football analogies. "When we start in fifth grade, we're starting in the fourth quarter, down by a touchdown, and the two-minute warning has been given. Every second counts, and there's no margin for error." Even starting in pre-K a school is "still down by a touchdown," he says. We look at him quizzically. "Look," he says, "there's a gap between our kids and the kids from the affluent suburbs who've been exposed to four million more words by the age of four. The uneven playing field is prenatal too." So KIPP Academies use the new school day to close the achievement gap. All—100 percent—of Houston KIPP's ninth graders passed the statewide reading test, as opposed to 82 percent of the district; 96 percent passed in math, compared to 43 percent of district ninth graders. KIPP's pre-K children enter before they've learned to read. Two years later, at the end of kindergarten, they are reading at the second-grade level in both English and Spanish.

Perhaps not surprisingly with these results, KIPP Houston is embarked on a city-endorsed, decade-long expansion that will take it from its current nine schools to forty-two, serving 21,000 students, 10 percent of Houston's school-age population.

Private Schools

The new school day is the norm for many children of the most affluent and highly educated families in the country. When these kids attend private schools, their parents have opted for academic, enrichment, and athletic time going well beyond the conventional school schedule. The oldest, most storied private schools in the nation, which have educated generations of political, business, and professional leaders, have always used a version of the new school day, in which students are engaged in structured, supervised academics, sports, clubs, drama, or homework from morning until dinner-time—or beyond for those who board.

Affluent Suburban Families

Many of the most affluent American parents, as well as those who sacrifice to live in more affluent school districts, send their children to suburban schools whose curricular and extracurricular offerings rival those of private schools. Even these schools, however, dismiss children between 2:00 and 2:30 in the afternoon, so many of these families have custom-built their own new school days by seeking out and purchasing a wide range of activities for their children. The result has been a boom in after-school programs, tutoring, summer camps, traveling sports teams, music lessons, and other expensive enrichment industries. Their children receive a far more extensive and well-rounded education than if they were simply depending on the standard school schedule.

Turnaround: Miami-Dade's School Improvement Zone

In Miami, students in the School Improvement Zone, in which the school day has been extended by an hour and partially redesigned, showed steady improvements in math and reading scores, both absolutely and by comparison to the entire district. They have begun, in other words, to close the achievement gap. But "Zone schools," as they are known in Miami, demonstrated something else as well, too often overlooked in the question of what helps children learn. Almost across the board, schools showed increased attendance rates and stunning reductions in suspensions and "serious targeted incidents." The new school day has improved the learning climate in the school, so children come to school more—and spend less time in disruptive behavior while there. Miami's experience helps answer a question also addressed by the Massachusetts experiment: can schools convert from a standard schedule to the new school day? Or do they have to start from scratch, as charter schools do?

Conversion: Expanded Learning Time in Massachusetts

The Massachusetts Expanded Learning Time (ELT) Initiative engages schools in extensive expansion and redesign of their schedule, adding 25–30 percent more time (an hour and a half to two hours) to the school day. And in just one year, the first ten ELT schools outpaced statewide gains modestly in math, noticeably in science, and dramatically in English language arts. What that means, in lay language, is that these schools actually *narrowed the achievement gap* in just one year—in the case of reading and writing, by more than a third. The Osborn Street School in long-depressed Fall River showed phenomenal results, entirely eliminating failures in some categories, such as fifth-grade math, when nearly four in ten had failed the previous year. In fifth-grade English language arts, 22 percent of fifth graders had scored at or above proficiency on the statewide test the year before conversion. After a year of the new school day, *69 percent of fifth graders scored at or above proficiency, an increase of 214 percent.* Yes, it can be done: standard public schools can switch to the new school day, and they can achieve results little short of astonishing in very little time.

So it's already plain that the new school schedule is making kids smarter—they learn more, they know more, they perform better. What about parents? How are they happier?

Making Parents Happier

Parents of students at new day schools think they've hit the jackpot. They see their children making academic gains ranging from modest to extraordinary. They see their children's newfound engagement with school through enrichment activities ranging from forensics to music production, robotics to martial arts. And they see their children completing the bulk of their homework in school, with teachers who can really help them.

They also know what happens all too often to children between school dismissal and the end of the workday. They know that the myth of children playing pickup baseball games after school has little relation to reality. Parents who work outside the home feel tremendous relief due to the new school schedule, because their kids aren't spending long afternoon hours in front of a television or computer screen or playing video games, or getting into trouble with other unsupervised adolescents. Parents who have been through this juggling act recall the complexity of managing drop-offs and pickups, baby-sitters, friends, and neighbors, all while trying to do their own jobs. Parents in the middle of it now probably don't have time to read this book. By matching children's daily rhythms to those of their parents, the new school day makes families happier, and it offers a simple, powerful, and far-reaching solution to a multifaceted problem.

Making Neighborhoods Safer

You don't have to be the parent of a school-age child to appreciate the difference on your local streets and sidewalks—and in malls and supermarkets and convenience stores—when teenagers are learning or playing in school rather than loitering in your neighborhood or driving their cars through town recklessly. All you have to do is read the local police reports in the newspaper, or see the results of juvenile crime on TV news, or notice your neighbor's teenage daughter and her boyfriend hanging out all afternoon while their parents are working, to appreciate why kids *and* neighborhoods become safer when schools adopt the new school day.

Out of the Rut: Making Change

But despite the overwhelming evidence that the new school day is needed to give poor kids a fighting chance of academic success, and to provide all kids with an education adequate to the demands of today's world—while offering huge benefits to teachers, families, and communities—mainstream public schools, responsible for more than 90 percent of all American children, remain stuck in the old school day. Only children lucky enough to land in a new day school or whose parents are resourceful enough to build or purchase the equivalent receive the benefit of an education that really meets their needs.

We intend *Time to Learn* to help change the terms of debate about public education in America, to help the country let go of a relic from the past that no longer works, and to provide a comprehensive guide to the new school day; to show what we know about it and what works, and to help parents, teachers, principals, superintendents, members of school boards, and public officials find the will and the ways to transform the conventional schedule into the exciting, reshaped, reinvigorated new school day.

We don't think it makes any sense to impose the new school day on teachers or parents. Let's say this again. *We do not advocate imposing the new school day on anyone.* A change of this order absolutely demands the willing participation of parents and teachers, as well as the active leadership of committed principals and superintendents.

Even so, we believe American society has reached the political and cultural moment for this transformation, and therefore this book. Why?

Parents, elected officials, and education professionals are hungry for ways to address the obvious and persistent inadequacies and inequities in public education—while American schoolchildren are falling behind their global counterparts. Political candidates know that voters consider education a critical issue, and the new school day is reaching the threshold of national debate. The new school day is a tangible, concrete proposal—already proven to work—that offers parents, politicians, educators, and policymakers something substantial to latch on to, and it is the prisoner of no political party.

You've probably figured out that we're idealists. We plead guilty: we do have ideals about how our children ought to learn, what an education ought to be, and what our country ought to look like. We believe that adopting the new school day is the most practical, realistic step schools and districts can take toward revolutionizing children's educational experience, raising academic achievement across the board, making it possible for teachers to both fulfill the mandates of high-stakes testing *and* enhance their feelings of professional accomplishment, supporting parents struggling to help their children succeed in school, and reducing juvenile crime. The new school day is not just another educational reform fad. Bringing about *time to learn* is, and will be, a fundamental structural transformation of American public education.

A GUIDE TO WHAT FOLLOWS

Much as we'd like it if you start reading this book and can't put it down, we know what modern life is really like—multiple, overlapping demands on your attention from many different quarters. As a result, you may well want to dip into different chapters as they strike your interest. That's why we've given you this guide to the rest of the book, and why we've tried to make many of the chapters stand more or less on their own. If you do decide to read straight through, you may find some key arguments restated, if in slightly different form. That's not an accident, merely an attempt to meet the needs of different groups of readers.

In Part One of this book, Chapter Two through Chapter Four, we focus on how this new schedule makes it possible for more children not only to learn but to master reading, writing, and math. At the same time, new day schools bring back such academic subjects as science, social studies, and languages, which have been pushed to the edges of the daily schedule in recent years. We take you into classrooms to give you some of the flavor of teaching and learning in these new day schools.

In Part Two, Chapter Five through Chapter Eight, we look at different kinds of subjects and activities, those that have more to do with the whole child. Here we describe how enrichment, the arts, and extracurricular activities play a part in the new school day. And since children come to school in the morning from very different backgrounds, home lives, and neighborhoods, we look at programs in social and emotional learning, sometimes called "character education," made possible by the expanded schedule. We show how the new school day encourages recess and physical education, both of which have declined in recent years as core academic subjects have taken center stage. Finally, we see how the new schedule offers some different ways of addressing the complicated question of homework. So these first eight chapters are mostly about kids and their world: what and how kids are learning as a result of an expanded school schedule.

Part Three, Chapter Nine through Chapter Eleven, is mostly about the adult world, and how adults' lives change for the better in the new school day, though it also shows how kids accept and often embrace the new day, much to the surprise of many people, including themselves. Also contrary to what most people think (and predict, for that matter), teachers tend to be thoroughly on board with the idea. They don't like it imposed on them (who would?), and they want to get paid for extra work, but why should that be a surprise or an insurmountable obstacle? It turns out that what's good for teachers and children is good for parents, because their kids spend more time learning and less time unsupervised. Most parents love the new schedule, again as long as they have the opportunity to buy in first. And what's good for parents turns out to be good for all taxpayers and residents of American neighborhoods, towns, and cities. This linchpin educational reform also proves to be an extremely effective crime-fighting measure.

In Part Four, Chapter Twelve through Chapter Sixteen, we get really practical. If we manage to persuade you, after all, we're not going to leave you high and dry. In Chapter Twelve we look at a number of alternatives people have suggested both for making better use of the time we have in the current school day and for expanding learning time by increasing the number of days kids go to school. In Chapter Thirteen we ask who would benefit most from the new school day, and show, step by step, how different groups of students and parents would benefit from transforming the schedule. Then you'll really want to read Chapter Fourteen, where we tackle the nitty-gritty of creating the new school day: what it costs, and what's involved in terms of research, planning, and public relations. We talk about interacting with teachers, parents, and school boards, and about predicting obstacles and how to overcome them. In Chapter Fifteen we lay out a dozen design principles to guide you in developing the new school day, and also raise some questions—such as summer terms and special high school issues—that need further thought and research. Chapter Sixteen ties together many of the themes of the book in a forward-looking conclusion and call to action.

This transformation may seem daunting at times, but it's completely do-able—and getting easier all the time! After all, our children's present education as well as their future lies in our hands.

PART ONE

TIME FOR CORE ACADEMICS

THE ABC'S OF SUCCESS

Reading and Writing in the
New School Day

*Expanded learning time is a tool. It gives you the
piece that you need to redesign the school day, but it
also gives you the time for teachers to change their
practice. . . .*
—Tony Caputo, former principal, Jacob Hiatt
Magnet School, Worcester, Massachusetts

"WHAT DO YOU LIKE ABOUT 'super-sentences'?" we ask
Jared, a first grader at the Jacob Hiatt Magnet School in
Worcester, Massachusetts.

He thinks. "When other people read super-sentences you can
see a movie in your head. I like when people use details in super-
sentences, and luscious language."

"Luscious language? What's that?"

"Luscious language is when you actually say more than like,
'I walked to bed.' You say, 'I ran to bed,' or 'I slithered to bed.' You
use more details, you go, like, 'I ran as fast as a cheetah. I jumped
as high as a rocket.'"

Yvette chimes in: "I slowly poured my toothpaste as slow as
molasses."

Although reading and writing make up the absolute center
of what children need to learn before they can learn anything
at all of an academic nature, nowhere is the stagnation of the

American educational system more evident than in how well—or poorly—most schoolchildren learn to read and write. The new school day offers a powerful, large-scale solution to this problem, giving classroom teachers the time to use an array of instructional strategies to engage and build their students' widely differing literacy skills.

In this chapter we show how a respected magnet school in Worcester, part of the Massachusetts ELT Initiative, uses two full hours and a dedicated literacy block to address student reading and writing. We also show how a district turnaround initiative in Miami-Dade County, Florida, uses an additional hour per day and some packaged reading programs to make real gains among low-performing students, and how a nationally respected charter school in the Mission Hill area of Boston uses significantly more time—not only to narrow the achievement gap but to beat it. But before we go more deeply into how students learn to read and write and how a new school day helps, here's a review of the problem.

THE LITERACY PROBLEM

America's predicament lies chiefly in the fact that despite massively increased spending (in real dollars) on public education in the past thirty-five years, the indices charting how well our children read and write have remained stubbornly flat. Some years they go up a few points; some years they go down a few points—an operational definition of stagnation. The National Assessment of Educational Progress (NAEP), also known as "the nation's report card," has tested many thousands of children throughout the country in reading and math at ages nine, thirteen, and seventeen (generally grades 4, 8, and 12) through its "long-term trend assessment" since 1971. As with any large body of data, people crunch the numbers in different ways. The U.S. Department of Education's National Center for Education Statistics (which reports the NAEP), for example, appears to be on a permanent hunt for the silver lining in the generally dark cloudbank of these "long-term trend" statistics. For thirteen-year-olds, it explains, "The average score in 2004 was higher than the average score in 1971"—true, but only by a hair's breadth—"but no difference from the average score in 1999 was found." In fact, out of a possible score of 500 on the NAEP test, the average reading score for thirteen-year-olds has fluctuated between 255 in 1971 and 259 in 2004 (with a relative "spike" all the way to 260 in 1992, when all ages experienced a similar bump)—a difference of *less than 1 percent*. Meanwhile, real education spending more than doubled.

This bears repeating: *During the past thirty-five years, while the United States has doubled real spending on K–12 education, the reading abilities of our students have shown virtually no improvement at all.*

In this period, seventeen-year-olds' scores show an even flatter trajectory: an identical average score thirty-three years after the first test. The only positive glimmer of hope in this picture comes from fourth graders, whose reading scores took a noticeable jump of about 3.3 percent between 1999 and 2004.

These long-term trends are confirmed by the test scores of the "main NAEP" (a different test from the same source) showing the percentage of students in grades 4, 8, and 12 scoring Advanced, Proficient, Basic, or Below Basic (we'll call it failing) on reading tests from 1992 to 2007. Since 2000, fourth graders' scores have definitely improved, if modestly. The failing percentage dropped 8 percent, while the percentage making it to Basic increased 3 percent, Proficient 4 percent, and Advanced by a single point. These hardly seem signs of educational transformation; nevertheless, since they represent the first nationwide advances in more than thirty years, they deserve some attention. We can only speculate about the mix of factors—more preschool and full-day kindergarten, better after-school programs, better-educated elementary school teachers, better use of computers—that produced these gains.

On the other hand, the fact that the increases are so small and that they have not translated into similar improvements at the eighth-grade level suggests that even a small achievement boost soon disappears; as a nation, we seem unable to come up with educational strategies that allow for a genuine achievement breakthrough. And while this stasis may not owe its existence to the old school day, consider how much children's lives in middle and high school are influenced by a school day ending at 2:30. Middle and high schoolers participate at much lower rates than younger children in formal after-school programs, and in general have less adult supervision in the mid- to late-afternoon hours. High school students in particular are more engaged in sports, while also being more likely to have jobs or other household responsibilities such as caring for younger siblings. While sports have many benefits for young people, they rarely boost reading and writing skills, and neither do most of the jobs and household responsibilities that fall to students after school. Nor does the group of activities associated with hanging out on street corners or at home, watching television or playing video games.

What sorts of skills are we talking about here? The National Center for Education Statistics describes the abilities of the most advanced seventeen-year-olds this way: "Readers at this level can extend and restructure the ideas presented in specialized and complex texts. Examples include scientific materials, literary essays, and historical documents. Readers are also able to understand the links between ideas, even when those links are not explicitly stated, and to make appropriate generalizations. Performance at this level suggests the ability to synthesize and learn from specialized reading materials." Sounds like college material, right? Perhaps, but only 6 percent of U.S. seventeen-year-olds reach this level today; in 1971, 7 percent did.

How ready for college are our high school graduates these days? After all, a college degree has come to mean what a high school degree did two generations ago: the basic credential for a middle-class job. Here's the distressing answer: nearly a third of those who get into college have to take remedial classes upon arrival because their institutions consider them underprepared for college-level work. And Goldstein, who teaches at the college level, can attest to the often disappointingly low reading and writing skills of many suburban high schools' graduates.

Leave schools for a while. How about Americans' literacy skills in the world at large? Well, a national survey called the "National Assessment of Adult Literacy" (NAAL) or, more simply, "Literacy in Everyday Life" is performed about once a decade. The most recent version, published in 2007 for 2003 data, surveyed about nineteen thousand adults randomly, and measured three practical aspects of reading comprehension:

- *Prose Literacy:* The ability to comprehend, search, and use sources such as newspaper articles, brochures, and instruction manuals.
- *Document Literacy:* The same skills applied to items such as job application forms, payroll forms, television guides, maps, and food labels.
- *Quantitative Literacy:* The ability to identify and perform computations on numbers embedded in situations, such as balancing a checkbook, figuring out a tip, and determining the amount of interest on a loan from an advertisement.

For each of these forms of literacy, researchers decided if respondents were Below Basic, Basic, Intermediate, or Proficient. To provide some context, on the Prose Literacy measure, a Proficient scorer is expected to generally be able to, for example, "evaluate information to determine which legal document is applicable to a specific healthcare situation," while an Intermediate scorer cannot do that reliably but can "summarize the work experience required for a specific job based on information in a newspaper ad." A Basic scorer can do neither of these things consistently but can "find, in a long narrative passage, the name of the person who performed a particular action." Finally, a Below Basic scorer can do none of the above effectively but may be able to "find information in a short, simple prose passage."

In 2003, 14 percent of all Americans tested (a proportion that would indicate 30 million people share the same result!) were Below Basic, while another 29 percent reached only Basic. In other words, more than 40 percent of Americans sixteen and older cannot summarize the work experience required for a job based on an advertisement. Only 13 percent of adult Americans scored Proficient. There was no improvement at all between 1992 and 2003. More than half of the high school graduates scored Basic or Below Basic on the Prose Literacy measure, and even among college graduates, the Proficient rate dropped from an already alarmingly low 40 percent in 1992 to just 31 percent in 2003.

These are shocking figures. Nearly 90 million adult Americans with Basic or Below Basic literacy skills! Less than one in three college graduates Proficient! No gains over the past decade and significant slippage even among those with better credentials.

We know the numbers aren't good, intuitively, but the NAAL went a little further and correlated literacy levels with some other aspects of everyday life. The results may be predictable; they nevertheless tell a depressing story. For example, only 35 percent of adults with Below Basic skills are employed full time, as against 64 percent of those who scored Proficient. Fifty-nine percent of working adults with Below Basic scores make under $500 a week, 43 percent of Basic skills people do the same, while only 14 percent of the Proficient fall into that category. And they know it. Seventy percent of those with Below Basic skills say they think their reading skills limit their job opportunities (35 percent say the effect is "a lot") and 38 percent of those with Basic skills agree—while 96 percent of those who are Proficient feel no such limitation.

Those concerned about civic and political participation in our democracy may find it of interest that while more than 80 percent of the Proficient claimed to have voted in the 2000 election, just over half of Below Basic adults said they had done so—and from what we know, both groups were probably exaggerating. Fewer than one in five Below Basic adults say they ever do volunteer work versus nearly three in five of the Proficient.

Over and above the impact of literacy skills on these adults' own economic lives, their skill levels have a large effect on their children as well. For example, 41 percent of Below Basic skills adults with children under age eight say they did not read at all to their children in the previous week, compared with just 14 percent of the Proficient. And while 12 percent of those with Below Basic capabilities reported that their children aged three to five knew the letters of the alphabet, 31 percent of the Proficient adults' children had gained that skill. Nor do those differences end when school starts. A quarter of Below Basic adults never help their children with their homework, compared with just 8 percent of the Proficient. Not surprisingly, only 60 percent of the Below Basic skills folks often saw their children reading—compared with 90 percent of the Proficient.

No more statistics for a while. We've given you all these dreary numbers—and there are plenty more where these come from!—to bring home a conclusion we think is fundamental to any honest discussion about where we are and where we are going: American schools have made virtually no progress on improving student reading skills for the past thirty-five years, a state of affairs for which adults and society as a whole are paying a very high price. No wonder we seem to be overtaken by other countries in the new globally competitive economy. We need nothing short of a revolution in our expectations about how well our schools need to teach our children to read and write—as well as some real results.

To their credit, most schools and educators know the problem is huge, and many are really grappling with it. We don't want to give the impression that we think teaching reading and writing is a simple matter, or that transforming flat reading scores for millions of students is subject to an easy fix. A tremendous amount of current research is under way about how reading skills emerge and can be taught, and about how various forms of instruction help (or don't), and about how to intervene when children struggle. Unlike speech, which comes fairly easily to most children without any instruction, reading is not a natural activity. We know that for many people—younger and older— learning to read is far more of a battle than for those who traditionally have advanced readily in school.

As educators and scientists have worked on the problem of reading and teaching reading, two rival schools of thought and pedagogy have emerged. One stresses phonics, "the science of sound," and emphasizes how letters, individually and in combinations, both represent and in turn create sounds. There's a good bit of research showing that children's ability to understand how spoken words can be taken apart into abstract sounds (a skill called "phonemic awareness") is a key building block for successful reading. That's why children benefit from rhymes and other exercises that teach them how to create words from individual sounds and what the patterns are among those sounds. Advocates of phonics approaches highlight the need for children to develop the basics of sounding words out before advancing to higher-level reading.

The competing school stresses a "whole language" approach to reading and generally puts more of an emphasis on meaning in texts and on student motivation in learning to read. Whole language methods downplay the mechanical elements of sounding out words in favor of developing sight recognition of words as well as appreciating texts as a whole. They focus on meaning at every level: meaning (versus proper sound) of single words and meaning of entire sections of text. Whole language proponents believe that children must become engaged with reading, eager to find the meaning that will draw them into reading more and better. They point to many studies that show a high correlation between reading skills and the time students spend reading on their own, and argue that good readers must have developed their own motivation to read.

There's been something of a battle between these two schools for much of the past twenty-five years. Although honest debate—and occasional ideological mudslinging—continues, much of the dust has now cleared, and most educators have settled on a balanced approach. They see the need for strong instruction, and for aggressive remediation where needed, in phonics. They also see the need for young readers to see meaning in texts and to gain motivation as readers. So they have children practice reading in small groups, practice reading out loud, engage in guided reading, and ultimately engage in independent reading. While there remains much to learn about what works best and how to teach students to read and to write most effectively, teachers now have a number of proven techniques and a variety of first-rate, off-the-shelf materials and reading programs available to help children with a wide range of learning styles and aptitudes strive to reach success. As we illustrate by visits to some new day schools, one of the principal advantages of expanding learning time for students is the opportunity to deploy different strategies more extensively and on a more individualized basis.

Literacy in Action: Jacob Hiatt Magnet School

Tony Caputo was explaining how he organized the Jacob Hiatt Magnet School in Worcester, Massachusetts, which he founded. "I felt school should be a place where, when you went into the teachers' room, there wasn't a lot of bitching and moaning about what was wrong, but a lot of talk about what you could be doing for the education of the kids," he began. "I'd spent a lot of time with teachers in their room listening to what they said. Inevitably when they got to talking about their practice, what you always heard was, 'if I only had another half hour when I could meet with this group, if I only had a little bit more time, I could have done this. If I only had a little bit more time.' I heard this all the time." So when he launched the school fifteen years ago as a public, non-exam, lottery-admission magnet elementary school whose student body demographics reflected the city's—now about 68 percent African American and Latino—Mr. C (as everyone calls him around the school even though he's now retired) asked the school board for an extra fifty minutes in the day.

"I came the second year," said Principal Patricia Gaudette. "It felt like a private school, with the high standards, extra subject matter, the full day. We were pioneers. Every new school after us was an extended day school—there were about ten in the city."

Patty Genese has taught at Hiatt for fourteen years, loves her job, and loves her school. "We have a common purpose here," she explained, "a climate of high expectations for our students and ourselves. We have lots of professional development and a special professional development coordinator." Hiatt teachers have learned "portfolio assessment," using a variety of students' work to track their progress. "We don't look at one test," she explained. "We look at the development of the child from beginning to end, rather than use just one standardized assessment." In 2001, Hiatt joined a select company as it became a National Blue Ribbon School, one of 266 nationwide so honored that year.

When the bottom fell out of the Massachusetts economy as the Internet bubble burst and state and local budgets plummeted in 2003, Hiatt, along with other Worcester schools, faced dreadful cutbacks. "We lost the extended day, went back to six hours, and lost twenty-four staff people out of sixty-five in a four-year period," said Caputo. Test scores declined, and staff morale suffered. "It freaked a lot of people out," said Genese. So when the Massachusetts Expanded Learning Time Initiative began, offering the chance for the new school day (which for them expanded upon an older ideal, one they'd lost), Caputo and his team of administrators eagerly applied. This time round, with the added resource of nearly two more hours, Hiatt's leadership chose to redesign the entire day and put their highest priority on a major increase in the amount and quality of time spent on literacy.

This choice—to spend significantly more time on reading and writing instruction—is one of the true hallmarks of new day schools across the country. We've found it in every school we describe in this book, as well as in every new day school we've ever heard of. In school systems looking for turnarounds in low-performing schools, the primary new school day strategy is to increase the amount of instructional time in the targeted subjects of literacy and math.

In Miami-Dade's School Improvement Zone, which we visited in the fall of 2007, the Superintendent's Office required all students in need of remediation—90 percent of students in Miami Edison High School, for example—to take an extra hour of math or reading instruction. Most of the new time got used for special intervention programs, such as the "Reading Plus" and "Read 180" curriculum for high schools, explained District Supervisor Diana Taub when we visited early in the 2007–2008 school year. Teachers agreed to spend extra time—fifty-six hours' worth—in professional development focused on using these new instructional strategies, including how to make best use of the Zone-wide "block schedules"—ninety-minute periods devoted to each academic subject. This was "very important, so that teachers felt the moral support was there, and they didn't feel out on their own, thinking 'now what?'"

Assistant Zone Superintendent Blanca Valle explained further. "What happens in extended time [she means the new eighth period of the day], doesn't look like another reading class; we don't use the same strategies. Student weaknesses are targeted, and teachers make the connection between those and the regular curriculum. These are highly interactive discussions."

We start here because the Miami-Dade turnaround initiative, the School Improvement Zone, is the simplest, most straightforward use of more time. The district office identifies the schools struggling the most, in which students score the lowest on the statewide tests, and figures out how to give them committed teachers and principals and one additional period in the school day, in this case an hour. The district purchases high-quality, proven curriculum packages along with the necessary equipment, and it gives the teachers extensive and focused professional development in how to use the new packages. It's in some ways a limited strategy, but it's also one that can provide genuine results, and it's working in Miami. The specific gains in terms of reading proficiency are modest but real.

While in much of this book we describe schools that use more time in a more varied manner, it's important to point out here that increasing numbers of districts all over the country are likely to try turnaround efforts. Especially for big-city systems with large numbers of low-performing schools, turnarounds are likely to be seen more and more as a core strategy for meeting NCLB standards. The Miami-Dade example demonstrates than even without customizing an expanded school day, turnaround initiatives relying on increased time can have real results.

On the other end of the spectrum, we have the individualized example of Hiatt Magnet School, where, according to Tony Caputo, "we started with the premise that we were accountable for the testing and achievement of kids in the school. We looked at our testing in the area of literacy and decided we needed to address it, especially because of our bilingual population. We felt the best way to achieve that was not only to increase the amount of time devoted to literacy but to make it uninterrupted time."

"Why was uninterrupted time so important?" we wondered. "Don't young kids get bored in a long block with no interruptions?"

"From an educational perspective," he said, "it's not only increased time, it's uninterrupted time that matters." Specialists such as the occupational therapy teacher or the speech teacher "were always pulling kids out" of the classroom. Teachers frequently complained that the time they could devote to literacy was chopped up. "So we looked at that. We figured if we're going to have 30 percent more time, we'll have uninterrupted time to teach literacy, and say to all the others, 'You can't touch the kids.' We told them, 'You can still have the last six hours of the day. You just can't start teaching till ten. But if you do opt into working the time between eight and ten in the morning, you become a reading teacher. If you teach art, music, physical education—it doesn't matter, between eight and ten, you're a reading teacher. You'll work with another teacher and teach reading.'" That way, most classrooms got two teachers during a two-hour literacy block.

Two hours of reading? We can almost hear you groan. "This is *elementary school,* for goodness' sake! How can first graders take a two-hour, uninterrupted block of anything?" That's why we visited Kim Langhill's first-grade reading class one Tuesday morning, just two days before the end of the 2006–2007 school year. We figured the kids would be bouncing off the walls, barely able to concentrate.

Instead, as we walk in, we see the thirtyish live wire of a teacher running what looks like a math class. "How many toes on seven people?" Hands shoot up. "Right, Laurie. You can start by counting your own toes. You know you have five on one foot, five plus five . . . right, ten. Now, what do you need to do?" More hands, as children lift out of their seats to answer. As they do so she nods, smiles, reinforces, mouths the numbers in an exaggerated manner as she counts with them up to seventy, and back down again, showing them that counting toes is counting by tens. She holds up a book showing this, asks them to look in their books.

We're confused. How is this a literacy block? Caputo leans over and says, softly, "Reading is everything. English language arts (ELA in the language of schools, a term we use a lot in what follows) is not strictly reading, since there's language in everything. There's lots of cross-curriculum work in the ELA period, like here, connecting math to reading. All the math curricula, Chicago Math, Everyday Math, if you even look at the MCAS [the statewide Massachusetts Comprehensive Assessment System], the math section is probably 60 percent reading."

The literacy block, in other words, doesn't stick the kids into a basal reader for two hours. They do lots of different things throughout the period: some guided reading—with the teacher, that is—in groups, some writing, some math, some social studies, and some days even science, using reading to tie the whole curriculum together.

Langhill follows a list she has on the board for the block, an eight-point program that begins with a conversation journal and then moves on to math boxes, then a math message.

Once she's done with the math message, which appears to be about counting by tens, she gives an assignment—she wants four "super-sentences" about what each child did before going to bed the previous night. What's a super-sentence?

"Writers pick the best writing words," she explains to the class. They don't just say, "I walk to bed. What's another word you can use? Brianna?"

"I walked as slow as a tortoise," says Brianna.

"I walked as slow as molasses," chimes in another student.

"Joshua?"

"I walked to bed really slow like a snail."

"Perfect! Those are things I can see in my head! I want you to think about just the right words so I can see in my head, to get me there with you."

"I walked as slow as the sand coming down. . . . "

She screws her face into a question, then gets it, "Oh, like in an hourglass?" The boy nods.

"I walked to bed as slow as a slug," says another. She repeats it, drawing out "slow as a slug," demonstrating the alliteration.

"I walked to bed drowsy."

More follow, and now that she's shown them "super-sentences," she turns the class loose to work on coming up with four on the same subject. "You can talk at your table. That's what your whispers are for. Off you go!"

There's so much going on here it takes hours to unpack it all. In this super-sentence discussion, maybe ten minutes long, she got just about every child to come up with a sample sentence. She had plenty of time, in other words, to make sure the whole class understood the assignment. This is what we mean by teachers and students alike getting "more time on task." At the same time, she was combining reading lessons with writing. She wanted students to say sentences, write them, and read them.

She turns to us: "Now I call reading groups back. They're at different levels, and the groups change. They're used to the groups changing every couple of weeks. They know if I call 'Sharita's group,' it might be different this week." Here we see, in action, a key advantage of the expanded school day: it allows teachers to institutionalize instruction at different skill levels for the wide range of students in just about any public school classroom.

She bounces to the back of the room, calls out for a group, and soon she's on the rug, kneeling down in front of five first graders, all of whom have their books open. She has them read in turn, while those not reading follow along. "Whenever the animals got together to talk . . . he has stomped on my house again." The boy is stuck on a word, turns to a classmate for help, gets it, moves on. Gets stuck again, and she helps him sound it out. But he says it very faintly, and she's on it: "This time I want you to push it out," which he does, and her eyes light up. Another student picks up the story and reads it fluently—but the pencil sharpener has been going loudly for a couple of minutes now not far away, and one boy's attention is wandering. (And why not?) She announces to the group at the sharpener, "If you need a sharp pencil, get it off the other desk," then turns to her reading group.

"OK, now, did Bear eat all the apples?"

They all nod vigorously. She stops them. "I know. You gotta prove it. I want to know for sure. Look up at me when you find the proof." She sits, kneeling, expectantly, radiating energy. Darren catches her eye, she flashes a smile. "Did he eat all the apples?" "Yes." "How do you know he ate them all—can you prove it?"

"Because it says . . ." He starts reading about the house, and she stops him: "Can you go just to the apple part?"

"Bear climbed up to get the apples," he reads.

"You're proving that he ate apples, but I want to know is, did he eat them all?" She holds off two others, focusing on the slightly slower boy. He looks in the book, the others wait patiently, but in the growing silence he's getting embarrassed.

She helps out. "Did you lose it?" He nods.

"Did he eat them all, Jared? How do you know?"

Jared zeroes in on the sentence. "He ate every one."

"So did he eat them all?" Nods all around.

"Yes, he did, and there's the proof! You know what I noticed that Darren did?" she then asks the group. "When I asked the question, he was looking through the page, looking for the word 'apples.' We've talked about that, how to look for the word. You don't have to read every single word to answer the question. OK, let's go to the next page. Allllll right! What happened *here*?"

We've mentioned that one of the main reasons the ELT Initiative is achieving such remarkable results is that it allows many well-known and tested reading strategies and techniques to be incorporated into the classroom for the first time. One example, illustrated right here, is the explicit strategy for going back to review a text. Sometimes skeptics worry that "more time on reading" means that teachers say the same thing over and over, or that students just have more time to read silently. Here we see the teacher using one of these new techniques, skimming the text for word clues, working to develop comprehension of the text. She's teaching her little group how to find information from a passage without rereading the whole thing.

Suddenly she sings out, "Miguel, you've got a warning because I can hear you talking all the way back here. That's not a whisper voice."

Back to the group: "He stepped on the house," says Jared. "OK, can you prove that?"

Reading the passage, Jared proves it again.

"Perfect. That's what I want you to do. OK, really nice job."

She's finished with this group, so we get to ask the kids some questions. "Which do you like more, being a reader or a writer?"

"What I like is being a writer."

"Why?"

"I like revising."

"Revising? Really?"

"Yeah, seeing if the words are spelled right or if I need to put some sentences somewhere else. My last book, I wrote about me and beginning first grade." We're thinking "my *last* book"?

"You were crying at first, right?" Langhill prompts.

"Yes, I was crying and I changed, and tried to be brave."

"Who helped you be brave?"

"Mommy and daddy."

"That was really great about the beginning of the year. Brianna, what'd you write about?"

"I wrote about when I went to my uncle Eduardo's wedding in Honduras. I got to see Grampy. I wrapped my arms around him."

It turns out the kids all write books, and then pick out the ones they like the best, and publish them, and go on "book tours" to the local hospital and around the school itself. They have "author's teas," with a special chair for the author, and tea and cookies.

This little exchange owes a good bit to some important changes that emerged in the past ten or fifteen years, as educators began to focus on the fact that it wasn't only reading that was in trouble—writing seemed to be in even worse trouble. After all, multiple-choice or standardized tests didn't do much to teach or evaluate student writing, which takes a lot of time, both for the child to learn how to do and to practice, and for the teacher to review. Educators have developed a whole range of new teaching techniques, and many students at new day schools—and others, to be fair—are taking pride in themselves as writers. Like this class, they are doing first drafts, revisions, and then publishing their best work so they have something to show around.

The SAT recently launched a writing section, and some statewide school tests, like the MCAS, are now assessing writing as well. As a result, more schools are putting more of a premium on writing instruction, which bodes well for the future of student writing skills. But perhaps more than any other single classroom activity, writing takes more time than most teachers and students can fit into a standard school schedule.

The little guided-reading group went back to their tables and picked up on their sentences, while Langhill brought another group back. All this took place in fifteen minutes, and all the children received genuinely individual attention, time in a group reading project, practice in reading comprehension, and five minutes talking confidently about themselves—and their writing—with outsiders.

Since it all flowed together so seamlessly, we had to look closely after the fact to see what this long block made possible. Langhill was able to give individual attention to just about every kid in the class that day—and we saw at least ten different activities during the hundred minutes or so that we were there. Everything was in motion, but when she needed to stop and focus on one group of kids, or just one child, or just one concept, she could and did.

Even though she kneels behind a low barrier to be on the rug with her group, the other kids, "almost second graders," she was calling them, seem thoroughly engaged in their work and unconcerned about whether the teacher has an eye on them or not. They move around the classroom; they amble back up to the board; they talk to each other; they work independently; they ask for help. Kids are writing their super-sentences. "Before I went to bed I ate my grapes," Jared says, then explains, "We're actually writing about what we did last night."

We've been looking at some of these super-sentences on paper, so we feel we have to ask about spelling. "We have separate conferences where we edit," Langhill says. "I use address labels, and put them over misspelled words, punctuation mistakes. My number one goal is to get them to focus on the joy of writing and beauty of writing, and so I don't want to stifle them by stressing about spelling. They are held accountable in spelling check, and on word wall, after we have them for the week, and if it's something that's going to be published on our bulletin board, they are responsible for it. Before they come to a conference, they check the word wall.

"There's a time and place for the more formalized writing; this is more free write, expression, word choice, luscious language; they do clearly know what more formal writing is. I kind of take it as a separate entity, and hope that 85 percent filters into their everyday writing so it's clearer to people that don't teach first grade. I do want it to be writing that the rest of the world can read, but I don't want them stress out so much about spelling that they're not writing from the heart. We don't formally publish every single thing they write." She breaks off, sees the period's almost over. "OK, almost second graders. We have seven or ten minutes left. Think about what you need to finish. Think about getting a sticker on your calendar!"

Caputo puts the literacy block in context. "What's the teacher going to do with the extra time? What does it allow teachers to do? How does it change what teachers are able to do in the classroom? It's what we just saw. Being able to sit down and do guided reading with four or five kids at a time, to set up a classroom management program where other kids know exactly what to do, while she sits down with one small group of kids. This is a systematic program with a nice flow to it."

READING IN THE ZONE

Before leaving Miami we visited a school in the Improvement Zone, the Jose de Diego Middle School near Little Havana, and began in a seventh-grade Read 180 classroom.

Read 180 is a combination of computer-assisted learning with whole-group and small-group instruction (led by a teacher) and independent reading of texts chosen carefully to be of interest to adolescents and "leveled" to students' reading ability. The entire program is designed for the older struggling reader. It uses computer technology to continuously monitor and adjust to individual students.

The curriculum is based on a ninety-minute block: twenty minutes of whole-group instruction; then three twenty-minute rotations: independent reading time with specific leveled books; small-group instruction with the teacher; then work on the computer, as students read and listen to themselves and the software; and a final ten minutes for wrap-up as a group. When we walked in, we immediately recognized the curriculum. In this well-organized classroom, we saw one group doing independent reading, another guided-reading group working with the teacher, and a third group on computers, with headphones, reading aloud softly while they answered questions based on what they'd just read. All the students were engaged in active reading instruction.

The Read 180 Web site explains why the curriculum needs ninety minutes, a block rarely available in the conventional school schedule. "The research is clear. We must invest sufficient time for instruction for students who are at risk of failure. Studies have conclusively shown that when schools implement and follow the ninety-minute instructional model, significant gains can be expected after one to two years of program participation." And in fact, 57 percent of all the students in middle and high schools showed midyear gains in 2006–2007 due to Reading 180. Jose de Diego had the second highest percentage in the Zone (of nineteen schools) of secondary students demonstrating Read 180 improvement: 73 percent.

Zone middle school reading scores not only improved markedly in the first two years—they also improved relative to statewide and overall district scores, thus beginning to close the achievement gap. It's worth remembering that the district chose these schools for a reason: the nearly 44,000 students (in twenty elementary, eleven middle, and eight senior high schools) had demonstrated extremely low academic performance for at least three years running. They had a long way to go in almost every category: school climate (as measured by disciplinary incidents), suspensions, attendance, and the grades assigned by the state of Florida.

We then visited Mrs. Cohen's seventh-grade Academic Improvement Period reading class. We sat down with Shonelle, Jessica, Desiree, and Allegra and asked about the play they'd just finished reading, and the girls couldn't stop interrupting each other to tell the story about a skinny boy who wanted to work out and get strong, and which girl he was going to pursue—which they thought was funny and true. They liked plays more than stories because "you can actually see it—it's different."

"I don't like to read," says Jessica. "I can only read something that I like. I like mysteries. This is a miracle that I read this. Normally when I read and I don't like a story my mind is like woooo. Once I finish I think 'What did I just read?' Last year we read this teen story, *Darkness before Dawn* [by Sharon Draper]. I can't believe I read two whole things like this—the biggest book I ever read!" Like a lot of teenage girls with their friends at the end of the day, she was so excited that she appeared to contradict herself. But look again. She's broadening her reading horizons beyond mysteries, reading new kinds of books, big books and teen books, and keeping her mind in them. There's no mystery here. She's also getting the time to read on her own as well as with her group: in other words, she's motivated and she has the time to practice—that's right, practice—her reading skills. She's even surprising herself, reading larger books, and her mind is wandering less.

She's an advertisement for whole language pedagogy, whose advocates argue that kids need lots of opportunities to read in circumstances where they can be successful. After all, struggling readers get little pleasure out of reading; the point is for children to enjoy what they read, so they'll come back for more. Listen to Shonelle, who interrupted her friend. "I express my feelings when I read," she tells us. "I saw this book. I got so curious, so when we didn't read it in class, I wanted to check it out. Our

teacher checked it out for us. And then we could read it in class."
She launches into the details of the story. She's made the connection between her own self-expression and the books she reads—if
the connection holds, she'll be reading her entire life.

"So what's cool about this school?" we ask.

They tumble over each other to answer: "It's fun! It's cool!
We have extra time to learn. It's like a free period. Each is ninety
minutes, but the time goes fast."

There it is. When kids are engaged, the time goes fast; when
they're not, even a fifty-minute period feels like an eternity. What
no one is saying here, though, is that by staying in school longer,
these girls are getting the chance to do something—read books
with fellow students and a teacher—that just wouldn't happen if
they weren't in school. Lots of them live in homes with few or no
books, with parents who don't read much, in smallish houses and
apartments where TVs are often on. How, without this period,
would these girls get the encouragement to read that they do
now in Miami's Improvement Zone?

At KIPP Academy, Houston, they build in a half-hour of free
reading at the end of each day, in books that kids pick out themselves. As Mike Feinberg points out, "Our kids are not going
home to read independently." The implication? "We've got to do
it here."

At Roxbury Preparatory Charter School, a middle school in
Boston (which we tell you much more about in the next chapter),
kids always have a "Drop Everything And Read" book—known as
a DEAR book—that they've chosen themselves. The technique
gets them reading lots and lots of books. "Reading is hard," says
eighth grader Sherise, when we ask her about her DEAR book,
"but I like stories."

Mrs. Cohen in Miami gets it, too:

"Before the Improvement Zone, where would these kids be?"
she asks? "Out the door at 3:40. Now they say, 'we're going to
another enrichment class!'"

"Does more time help?" we ask.

"Absolutely!"

What about parents?

"Parents don't complain."

"They like the longer time?" we press.

"I haven't heard anybody object."

EVEN YOUNGER READERS

Patty's Playground

Back in Worcester, before heading to pre-Kindergarten, we're invited outside to take a look at the playground—recess, we figured, with noisy games of four square. Instead, children are sitting in pairs all over the benches, the asphalt, climbing apparatus, everywhere, and they're reading—together. Even odder, the pairs are mismatched, one kid is much older than the other. "We call it Patty's Playground," says the principal. "We pair up class to class, second grade with sixth, first with fifth, and they read to each other back and forth, for about forty-five minutes. It's like a book marathon; they can go through three books in a period."

"And sixth graders are nice to the little ones?"

"Oh, our sixth graders are so sweet: we have the best kids: thoughtful, kind, helpful. Listening to one of the older kids you hear, 'this is what you have to do, read like this.' And the younger kids will say, looking at the older ones, 'she's a great reader!' And she's thinking, 'I want to be like that.' So you see we've got a role model, mentoring situation." Patty's playground takes place inside the literacy block, "and it's something we lost when we lost the extended day," says Caputo, "when we ran out of time. We had to cram math and ELA and social studies and science into x number of minutes and had time for nothing else in the day.

Pre-K is half-day at the Hiatt School, and Ann McPartland is deep inside her own literacy block, helping four-year-olds recognize and sound out letters and little words. They get it, and she starts on little sentences too. "The gum is in the bag." "I was wet." She gets her kids to answer the question, "Why are vowels important?"

"What difference has the expanded school day meant?" we ask her.

"My day is longer, almost forty-five minutes per session; what it has given me is the chance to do a nice group time with the kids. I also get to add in free time, and can go around to other centers in the classroom. I take kids into small groups reiterating what we've done in large groups. It's given me enough time. I was so rushed before; when we lost the extended day and went down to six hours, it was extremely rushed. I couldn't get in everything the kids would benefit from.

"Look, we're studying Vincent van Gogh right now, they really get it, they're getting to do the sunflowers, they're doing 'Starry Night.'" *Starry Night?* We turned to each other. We didn't even know the painting *existed* till high school or college.

She sees our skeptical looks. "Yes, They're painting a picture of 'Starry Night.' We add to it. Lights are on in the houses. We did the story of 'The Yellow House' [we had to look up the story, having thought we knew something about Van Gogh], and they can name some other paintings. I never had enough time to add this stuff in. I know it sounds like a lot, but it's not too much for kids. Their energy level is unbelievable as long as you have enough free play and let them talk."

"So it's not exhausting for them to go to school longer?".

"Kids are going to be up during the day anyplace. When I worked in a nursery school, we used to do full day. If you had a child at home, you'd set the day up, and we'd do the same thing in school. If you have enough time for active play, quiet play, rest if needed, no, it shouldn't affect what they're doing; because you're doing the same thing as you would at home or in a small child care center. It's all in setting up the day."

She adds, "I share what I do with the parents. I do portfolio assessments, in September, in the middle of the year, and I teach off the assessments. But I individualize with each kid."

Broader Lessons

The experience at Hiatt suggests that when teachers have significantly more time in the classroom, the need for taking sides between phonics and whole language approaches simply dissolves. McPartland does phonics instruction in pre-Kindergarten, getting children to recognize letters and the sounds they make, and how they fit together into words. A grade later, Kim Langhill has a class full of writers publishing books, talking about "luscious language," going on book tours, and starring at author's teas. The two systems of reading instruction coexist smoothly when there's enough time for both.

Increasingly, too, literacy specialists are arguing that children achieve greater reading and writing fluency when their explicit "literacy" lessons are reinforced throughout the curriculum: in math class as well as science and social studies. That's what happens in Kim Langhill's class; it's what happens in Jennifer Spencer's math class at Roxbury Prep, as the teacher asks a student, "Can you put it in a sentence? Yes, now answer the question with a complete sentence, using a proportion to solve the problem." That's what the foundational nature of literacy really means.

At Roxbury Prep, reading causes deep concern for several reasons. Among high-performing urban middle schools, reading is *the* question. "Our students love math and hate reading," says co-director Josh Phillips. "We're killing the suburbs on math, not on English," says his co-director Dana Lehman. The scary nationwide statistic is that 80 percent of students who aren't proficient readers by eighth grade will never be proficient readers. Third-grade reading levels predict ninth-grade reading levels. And as Phillips insists, "Reading is life." No wonder each student has two language arts classes per day.

Whatever they're doing about their concern seems to be paying off, at least some. In the 2007 MCAS, their English language arts scores showed real single-year gains in grade 7, in which 86 percent of their students scored either Advanced or Proficient (an increase of 12 percent over 2006), and grade 8 (92 percent in the top two tiers). The percentage of eighth graders scoring Proficient doubled from 2006.

It is not enough for students learning a skill to learn how to do something once and then move on. Since so much of reading, writing, and mathematics, as well as music, art, and athletics, depends on mastery of particular skills to make the next step come more easily, it ought to be clear that students need time to practice what they learn.

Take Ann McPartland's pre-Kindergarten class at the Hiatt School, the same day we visited the first-grade class. She was going through the entire alphabet with the children, all in a semicircle at the front of the room. She had already gone through the alphabet, in pieces, then all at a time, dozens of times during the school year, but she knew just how much practice it takes to truly absorb and master a new level of learning.

Consider the amount of practice a first-rate basketball or tennis player gives to numerous points of the game. Basketball players will shoot hundreds of foul shots a day in order to develop rhythm and consistency and memory and skill—so that these do not need to be rediscovered in the middle of a game when the team needs the points. Similarly, tennis players will practice hitting cross-court backhands into a very small area of the court for hours on end—all in preparation for the match situation, when the shot looks effortless. Musicians practice, actors practice, writers practice. Practice may not make perfect, but it does help anyone learning a new skill get better at using it. It also takes time, one of the most important reasons the new school day offers such far-reaching educational opportunity to American schoolchildren.

In the first year of the ELT Initiative, at ten schools across Massachusetts, overall English language arts gains were extremely impressive and promising. The percentage of students reaching the Proficient level on the MCAS jumped 39 percent above the previous five-year average. In just the first year of the long-term battle to close the achievement gap, the ten ELT schools (whose combined poverty rate is 75 percent) narrowed that gap by about 40 percent.

Researchers will want to see years of data to make sure such changes are genuine as well as ongoing. And while these ten schools employed a broad variety of approaches to using the new school day, it remains to be seen whether such extraordinary gains can be achieved and sustained at dozens of schools. On the other hand, new day schools may well improve their use of the expanded day, and gains achieved in the first year may start students at a higher level the following year and lead to even greater cumulative improvements. In other words, first-year English language arts gains are so exciting and promising that they fuel our confidence that the new school day is going to deliver on its promise in Massachusetts. It's already delivering in hundreds of schools around the country—why should we be surprised?

3

"MISS SPENCER, CAN I HAVE TUTORING?"
How the New School Day Adds Up for Math

The pigtailed eighth grader smiled a little nervously, but her answers came back just as fast as the questions.

What's your favorite subject, Keisha?

—Math! (She laughs.)

Why?

—'Cause math is so easy!

Easy? What's your favorite number?

—Nineteen [no hesitation].

Why?

—'Cause it's prime.

What makes a prime?

—Only divisible by one and itself!

What's the next one?

—Twenty-three.

And the next?

—Twenty-nine.

What about twenty-seven?

—Not prime. [A look: *Thought you knew stuff!*]

Why not?

—Divisible by three and nine! [Triumphant smile.]

This exchange took twenty seconds. We looked at each other, incredulous. We'd heard the stories, but we also knew the research on girls and math, especially the well-known data that so many girls turn off to math and science right at puberty. What was going on here?

The answer was Keisha's school, Roxbury Preparatory Charter School, known as Roxbury Prep, the highest-performing urban middle school in Massachusetts, whose 100 percent African American and Latino eighth graders posted the single highest math scores of any school in the state in 2007. Four years earlier, in different schools, more than four in ten of these same students had failed the fourth-grade test.

As the world has become more scientifically and technologically complex over the past couple of generations, the need for mathematical literacy has increased dramatically. Unfortunately, American math education has remained the prisoner of a long-running war between traditionalists (who stress fundamental facts and skills) and those promoting different versions of "whole math" or "new math," who push for more open student exploration. Both swings of the pendulum have failed American schoolchildren, who score further below their peers in other countries the longer they stay in school, no matter which philosophical combatant is temporarily ascendant.

Test Yourself

The following question appears on the NAEP test for twelfth graders:

In a school fundraiser, 10 students in class A sold an average (arithmetic mean) of 4 boxes of cookies. In class B, 15 students sold an average of 9 boxes. What was the average number of boxes of cookies sold by the 25 students?

A)   13/25
B)   1
C)   6 ½
D)   7
E)   13 6/13

Just 24 percent of American twelfth graders answered the question correctly (D), 11 percent of African Americans, 15 percent of Hispanics.

Here's another:

A car costs $20,000. It decreases in value at the rate of 20 percent each year, based on the value at the beginning of that year. At the end of how many years will the value of the car first be less than half the cost?

Answer: ___ years. Justify your answer. Did you use a calculator?

26 percent got the correct answer of **four years** and showed their justification

THE THEORY

Founded in 2000, Roxbury Prep is jammed into most of a narrow corridor and about fifteen classrooms on the third floor of a nondescript brick building up a steep hill off Huntington Avenue, in the Mission Hill area of Boston. Comprising grades 6 through 8, its student body consists of two hundred black and Latino students, most from single-parent households; two-thirds poor enough to qualify for free or reduced-price lunches. Roxbury Prep has a mission: helping its graduates "gain admission to outstanding public and private college preparatory high schools." Fifty students graduated (completed eighth grade) in the class of 2006, and all fifty went on to high schools "with an explicitly college preparatory mission," including the nationally renowned independent schools Choate Rosemary Hall and Milton Academy, as well as two of the finest exam-selective public high schools in the country: Boston Latin School and Boston Latin Academy. Fully 70 percent of Roxbury Prep's first graduating class enrolled in college four years later. If these students had followed national expectations, just 23 percent of the black graduates and 20 percent of the Latinos would have graduated from high school and promptly enrolled in college.

Roxbury Prep succeeds for a variety of reasons: teachers want to work there; families choose to enter the lottery (except for siblings of current students, all students are admitted by lottery); the school insists on high academic standards, a strong work ethic, a dress code, and a strict conduct code—and the school day runs from 7:45—4:15 (eight and a half hours) Monday—Thursday. Fridays end at 1:20 for students, 4:20 for staff. Close to half the students stay in school until 5:30 or 6. "We don't push it," says co-director Josh Phillips, but the homework center is open till six, and teachers are usually around till six or seven. And a growing number of classes meet on Saturday.

When Roxbury Prep opened, students got one period of math a day, like most kids. Soon, teachers saw that they just couldn't get it done in that period. Why? Because, to put it bluntly, the children who began sixth grade at Roxbury Prep had dismal math skills. Teachers had to spend too much time helping kids catch up to grade level before they were able to take on sixth-grade math. So they quickly concluded, along with former Secretary of Education Richard Riley, "You need to provide the traditional basics, along with more challenging concepts, as well as the ability to problem solve, and to apply concepts in real-world settings." Rather than choose one side of the math wars (according to the school's published curriculum guide, *Calculated Success*) and "focus on procedures or focus on problem solving, at Roxbury Prep we stood at this fork in the trail and decided our students would not take one or the other, but rather both at the same time."

By the time the first class (of 2002) reached eighth grade, they were getting "double math" periods, and the school had begun a regime of two fifty-minute math periods per day for *everyone.* As *Calculated Success* puts it,

> Each day, students build their facility with numbers and pro-
> cedures, while also pushing their conceptual understanding
> of those procedures with more involved, multi-step problem-
> solving. With two math classes, students are also able to get
> more of the all-important *time* they need so that, even if they
> begin the year several years below grade level, by the end of the
> school year, their on-grade goals are within reach.

These goals are not achieved simply. Teachers begin the year with a detailed and personalized yearlong plan they name the "Curriculum Alignment Template," or CAT, which they've developed or revised in the weeks before school starts. Teachers analyze the latest versions of the high-stakes tests their students will have to take at the end of the year, identifying the skills required by these exams, grouping them into categories, and figuring out overall standards (say, "students will demonstrate proficiency with decimal multiplication without a calculator") to guide their teaching of specific skills (multiplying decimals by powers of ten, for example). They then develop a very broad range of assessment tools (quizzes, tests, homework, review drills, projects) designed to make sure they know just how well each student is doing toward mastering the skill in question—on any given day. Only at this point do teachers write their daily lesson plans, making sure that each day's class contributes to meeting the larger goals.

It almost sounds as though the "Prep" in Roxbury Prep stands for all the preparation teachers do before they even walk into the classroom. And this is just the beginning!

WHAT IT LOOKS LIKE IN PRACTICE

We probably shouldn't admit it, but we'd both wondered what our visit to Roxbury Prep would be like: a couple of middle-aged white guys, after all, in an inner-city public middle school. We knew teenagers. Would these kids even talk to us? How comfortable would we feel in the halls? How much jostling, how much testing of the newcomers would there be?

Instead, we encountered one of the politest, friendliest bunches of middle schoolers either of us had ever seen! They told stories, talked about themselves openly, shook our hands, asked us questions, and answered ours. They changed classes without a sound (one of the school's hallmarks), paid attention in class, raised hands eagerly to answer their teacher's questions, got down to work (known as a "Do Now") as soon as they sat down in class, and treated each other with respect.

We know what middle schools are like in most cities—this was simply astonishing. Afterward, we struggled for metaphors. Were the children like a garden whose fertile soil and parched plants had finally gotten the water they needed? Were they natural athletes who'd found the right coach? No, we concluded, they were simply children who were receiving the adult attention to their academic and character development they needed and deserved. Conventional wisdom—backed up by reams of research—has it that "middle school is hell." The teachers and children at Roxbury Prep have created a very different kind of middle school, the foundation of which is the new school schedule and day.

Now we were listening to three young women—Jennifer Spencer, Kathryn McCurdy, and Jami Therrien—all math teachers, all under thirty, all animated, interrupting each other to explain what they do and how they teach—and why Keisha (they all knew her immediately) liked math so much.

"You want to know what's the key? Look at the excitement on our faces; we're excited about math!" We told them our story about Keisha; Spencer was a little disappointed. "Oh, I wish she'd picked 0 or 1. We're doing lines, graphs, what happens when you graph a line that has a zero." She brightened. "How cool is that? Oh, yeah!"

"Look at us," she picked up, happily. "We're dorks. We definitely show our excitement about math—and it helps. Kids are so excited to learn new things."

We were joined by Jason Armstrong, a sixth-grade math teacher with a Harvard degree in music (he's a percussionist who teaches enrichment as well). "Look," he said, "When they arrive, there's a wide range in level of skill and attitude. Some are excited and want to make it to "exam schools," and some come in way below grade level and have struggled for years. We try to provide enough opportunities outside the regular classroom setting: lots of time with tutors, to build skills and confidence. If they don't get it, we don't make them move on. They come to tutoring, and school on Saturday. If they don't get it all in sixth grade, then they get it again in seventh. They're given the opportunity and support to be successful."

The secret to the Roxbury Prep miracle turns out not to be a secret at all. "Double math" works because the teachers are providing carefully coordinated math instruction for the same students, developing new skills (multiplying fractions, say) in one class one week, and practicing those skills (multiplying fractions in a range of problems) in the other class the following week. It also works because when the formal school day is over, teachers meet at 4:15 to discuss their students—and on Friday afternoons they often form "inquiry groups" to research ideas that might help their students learn better. And it works because the two teachers for each grade develop their CATs together and triangulate on their students, whom they both know very, very well.

"We teachers also spend a lot of time in conversation," says McCurdy. "Jen's class is more about problem solving. Mine is more pre-algebra. We spend a lot of time making sure there are as few inconsistencies as possible. What they learn here in my class carries over to other classes. We are reinforcing that. Students can't compartmentalize." In fact, *Calculated Success* describes how all the math teachers bring writing into their classrooms, so that learning to frame math problems and answers in complete sentences constantly reinforces what students learn in English classes.

When students fall behind or struggle with new concepts or problems, "I have three potential times during the day for tutoring," says McCurdy, "during computer class, gym, and enrichment time. I also have four tutoring slots per week, and I get a second shot at them in after-school time. Some are on a regular schedule, an additional fifty minutes to an hour every week."

"But there must be some stigma about tutoring," we insist. "Doesn't it force kids to admit they don't get something?"

She shakes her head vigorously. "No, the culture of the school is such, they know we want them to be academically successful, and they want to see themselves as successful academically as well. We use these clues in our speech, so tutoring becomes one of the tools they can use. There's a progression from sixth to eighth grade, in how they use tutoring. In sixth grade we make lists of students we need to see, whereas in seventh and eighth grade, they are more apt to ask us." Spencer breaks in: "One way Keisha shows how much she loves math, is 'Miss Spencer, can I have tutoring?'"

RESULTS

Some may bemoan the fact, but at this historical moment we cannot escape the reality that the proof of any educational theory or teaching strategy must lie, at least partly, in eating the pudding of standardized tests. So here's a look at Roxbury Prep's results. The Massachusetts test, the MCAS, has four outcome categories: Advanced, Proficient, Needs Improvement, and Failing. Seventy percent of the entering class of 2002 scored in one of the top three categories by the time they reached eighth grade. Then 98 percent of the next class passed, as did 100 percent of the one after that.

But face it. Passing grades on state tests, even though they are a 50/50 proposition statewide for students with Roxbury Prep's socioeconomic profile, should be nothing to crow about. While it's difficult to show what Proficient means in terms of math ability (since the MCAS category is based on how many questions get answered correctly), it's useful to look at a few sample questions, to get some idea of the material.

Two Questions from the 2006 Eighth-Grade MCAS

15. Sandra bought $2\frac{5}{8}$ pounds of apples. Which of the following shows $2\frac{5}{8}$ written in decimal notation?

A. 2.375
B. 2.580
C. 2.625
D. 2.875

Just 59 percent of students statewide answered this question correctly—as opposed to 100 percent of Roxbury Prep students.

36. Which of the following is equivalent to the expression below?

$$(-a)(b - c)$$

A. $-ab - c$
B. $-ab + c$
C. $-ab - ac$
D. $-ab + ac$

Just 32 percent of eighth graders statewide chose the correct answer; twice as many Roxbury Prep students (65 percent) did so.

As Roxbury Prep teachers improved and refined their approach to math—the double-math curriculum, supplemented by tutoring, extra help, the homework center, and a school atmosphere in which "it's cool to be smart"—they reached much more dramatic results, with kids that started, to put it mildly, far, far behind.

Take the class of 2004, Roxbury Prep's third graduating class. On their fourth-grade MCAS (two years before they came to Roxbury), just 11 percent scored Advanced or Proficient, fully a third failed, and the remaining 56 percent scored in the lowest passing category. Most of these students were likely to be headed for failure: persistent, cumulative, painful, consequential failure.

But after less than one full school year at Roxbury Prep, the tide had already begun to turn. The failure rate dropped two-thirds, from 33 percent to 10 percent. Those scoring Advanced or Proficient *quadrupled,* to 45 percent. By the end of eighth grade, 72 percent of the class scored in the top two categories, while none failed.

The change was even more dramatic in the class of 2006, *none* of whom had scored Advanced or Proficient in fourth grade, while 42 percent had failed and 58 percent barely passed. Two years later, the proportions had reversed: none were failing, 60 percent got to Advanced or Proficient, while 40 percent

Needed Improvement. By graduation time, two years later, 94 percent scored in the top two categories and none failed.

That year, 2006, on that test, Roxbury Prep students beat every school district in Massachusetts, ranking second out of the state's 458 schools. They scored Advanced or Proficient at the same rate as the celebrated Boston Latin School, and at a higher rate than students in the wealthy suburban school districts of Wellesley, Wayland, and Weston. (Just for the sake of a quick comparison, Wellesley's median annual family income, according to the 2000 census, was over $113,000, 2.7 times the national figure, while the percentage of adults in the town with at least a bachelor's degree was 77 percent, more than three times the national average.)

The most recent MCAS show continued gains. Fully 76 percent of Roxbury Prep sixth graders scored Advanced or Proficient, more than any group of sixth graders in the past four years. And the class of 2007, the eighth graders, took a giant leap from 62 percent Advanced or Proficient in 2006 all the way to 94 percent the following year—and more than half of these scored Advanced.

For the past few years, Roxbury Prep students have been taking the Secondary School Admissions Test (known as the SSAT), the type of test most private schools—including the most famous and selective, such as Philips Exeter, Andover, and Groton—require as part of the application process. The class of 2006 first took the SSAT as seventh graders, and scored in the 81st percentile in math; a year later the same students scored in the 90th percentile. It's hard to overstate the magnitude of this achievement. The middle-school students taking this test across the country (and the world) are applying to the most difficult schools to get into in the United States—already a high-achieving self-selected population. And a few dozen of Boston's black and Latino kids, predominantly from low-income, mostly single-parent homes and with just two years of a public middle school making use of the new school day, scored better than nine out of ten students on the math section of the exam.

In her own classroom, Jennifer Spencer is no dork. Tall and thin, she wears heels that make her taller, and her face turns serious. Class starts—all classes start—with a Do Now: kids start working immediately on warm-up math problems while she hovers from desk to desk, looking over homework. "No, I don't grade every one, but I do check and make sure it's there, and right," she had said earlier. "We also teach kids to see what they're not good at, and how to ask, 'What did I mess up with? What do I still need help on?' Everyone still needs help with something.

"Part of it's about adult attention," she had explained. "Most people believe that middle school students don't want to be with adults. We know that's wrong; they still want to be with adults, so we each have lunch once a week with students.

"Oh boy," she mutters now, "no homework. Oh boy."

Then to the board. She recaps the Do Now. "So what's the fraction for 28 percent? Austin says 7/25ths; do you agree? Hands?" All go up. "Disagree? Hands?" None go up. "Marvelous! Nice job!" She moves on to the next question, and the next. Lots of hands shoot up, and the pace is fast. The next answer is 30. A hand stays up, from the back, big kid, waving. We're thinking *troublemaker.* "What is it, Emmett?" "Thirty pencils!" "Right!" she calls out. "Not just thirty, gotta have the units too." Next question, there's an answer, but Emmett's hand is up again. "You disagree, Emmett? Really disagree?" She calls on him, he explains, and she congratulates him; she smiles for the first time. "Way to go, Emmett!"

Next stage: the mini-lesson starts. All about parts and wholes. "Ezra, talk a little louder. Pretend I'm ninety-five." Gets an answer, "Yes, awesome. Oh, you guys are *good.*" The next problem has to do with a comedian getting paid some portion of his salary before starting work. "Wouldn't that be great? Before you do any work? A check for $375? Whoo-hoo, that'd be great!" If the comedian gets 25 percent of the salary before he goes to work, how much does he get for the whole performance? They set up the equation, put it into fractions, then, "Emmett, nice job recognizing your mistake." They're looking for patterns. "Yes! You discovered my pattern. Yes!—Stop conversation please." (She slips this last in; no question about whether she means it, the side conversation stops, and the class moves on.) "Marcus, can you put the answer into a sentence?" "Yes, Jefferson earns $1,500 total for performing." "Now, is there another way we could have solved this?" She fixes her gaze on a student who's been messing with his notebook. "Can you stop organizing now, Daryl? I've been watching you for the last five minutes and I'm kind of done with it." She moves on.

She fills the time, combining review, new lesson, practice time, looking at the problem in a new way, working different angles, keeping focus, moving around. Kids are engaged, just about all of them, just about all the time. And they are fast.

"This is my favorite class," Latanya tells the visitor in a low tone while the rest of her eighth-grade classmates are solving homework problems.

"What about math before you came here?"

"In fifth grade," she remembers, "the teacher wrote on the board and I had to copy it over. I didn't get very good grades then. I never took math seriously."

"What happened when you came here?"

"I decided to take all my classes seriously. My brother came here first. They said I wouldn't make it because I talk a lot. [She grins.] So I decided to prove my brother wrong and I took my classes seriously."

"Did everything come easy or just math?"

"I'd say math. I discovered I like math. I would have to say that in elementary school I wasn't so focused that much. I didn't really understand. I didn't really ask questions. I didn't get the explanations that much. Maybe like a couple of times, but not like the majority of the time when I should have. It's different here.

"Here they explain it way more. And I guess here you can actually raise your hand and ask a question. Here I could say after sixth grade I just liked math."

"Teachers like it when you ask questions?"

"It's not like they make you, or tell you to put your hand up. But they like it when you show you're learning more. Yes, definitely."

"It's kind of challenging, learning stuff ahead," says eighth-grade Kalina, when we get a chance to talk to some students away from their teachers after school. "When you go to another school, you already know stuff. I went to shadow a student at a high school. When we got to math class, we were already past that stuff." Jessica breaks in, "My sister's in tenth grade, and she's doing the same stuff we're doing in pre-algebra!"

"Hi, my name is Randall," says the tall, thin eighth-grader, shaking our hands confidently. Think about the last time you shook hands with an eighth-grader, one who not only took your hand firmly but also looked you in the eye calmly as he did so.

"Well, Randall, what can you tell us about math here at Roxbury Prep?"

"Math class is fun sometimes. Both teachers make it easy for you to get the gist of it. They use scenarios that we're used to. Maybe going to the corner store and buying candy. Maybe stuff like we've heard in the news, moneywise, like America being a trillion dollars in debt. How tall would it be? As tall as the Sears Tower?"

"Where's the Sears Tower?"

"Chicago."

"What was math like before you came here?"

"We just did stuff from textbooks. I didn't like math in fifth grade. It was boring. It was bland; it wasn't really exciting to be in. I didn't feel like I wanted to come to school. And now I feel like I want to come to school because now I feel like I'm gonna learn something new.

"In these classrooms there's always something new I'm looking at, and you see other students' work, and that motivates you. They only post up work that's ninety and one hundred and that makes you want to do better yourself. The boards are overflowing. You want your work up there. Some of my work is up there, and you want more.

"We're learning stuff like, if you have a budget, how much can you spend? We've learned about interest, and bank accounts. Last year in history class we learned about managing money, and about growing up and maturity in the world." How many adults know how to read or create a budget, that basic document of economic and civic life? In the new school day, middle schoolers are learning math they will use the rest of their lives.

"I've grown up a lot here," Randall continues. "When was in sixth grade, I was frivolous. My actions were always based on fun, and now I think deeply and maturely about some of the decisions I make. We have something here called enrichment. I always used to pick sports, but now I pick things like maybe singing or the musical because maybe it could help me applying to high school, Boston Arts Academy. I've picked those kinds of enrichments. Maybe at the end during the spring, I might pick sports enrichment."

MASSACHUSETTS, MATH, AND EXPANDED LEARNING TIME

Helenann Civian has seen public education from a lot of different sides. A former math teacher, principal, and juvenile probation officer, she has also worked for the Bill and Melinda Gates Foundation consulting with schools starting "small learning communities" all over the country. Now she spends her days with teachers and principals in the Massachusetts ELT Initiative, helping them plan, launch, modify, and evaluate the new school day at schools that convert from the standard schedule. She's tough, opinionated, and utterly committed to public education.

"The exciting part is at the student level," she says. "I've seen it firsthand. Students are engaged now at the Kuss Middle School in Fall River." About six years ago, she was "very involved" in the Fall River public schools math assessment. The school was in jeopardy. "The teachers weren't talking to each other; there wasn't good leadership; there was absolute mayhem in the school. My recommendation to the state, honestly, was to just start from scratch." In fact, Kuss was the first school partially taken over by the state after being declared "chronically underperforming."

"Now there's a new principal who's embraced the new school day, who is using the extra time to have teachers talking to each other; there's more enrichment, more hands-on experience with mathematics—and the governor went to visit!"

"Because I was there before, I can compare," she says. "It's the same teachers, different leadership. I walk into a sunny place now, and let me tell you they didn't add new windows! It's just the culture of the school. So I ask the principal, 'Is it you?'

She says to me, 'Now, Helenann, I have the time to do what I need to do to make the school what it needs to be. Now I have the time!'"

Civian nods. "I've seen it. She provides her staff with the time and opportunity to build a collaborative culture in the building. They're an actual family now. Look," she says, "I want to tell you a story. There's one teacher there, a math teacher for years [she means decades], very traditional, older, never veered off, never did anything offbeat. This enrichment piece came along with the longer day, so the principal surveyed the staff and asked, 'What would you find interesting if you had the time to teach it?' Well, no one had ever asked her this question before, and she said she was very interested in weather, and would like to teach an enrichment program on weather. Now she's teaching this unbelievable weather program with kids, doing group work and projects, all these different techniques that she never used in her regular math class!"

She pauses, then adds, "My heart goes out to the math teachers."

"Why?" we ask. Because, she explains, the curriculum for many middle-school math teachers is the Connected Math Project, known as CMP. "It's a wonderful program if you do the lesson from beginning to end, but it takes ninety minutes. The last piece is the culminating piece of the lesson, the assessment piece, when the teacher gets real data about which students got it, and which didn't. That's what teachers never, ever had time to do, so it got cut out on behalf of making the lesson fit the available time. Since that piece was always missing, they always said CMP wasn't so good. Now it's totally different. They're getting to the end, and that culminating activity is now driving their entire instruction—and they're saying that it's a pretty impressive curriculum!"

"Plus there are all these extra benefits," she says. "Because of the time kids get out of school now, more parents are picking up their own kids. No matter what kids may tell you, they like being picked up." Exactly. Kids like adult attention; they like being picked up; they like having lunch with the teachers—they thrive when they get the right kind of attention. Communities like it too, since the standard schedule literally forces kids to hang around all afternoon, unsupervised, when it's easy to get into trouble. Civian is betting that this will make a difference. "[We'll see] an impact on the community at large, in terms of police records, suspensions. I used to be a probation officer, so I'm really interested in that data."

She's been through a lot of so-called reforms over the years. Some might even call them fads. How is the new school day different?

"In the beginning I might have said, 'the jury's out,' crossed my fingers, and hoped for the best. But now, when it's not even two years since we started this new expanded schedule, I'm totally persuaded that this is the linchpin issue—because I'm there on the ground level. I've seen schools transformed from September to March. It's all about how students are engaged. You can't capture this unless you go visit the schools, and go outside and talk to a parent. You get this sense of 'wow, this place is a place to be,' when before, they really weren't."

MATH IN THE ZONE

Now here's a look at math teaching in a different version of the new school day, this time in a big city public school once widely known as one of the worst schools in Miami-Dade County, Florida, in the poorest big city in the United States.

Jean Teal of Miami Edison has responsibility for one of the lowest-performing high schools in the entire state of Florida, and she is on a personal as well as professional mission. Her intense eloquence filled her office, and drew us to the edges of our seats. "I went to a public high school, Miami Northwestern Senior High. Back *then* it was in need of improvement. Since I was in AP classes, I was somewhat isolated from the population. All of our classes were in one wing of the building, so I only interacted with other AP students and teachers. Now it's in the Zone. I knew the location here, in the inner city. I know the most challenging high schools are low-performing. But I grew up here; my family still lives here. My first principalship was where I was a student, and then a teacher."

She knows how hard the work is and recruits teachers ready for a challenge. Her first year in the Zone, twenty-five of her teachers (out of just over a hundred) were brand new—only four were new this year. "Working in a low-performing high school is very difficult," she says. "Burnout is high. It's very demanding and challenging. Retention is key."

Miami-Dade didn't redesign the entire day for schools in the Zone. It added an extra period, so kids who need help get an extra class. Kids doing pretty well get an extra period of enrichment in addition to the two electives in the regular day, but "if I'm a ninth grade student, and scored 'level one' on math [the lowest]," explains Teal, "I get an additional period of math instead of an elective. If I score level one or two in ELA, I get English plus intensive reading, every single day." And a student who scores low on both loses one of the electives during the regular day, so as to have extra classes in reading and in math.

Miami-Dade made one of Roxbury Prep's choices, but tried a different tack. "We try to keep the same teacher linked to the class, so it's not a separation, just a continuation of instruction. The kids always get the same teacher, which is important, building on the same curriculum, with no break in the instruction. What better than to have that same teacher, using that data to drive instruction, who already knows the kid's strengths and weaknesses? Teachers prefer it because the kids see you every day. The kids don't like it because it restricts them from their electives: they can't take computers or chess or home ec until they score level three or above."

Scott Miller is one of those teachers. Lean, filled with energy, speaking with a slight southern accent that occasionally slides into preaching cadences, he moves constantly around his tenth-grade classroom. His outline for the day is on the board, so the students know what's coming. Point II is the "Fantastic Five." "I need to expose students to all five math strands," he says, "every day, every week: number sense, geometry, algebra, data analysis, and measurement."

He's acutely conscious of the FCAT, the Florida Comprehensive Assessment Test. He's given the kids a problem, strides around and through the jumbled desks—no straight rows here!—as they work. "Remember, time is a factor this year; we've got to get this down to three minutes. Remember, I'm not going to be there for the FCAT."

"Oh!" exclaims a girl happily.

He leans over quickly. "I see at least one right answer," he says. "Remember when you weren't getting any of that fantastic five? Now I see a few of them!" He walks them through a graph,

plotting a class's test scores. The fourteen students laugh, inter-
rupt, raise hands, answer questions, study—he's got them
hooked.

"Suppose they change the number? How might they change
it for the FCAT? Could they ask for mode? Mode is eighty. They
could ask for the range, right? What's that? Right—the difference
between the greatest and the least number." He discusses range
for a while. What does it mean? Is the class doing well? "How
could they change this problem without changing the graph?
Suppose the question was 'think, solve, explain?' If you just memorize your answer, is that going to help you?"

"If you understand concepts, you are going to do better on the
test. I don't like teaching to the test, but the reality is, you guys are
in this class, intensive math this year, because you didn't get to level
three last year. Do you want to be taking a tenth grade test in elev-
enth grade? No. Twelfth grade? Thirteenth grade? Do you want to
be in this class?" Somehow he's got their trust, and they're all on
the same side here. He gives them a problem and comes over to us.

"With most of our tenth graders," he says, "we do test prep
and then geometry; if you have two different teachers, they don't
retain concepts as well. My suggestion this year was to have one
teacher do both. I've seen a big improvement with colleagues'
doing the same thing. Some teachers didn't want to see the same
students every day. Students too. But it works much better to
see students every day, rather than every other day. Double math
is really good for everyone." He goes back to the kids.

"*When in doubt, write it out.* I'm going to say that so much that
you're going to wake up in the middle of the night in a cold sweat,
saying, 'When in doubt, write it out.'" He starts showing how to figure the area of a trapezoid. "Does it matter if we change the order?"

They chorus, "No!"

"No," he confirms. "Commutative property of addition." He
spies a kid drifting off, nails him: "You know, I got your parents
on speed dial, you know that? Not enough to give answers! You
gotta show how you got it!" He gets two kids to sit up, gets a
girl to give up her gum. Then, "I want B and A work from you.
I'm getting tired of C and D work. I work too hard in this class.
Remember we had that really good day last week where you did
really good? Let's double it up!"

He goes to collect homework. "'I wasn't here so I didn't finish it?' Now whose responsibility is it to finish the work? If I give you another day will it really make a difference? If a day will really make a difference, then you can take it home and give it to me tomorrow. If you don't give it to me tomorrow you will get a Z. Z is below an F.

"Don't complain, use your brain."

He gives new homework, calling it "home learning"—what an interesting riff on an old standard! "You can either copy the problems down, or I'm here after school, and you can come here. Get as much done now." He wants as much "home learning" done in class as possible. He talks about the class. "With average gain half would pass the test, with exceptional gain all would pass. My goal is 75 percent. You know," he says, "I taught the honor students last year: all 100 percent had passed the test, some with a minimal passing grade. It's critical even for those on the border that they all take both classes. But these only had one. Not having that second math class really hurt them. They were supposed to make a forty-nine-point gain, and only made a thirty-point gain. But the lowest level's gain last year (with double math) was over a hundred points." After a few minutes, he spies restlessness. "For those of you that finish, I've got our math calisthenics."

After class, he's done for the day. Except for homework tutoring, and maybe an enrichment class. Physically he's starting to drag, but his eyes stay lit. "The worst part about the school when I got here," he says, "was the culture of failure. I mean this was the lowest-performing school in the state. It was so bad that when we had the highest gains in the state, we were *still* the worst in the state. I'm a former social worker. When I tell people I work here I get one of two reactions. Either 'What did you do to the superintendent?' or they think there's something wrong with me. And here's what I say to the kids: 'You're not in a D school! You're not D kids! You're A kids, so let's show 'em what we can do!'"

Now, Scott Miller is using the new school day and double math and his energy and how much he cares for these tenth graders to pull them into achievement levels they didn't know they had in them. The new school day makes it possible.

4

BACK FROM EXILE

The Return of Science, History,
Languages, and Social Studies in the
New School Day

Science is back!

—SCIENCE TEACHER, MASSACHUSETTS ELT SCHOOL

W HEN WE BEGAN WRITING THIS book, we planned chapters on science and technology as well as on history, social studies, and foreign languages to show how the new school day matters to all of these academic subjects. But the more we thought about it, the more we became convinced that all of them are in pretty much the same boat. Reading, writing, and mathematics are at the core of the standards-based accountability movement, and as a result the amount of instructional time devoted to them has increased significantly over the past decade, while the time for other subjects in most public schools has diminished.

A wide range of federal and nonprofit organizations have been collecting data on this question. The U.S. Department of Education carries out a "Schools and Staffing Survey" that allows us to compare the amount of time spent on particular subjects in different years. Between the 1991–92 academic year and that of 2003–04, for example, the amount of time spent on reading and math instruction in grades 1–4 increased ninety-six minutes per week, nearly fifty-eight hours per year, while the amount spent on social studies and science decreased by forty-eight minutes, twenty-nine hours per year, over the same period.

The Council for Basic Education surveyed principals in four states—Maryland, New Mexico, Illinois, and New York—in 2004 to find out how their schools had changed since NCLB went into effect in 2002, producing a report chillingly titled "Academic Atrophy." In just two years the principals described substantial adjustments. Three-quarters said their schools had increased instructional time in reading, writing, and math. At the same time, 29 percent of elementary school principals overall, but 47 percent of those in "high minority" schools (more than 50 percent nonwhite, usually a majority African American and Latino) reported decreases in time for social studies, civics, and geography. Across the board, schools with majority nonwhite populations experienced the greatest decline in instructional time devoted to the arts, foreign languages, and social studies.

This ought not to be surprising. Since the achievement gap is real, and schools with larger African American and Latino populations are generally in poorer cities and neighborhoods and tend to perform less well on standards-based tests, it makes sense that they would increase the amount of instructional time devoted to reading, writing, and math. Nevertheless, these figures suggest an additional dimension of educational inequity. As the authors of "Academic Atrophy" argue, "Though we must certainly strive to close racial achievement gaps in mathematics and reading, we run the risk of substituting one form of inequity for another, ultimately denying our most vulnerable students the full liberal arts curriculum our most privileged youth receive almost as a matter of course."

As the Center on Education Policy (CEP) found in its annual, nationally representative survey of 349 school districts ("Choices, Changes and Challenges: Curriculum and Instruction in the NCLB Era," issued in July 2007), those that have increased time for English language arts and math have on average augmented ELA by 46 percent and math by 37 percent. The consequent decreases in other subjects or activities (social studies, science, art and music, PE, lunch, and recess) added up to nearly thirty minutes per day, a reduction of roughly 31 percent in the instructional time devoted to these areas since 2001–02, just before

NCLB went into effect. In 2006–07, districts reported that, on average, they "spent nearly three times as many minutes per week on English language arts (503 minutes)—the greatest share of time of any subject—as they did on social studies and science (178 minutes for each). Elementary schools spent nearly twice as many minutes per week on math (323)—the subject with the next greatest share of time—as on social studies or science. As soon as the district had at least one school "identified for improvement," these numbers zoomed even more wildly out of proportion, as ELA jumped another 65 minutes a week, paid for by decreases in social studies, science, art and music, PE, and recess.

The CEP survey clearly shows the differential impact of efforts to meet No Child Left Behind and state standards, particularly between elementary schools in high-performing districts (those with no schools identified as being in difficulty) and those in less successful districts. Less than a third of districts with no identified schools reduced time devoted to social studies; less than 25 percent trimmed science minutes, only 12 percent cut arts and music, and just 7 percent reduced PE. In more challenged districts, half decreased social studies, 43 percent cut science, 30 percent art and music, and 14 percent PE. Nor were all cuts equal. The districts that reduced everything but ELA and math also made the deepest cuts into the time allotted to these other subjects.

Again, the point is not to accuse school officials of choosing educational inequity or a thoughtlessly narrowed curriculum. It is rather to document what has been happening to public education since the advent of high-stakes testing, and to identify one of the greatest barriers to educational equity—the prison of the six-and-a-half-hour day. Faced with the reshaping of their instructional week, the CEP report found, just 9 percent of districts have expanded their elementary school day, for an average of a wholly insignificant eighteen minutes. The changes that really matter took place in, for instance, Ann Arundel County (Maryland), which cut twenty-three middle school art teachers in mid-2003; in one Oregon district that eliminated foreign language classes in grades 7–8 that same fall; while Providence, Rhode Island, simply did away with elementary-level science and technology enrichment classes that year.

The RAND Corporation studied the results of standards-based accountability under NCLB in California, Georgia, and Pennsylvania, issuing a report titled "Standards-Based Accountability Under No Child Left Behind: Experiences of Teachers and Administrators in Three States" in 2007. When its investigators zeroed in on individual schools, "teachers and principals described a wide range of efforts to capture more time for reading and mathematics instruction, including eliminating an instrumental music program, decreasing the number of physical education classes offered each week from five to two, eliminating chorus and assemblies, and refocusing summer school from enrichment opportunities to academic instruction in tested subjects." In other words, the very "activities that teachers believed kept students in school and engaged in learning were exactly those activities that schools cut due to time constraints from increased pressure to focus" on ELA and math. One principal reported that "kindergartners' nap time was eliminated, reportedly to provide more time for academic instruction, although some teachers noted that some kindergarteners could not stay awake to benefit from that instruction."

SCIENCE

"All we hear is literacy, literacy, math, math, math," one longtime science teacher told *Education Week*. "In my classroom I started to see that for things you would assume kids would know when they get to middle school—like cloud structure, how to read instruments, basic parts of the cell, animal classification—they just don't have that background any more."

The science teachers may soon be looking at differently prepared students. NCLB requires states to begin testing in science beginning in the current school year, at least once in grades 3–5, once in grades 6–9, and once in grades 10–12. Most states have set science standards in preparation for science being included in NCLB testing, but whether their curricula are aligned with these standards appears to vary by state and school district, according to "Critical Issue: Science Education in the Era of No Child Left Behind—History, Benchmarks, and Standards," a report produced by Learning Point Associates.

The question that school districts will have to answer is simple: How are they going to find the time to add a third substantial subject to the core areas subject to annual statewide assessment? Especially a subject that requires, in the words of the National Science Teachers Association, that laboratory investigation be "an integral part of the science curriculum." The organization's February 2007 position statement elaborates on this time-intensive principle. "Inquiry-based laboratory investigations at every level should be at the core of the science program and should be woven into every lesson and concept strand. As students move through the grades, the level of complexity of laboratory investigations should increase."

The experience of the last five years suggests only one solution: schools will gradually increase the amount of time given over to academic instruction in science (moving slowly because the consequences of not demonstrating Adequate Yearly Progress do not kick in immediately), and reduce the time devoted to everything else: social studies, arts, history, foreign languages, PE, and recess.

We have no intention of arguing that science doesn't need to be a core academic subject for American schoolchildren. As the digital revolution spreads its reach ever further, and the boundaries between biology, engineering, technology, and mathematics break down even more—giving rise to such exploding fields of inquiry (and occupations) as biotechnology, nanotechnology, and alternative energy sources—children need more of a grounding in scientific and technological thinking than ever before in our history. Being able to make intelligent choices about such public-policy problems as those posed by global climate change, fossil-fuel dependence, genetic engineering, and stem-cell research, to choose just a few, demands that the citizens of the future have a much broader, deeper, and relevant science education than did their parents.

Fortunately, we can point to an answer to this otherwise insoluble problem: the new school day, which is already opening up a formerly zero-sum problem in schools across the country. In the Miami School Improvement Zone, middle and high school students study science in ninety-minute blocks every day, a recent increase over the standard fifty-minute periods allotted for most subjects in the standard school day in the rest of Miami-Dade.

In Massachusetts ELT schools, academic subjects have made a comeback in the last couple of years. In fact, according to the Cambridge fourth-grade teacher quoted at the beginning of the chapter, the single biggest change in the new school day could be summed up as, "Science is back!" Even more than most subjects, science benefits from longer classes, because labs take time to set up, clean up, and interpret. After all, teachers need to relate experimental results to the larger concepts at issue. One science teacher at a school forced by budget cuts to shorten its day described her formerly expanded day as "a dream come true. You can do lots of labs. Now, it takes three days to complete a lab that we could have completed in one class!"

At the Kuss Middle School in Fall River, students study science two additional hours each week, through such subjects as robotics, forensics, and the environment. At the Timilty Middle School in Boston, all students submit a project to the citywide science fair. By contrast, at most city public schools, science fair projects are optional, and as a result, only a small percentage of students participate. "The Timilty School faculty believes, however," researchers David Farbman and Claire Kaplan report, "that these hands-on projects offer critical learning opportunities that engage students more deeply in the science curriculum, and build skills, confidence, and knowledge. Thus, students spend time in science class planning the projects and exploring the concepts they are trying to demonstrate."

First-year test results in Massachusetts showed an immediate gain for science among the new ELT schools. Even though most of these schools focused far more on literacy and math, science scores also went up—with an especially impressive increase in fifth grade science: 33 percent more students scored Proficient than the previous year. Overall, science results in the ELT schools narrowed the achievement gap—that is, the gap between these formerly low-performing schools and the statewide average—by a third.

SOCIAL STUDIES AND HISTORY

But what if we produce technologically sophisticated students who know nothing about the history of human cultures, and who have no appreciation for differing points of view or values in religion, politics, or art? That is the dilemma that schools will soon face as they again move to reshape their curriculum inside the box of the old school day.

Science, after all, is far from the only subject that benefits from more time. Goldstein has taught U.S. history for a living for twenty years, and we both have a special interest in seeing how teachers and students in today's elementary, middle, and high schools are approaching social studies and history. What most college teachers know is that most students graduate from high school knowing appallingly little about the history of their own county, without even considering that of the rest of the world. As one historian puts it, "In order to teach world history, I used to have to teach students the rudiments of religions other than theirs—now I have to teach them the rudiments of their own religion as well."

NAEP scores—the nation's report card—suggest stagnation rather than decline, but the absolute numbers are still disturbing. Only 14 percent of twelfth graders and 18 percent of eighth graders scored Proficient or Advanced on the 2006 U.S. history assessment. About 40 percent of high school seniors scored "below basic"—they failed. In the dozen years between 1994 and 2006, average scores on the eighth and twelfth-grade NAEP tests did increase—but only between 1.4 and 1.5 percent.

The more that instructional time available for history and social studies is reduced, the greater the natural tendency of teachers to use the time they have to stress rote memorization of dates, names, wars, treaties, dynasties, and other facts. As a result, even those students who pass some standardized multiple-choice tests may learn little of substance and end up "hating history," or feeling "I'm terrible at history" (the two most common things they tell college history teachers).

When they have more time, teachers can respond to students' interest in a particular historical event or character by going into more depth. Hands-on historical projects and field trips that teachers have the time to prepare students for make the otherwise dry bones of the past come alive. As a Timilty School teacher put it, "There is less pressure to move on to the next lesson." All experienced teachers know that, confronted with a choice between coverage and depth, they prefer depth. Why? Because it's what students respond to; it respects natural human curiosity, and most people's gut-level understanding that the world is more complicated than it appears on a multiple-choice exam. "The amount of material I could get through was amazing," said a teacher of her ninety-minute classes. "You could introduce a concept, introduce primary sources to study it, have kids explore it in a group, and then come back and discuss the subject more in detail." The Jacob Hiatt School used its community partners enrichment program to supplement students' in-school curriculum, so students' social studies learning—national monuments and quilts, tin lanterns and colonial Massachusetts—deepened.

When KIPP co-founder (and founding Houston principal) Mike Feinberg moved on to the nationally oriented KIPP Foundation, Sam Lopez first took on the thankless job of following the hard-charging visionary for a couple of years. He now coordinates testing and teaches social studies at KIPP Academy, Houston. A gentle, large-featured man with a smile playing constantly about his lips, he had come to KIPP from a local public school.

"The big problem in the old school district, where I taught fifth grade, was that we didn't start till 8 AM and were dismissing at 2:45 or 2:50. We had to squeeze in everything, and kids wouldn't get all the class they needed. I had to teach science for six weeks, then social studies for six weeks, sometimes one week of all reading, one week of all math, depending on what was being tested on the grade level—and then teach test prep for one period. That's right. Always, the first period you did was test prep. The principal would walk around and check on you. Something had to give.

"Here, there's built-in time to do stuff. I have an hour-and-fifteen-minute class. I can reinforce a lot of reading and writing. We have that time. Every single day they have math. Including problem solving. In English, there's independent reading time, 4:00–4:30, silent reading time, everyone across the board reads, while the math teachers are tutoring, English teachers are tutoring."

Lopez's own social studies class, coincidentally, was preparing for a test when we visited, but the class didn't resemble any test-prep we'd ever seen. He'd divided the class into teams, with names like "Culture," "Politics," and "Economics." Each team sent a representative to the board, and Lopez posed a question. The kids wrote furiously, and when they finished they knelt down; he gave a point (or two or three, depending on difficulty) to each winning team. The questions came fast, and began with definitions: "A period of time between 20,000 B.C. and 10,000 B.C."—"Old Stone Age."

"Next group," he sings out. "Raising of crops and animals for human use." They scribble, feverishly, barely legibly. The "Culture" team wins: "Agriculture." New contestants scurry to the board, pick up their markers, and wait, expectantly. "A diagram showing when events took place in a period of time." Six markers hit the board, while one somehow beats the rest. "Come back, next round!" The winner high-fives her whole table, as her replacement races up. And on it goes, for better than half an hour. Who was Charles Darwin? What are the Bering Straits? What are four benefits of trade? What is evolution? Two reasons we think the Neanderthals buried their dead? What are four uses of fire? These fourth-graders were physically as well as mentally engaged in showing, practicing, expressing what they'd learned, so the test would be anticlimactic. Lopez was not only using a large block of time that would have been impossible in a conventional school day, he was also getting his students ready to take advantage of every minute they had.

"Tomorrow when you come in you're only going to have forty minutes," Lopez explained. "You're going to have vocabulary, multiple choice, and five short answers. And everything I asked you today, I got from the test—not in the same way, but the general idea. So you already know what's going to be on the test. You won't need to do your essay until Thursday. You still have about ten minutes. What I would do is go back over your notes silently or you can practice how you would answer your paragraph. To study vocabulary you can use flashcards, but you cannot do other homework."

There had been so much energy in the classroom that Lopez had to ask them to calm down, or be quieter, literally dozens of times. From a teacher's point of view, though, harnessing energy is far superior to having to generate it against resistance. Still, we wondered a bit about all the pat answers. So when we got a chance, we asked him, "Had they come from a textbook?" "No," he said. "The kids developed those answers themselves from the classes."

FOREIGN LANGUAGES

The global economy is not only a reality in terms of manufacturing, finance, transportation, and telecommunications—it also moves people around the planet in search of freedom, work, natural resources, labor, and tourism. The demographics of American cities and rural areas alike are being transformed by the largest wave of immigration in generations. At the very moment, then, that the United States is playing a newly global economic role, with partners all over the world, American study of foreign languages is plummeting.

This decline had begun well before the advent of the No Child Left Behind Act in 2002, and though a real upsurge in the number of children studying Spanish since the early 1980s has accounted for most of the growth in enrollments across the county, the truth is that many colleges no longer require a foreign language, either. Instead of seeing globalization as a spur to learning more languages, most Americans have responded by expecting residents of other countries to learn English. Thanks to the efforts of national education systems around the world, from France to China, Turkey to South Korea, more and more of the world is indeed learning English. The ignorance attached to those who refuse the effort to learn about another culture by learning its language is a national scandal and a worldwide joke. "What do you call someone who speaks three languages?" it begins. "Trilingual. What do you call someone who speaks two languages? Bilingual. What do you call someone who speaks one language? An American."

But again, what are principals supposed to do when their need to strengthen children's understanding of *English* language arts—reading and writing in this country's dominant language—and other subjects on which their students and teachers get publicly evaluated runs up against their desire to expand students' appreciation for other cultures? They feel this dilemma all the more strongly because dozens of those very cultures are represented in nearly every urban school in this country.

By now it will be obvious that we think the global solution to these quandaries is the new school day—but it's not simply our opinion on these matters. It's what we see when schools have the time to devote to more and broader learning. Timilty Middle School in Boston, for instance, offers Japanese and Chinese among its enrichment electives. And Martin Luther King, Jr. School in Cambridge has decided to make Mandarin Chinese obligatory for all students.

WELL-ROUNDED EDUCATION DEPENDS ON THE NEW SCHOOL DAY

The only way a well-rounded education can coexist with a standards-based accountability movement focused on a few core academic subjects is by expanding the amount of time children spend learning. Otherwise, we risk becoming a nation of narrow, competent workers technically proficient in reading, writing, math, and now perhaps in science, while lacking the most basic understanding of what makes the country tick, of how human beings have lived in and struggled with their world since the beginnings of civilization, and of what life is like for the 95 percent of the world's population living outside the United States of America.

PART TWO

TIME FOR A WELL-ROUNDED EDUCATION

5

DANCE, DRUMMING, AND DEBATE

Time for Enrichment and Extracurriculars in the New School Day

The only reason I stayed in school was the music!
—PUBLIC SCHOOLS SUPERINTENDENT, BOSTON

ONLY FOR THE MUSIC—THAT'S A telling anecdote. You may have one too. One of our children got hooked by Model UN, and surprised himself—as well as his peers and parents and siblings, around whom he'd been a boy of very few words—by becoming a prize-winning public speaker. As essential as a solid grounding in reading, writing, math, and science are, providing opportunity to experience, and in some cases to relish and master, other fields and activities is a central role for schools. Arts, music, drama, crafts, chess, robotics, photography, cooking, martial arts, debate, journalism, and so much more like them together offer a kaleidoscope of experiences and challenges that belong in the catalog of every student's total opportunities.

BEYOND THE CORE

The whole question of the proper place of enrichment and extracurricular activities in the new school day—or any school day, for that matter—turns on what people consider a "well-rounded education." Most of us—teachers, parents, school and other public officials, employers, and members of the general public—seem to agree on the principle of core academic subjects that lead to students' gaining fundamental skills: reading, writing, and math. English and mathematics instruction, we think, ought to develop literacy and its companion, numeracy, in our children. More recently, educators and public officials share a growing consensus that science ought to be among the core academic subjects as well. As a result, the standards and accountability movement of the past decade, including No Child Left Behind, has focused testing on these core areas.

But few of us think that children's education ought to stop with the core. Most conceptions of the liberal arts, of well-educated children, maintain that students also need to learn some history and social studies (such as geography and civics), foreign languages and something about other cultures, some art and music, and to receive some instruction in physical education and sports.

In practice, schools have tended to divide these subjects into two basic groups: those deemed academic or indispensable, which must be part of the school curriculum—English, math, science, social studies, foreign language (occasionally)—and those considered enrichment, which generally seem less essential—art, music, drama, physical education—needing less regular or intense instruction. Depending on the school, the district, or the state, only some of these enrichment subjects are incorporated into the standard required curriculum.

Increasingly, however, the reality is that schools and parents often expect that these belong chiefly, if at all, outside the school's core academic mission. Over the past decade of up-and-down budget cycles and the advent of high-stakes testing, many non-core subjects—considered fluff or extras by far too many taxpayers, school boards, and school systems under the budget guns—have been dramatically reduced in primary and secondary education across the country. Surveys by the Center on Education Policy show that a majority of schools across the country have significantly reduced school time for one or more of social studies, science, art and music, physical education, and even recess and lunch in order to free up more time to devote to English and math.

While many schools still offer art classes in which students learn the basics of drawing, color, painting, and crafts, these are limited, poorly funded, and easily cut back. Some schools still offer music, but very few offer instruction in a musical instrument. Many high schools offer plays, band, or orchestra as extracurricular activities, but very few middle or elementary schools have a regular after-school drama or music program. While high school sports remain very popular, elementary and middle school sports are generally left to town basketball and soccer leagues, along with such venerable institutions as Pop Warner football, Little League, and Babe Ruth League baseball.

Many parents and educators have decried the transformation of the school day into what sometimes looks like one long math and English (and occasionally science) class, as the subjects not tested on statewide proficiency exams get squeezed out of the curriculum. But school officials feel caught between a sharp rock and a very hard place. How can they justify dedicating scarce resources (and the very few hours kids are in school comprise their main resource) when their schools are being publicly tested and scored in English and math, not drama or painting or kickball or musical notation?

This excruciating dilemma becomes even more intense when we understand how much enrichment and extracurricular activities bring to the educational table for all kinds of students. Numerous studies conclude that in-school enrichment and structured after-school activities are not only good in and of themselves but also have a carryover effect, helping students better their academic performance. As one summary of a group of studies put it, "students engaged in extracurricular activities—including sports, service clubs, and art activities—are less likely to drop out, and more likely to have higher academic achievement. Of particular importance, students at risk for school failure appear to benefit even more from participation in extracurricular activities than do children who are normal achievers."

How does this mechanism work? It's simple, really. By increasing kids' connectedness to the school and helping to build on their strengths instead of focusing on their weaknesses and failures, these activities help them feel better about themselves and more attached or committed to their school. Teachers and parents may not always have the research data at hand, but they know these things from their own experience with schoolchildren.

HOW ENRICHMENT WORKS IN THE NEW SCHOOL DAY

One of the most important advantages of the new school day is that it offers a simple and powerful solution to the problem posed by the massively increased attention to math and English performance, making it possible to apply educators' knowledge and conviction that children learn better if they're more engaged in school. New day schools can consciously incorporate enrichment activities into the school day, engaging teachers and students in brand-new ways.

In fact, while some parents worry in advance that expanding the school day will simply tack more instructional hours onto an already rushed and pressured environment, the actual experience of new day schools couldn't be further from this grim picture. In reality, parents see and appreciate a dramatic expansion of their children's participation in activities that have traditionally only been available sporadically to them—if at all—well outside the school day and walls.

Sometimes enrichment activities have explicit academic underpinnings and benefits, as in robotics classes that combine science and math, or debate, which brings together English, public speaking, and competition. Others are less academic. At one of the Expanded Learning Time (ELT) schools in Cambridge, Fletcher-Maynard Academy, the principal recruited a community-based "Jamnastics" program, a blend of hip-hop music and gymnastics, while the Kuss School in Fall River instituted martial arts, and Martin Luther King, Jr. School runs City Sprouts, a gardening project for kids. So many kids have been so alienated from school for so long that the most important purpose of some enrichment programs is for kids to feel that fun can happen at school, that there's something to look forward to beyond academic learning that they know will be tested and graded.

At the N.B. Borden Elementary School in Fall River, the principal launched a "Kids' College" as part of the newly expanded school day, in which students get the "college" experience of choosing an elective course—such as dance, cake decorating, book club, or arts and crafts—each term. At the Mario Umana Middle School in East Boston, another Massachusetts ELT school, a seventh-grade math and science teacher started a journalism program that puts out a school newspaper, while one of his colleagues got a chess club going; two others (in English and drama) combined a couple of periods to teach theater production. Each student chose two electives, drawn from a varied menu including keyboard lab and music composition, ceramics, drawing, digital photography, yearbook, swimming, tennis, guitar, Afro-Cuban percussion, computer study, karate, and seminars on healthy lifestyles.

At the Kuss School in Fall River, according to the *Boston Globe,* "The once hit-or-miss drama program now regularly puts on major productions. Students must sign contracts of commitment and maintain good grades to participate. Aided by local business contributions, the troupe last fall staged a production of *Macbeth,* with the performers in professionally made costumes." They went on to *You're a Good Man, Charlie Brown.* Eighth-grader Markus Watson, who played the lead in *Macbeth,* also learned to operate a ham radio. "We're learning more than we usually do from teachers," he told *Newsweek.* He added that the expanded day "keeps me out of trouble."

At Roxbury Prep, enrichment programs begin when academic classes end at 3:10—and all students stay until 4:15. The day we visited, we saw engaged students in the classroom, to be sure, but at 3:10 the energy level in the building seemed to jump up a notch, and it's no wonder. These middle schoolers, who'd been focused on academic subjects since 7:45 AM, were headed for a whole range of offerings organized around athletics and visual and performing arts: from dance to basketball, double dutch (jump rope) to percussion, soccer to musical theater, computer Web design to guitar, photography, softball, yoga, and Tae Kwon Do.

In the KIPP Academy in the South Bronx, New York City, where students attend school from 7:25 AM until 5:00 PM on weekdays, half days on Saturdays, and three weeks during the summer, fifth graders get two periods of physical education per week, two periods of music, and two periods of electives (choices include sports, technology, art, and African dance). All students partici- pate in the school's 180-piece String and Rhythm Orchestra, con- sidered one of the finest middle-school orchestras in the nation. Middle schoolers (grades 6–8) take music lessons or orchestra practice from ten-and-a-half to thirteen-and-a-half hours weekly, and *everyone* has four hours of orchestra on Saturday mornings. Of the many hundreds of children who have gone through this school, fewer than one in a hundred arrived knowing how to read music or play an instrument. Every graduate has learned to do both.

At the Edwards Middle School in Boston, students receive up to four hours of arts and music instruction weekly as a result of the Massachusetts ELT initiative. Edwards now bills itself as "the school of choice for students interested in the Arts." The curricu- lum includes instrumental and vocal music, visual arts, theater, and dance, while specific classes include songwriting, band, digital- video and audio recording, and photography. To put these num- bers into context, the ELT initiative also enlarged the curriculum by four additional hours of math per week, including a second math class for all students, and up to four additional hours of literacy, science, and social studies per week. At the Dr. Martin Luther King, Jr. School in Cambridge, student elective courses include filmmaking and journalism. Salemwood School in Malden, Massachusetts, a 1,200-student K–8 school, is using its new school day to integrate arts experiences "across all other cur- ricula as we strive to bring alive our school's theme of Visual and Performing Arts." Three of the eight fifty-minute elective periods at Timilty Middle School in Boston (of which students choose two each semester) are dance, theater, and art.

At KIPP Academy in Houston, says co-founder Mike Feinberg, "we have plenty of athletics; we have a band, it squeaks." KIPP middle schoolers' extracurriculars include a "rock band, school play, kickball, Ultimate Frisbee, martial arts, a step team, a power dance team, cooking, storyboarding, and technology." Lots of these take place during "Saturday school," which kids attend at least twice a month.

Even at the turnaround schools in Miami's Improvement Zone, where only an hour a day has been added and the focus is on lifting very low-performing schools' academic performance, enrichment is offered to those who have shown by past test scores that they do not need as much extra time on academic basics. We walked across the hall from a classroom full of students getting a second literacy period in the day to watch higher-performing students deeply engaged in chess, and heard the principal boast that some of these students were already winning regional chess tournaments.

New day schools use three different approaches to bring enrichment into their school day. Most add a period or more a day to the schedule to allow for these activities, often dubbed "electives." In one approach, nonprofit community-based organizations partner with the schools and deliver programs during those periods. A different way to offer these courses is to recruit teachers to develop and lead the classes. Finally, at least one new day school has developed a strategy to embed some of its added enrichment into the fabric of core academic classes.

COMMUNITY-LED ENRICHMENT

In the past fifteen to twenty years, a growing number of non-profit organizations have developed content and expertise in offering after-school programs to young people. Most of these groups have been started either out of concern that young people need more constructive activities to pursue in the long, unsupervised hours after school, or by people with a passion to share their skill in extracurricular fields, such as the arts, with students who have little to no exposure to them during the regular school schedule. The former tend to develop comprehensive programs to fill the after-school hours with a blend of homework help, enrichment activities, and time to relax. The latter often run programs that meet less frequently or for fewer hours and focus on their specialty. Both have developed a great deal of capacity, and as a result, many organizations are very well prepared to provide specialized enrichment during elective periods in new day schools.

Citizen Schools is a good example. Founded in 1994 in Boston by two charismatic and driven social entrepreneurs, Eric Schwarz and Ned Rimer, Citizen Schools now serves three thousand middle-school children in five states and is widely considered one of the nation's superstars of after-school programming. Its hallmark is hands-on apprenticeships: projects led by volunteer adults, generally based on their jobs or hobbies. For example, lawyers and judges often lead apprenticeships that take the form of a moot court trial in which students serve as lawyers and witnesses and real judges decide the case. Engineers usually help students build solar-powered cars or robots, and entrepreneurs teach students to start their own small greeting card or food businesses. Students, who get to choose their apprenticeships, learn by doing concrete things.

The first Massachusetts schools to contemplate converting to a new school day included three that already had experience with Citizen Schools. But where it had been offered as an optional after-school program attracting 10–20 percent of students, these schools saw the opportunity to take the most original and exciting element of the broader after-school program and make it a standard part of every student's regular schedule. For example, at the Edwards Middle School in Boston, every sixth grader now participates during the school day in a Citizen Schools apprenticeship.

Partnerships with community-based organizations are commonplace among Massachusetts ELT schools. Many schools use multiple partners and some even use off-campus partner facilities—for example, the Kuss Middle School is providing swim lessons at the Fall River YMCA this year. Arrangements with partners vary but generally include at least some funding from the school out of its state allotment, with community partners sometimes supplementing that with some of their private funding. While the partnering process adds some complexity, it offers at least three key benefits. First, these organizations are often extremely accomplished at their specialty and bring experience and passion that would be hard to duplicate. Second, they often bring a whole new set of adults into the lives of the schoolchildren. Some of those adults are young recent college graduates while others are community residents; in both cases, the opportunity for inspiration and bonding between student and adult adds a valuable dimension to middle-school education. Finally, while the community-based organization runs its class, teachers are freed up to work together, pursue professional development, prepare for other classes, or get some needed downtime.

TEACHER-LED ENRICHMENT

A different strategy to add enrichment to the day is to turn to teachers. At the Kuss School in Fall River, the ELT effort started too close to the beginning of the next year, and the number of community-based organizations ready to step in was too small to consider any other path. While major cities such as Boston can often draw on a number of traditional groups like the YMCA and the Boys and Girls Clubs, as well as a bunch of new organizations such as Citizen Schools, smaller cities and towns rarely have anywhere near as much opportunity. What starts out as necessity—turning to teachers—can turn into reward. Many Kuss teachers had ideas, often related to their own hobbies and passions, for elective classes. For example, one math teacher turned out to be a martial arts expert. When the governor of Massachusetts visited the school, he saw many students' eyes light up as they discussed their enthusiasm for martial arts—including one girl who talked about how much more self-discipline and ability to control her anger she had gained. The math teacher seemed delighted to pursue his personal interest with his students and his skill level seemed as high as could ever be brought in from outside. One huge advantage also stood out—the relationships developed under this very different activity benefited his ability to teach math. No longer was he just the guy who made students suffer through algebra, he was also the cool guy who can split boards with his head! The teacher reported a considerable improvement in some students' attitude toward him and toward math, and he also reported a newfound respect and understanding for young people with whom he had worked effectively in martial arts. That sort of different and valuable teacher-student interaction is exactly why most private schools insist that teachers coach sports and lead extracurricular activities.

The Hiatt School's enrichment coordinator saw the Massachusetts ELT Initiative as an opportunity to add enrichment, but also to do it in a whole new way. The school launched an "eighth hour" for enrichment and offered some activities in-house, like cooking and yoga, Lego robotics, digital photography, and basketball, which teachers were "passionate about doing." And they used the extra time to do some tutoring.

INTEGRATED ENRICHMENT

In addition to adding the freestanding enrichment time, Hiatt School's leaders considered whether they could enhance regular class time. "When we redesigned the day," explained Enrichment Coordinator Patty Genese, "we looked at the whole issue of enrichment, and said to the community, 'there's no bad idea. Give us all your ideas.' But we also said, 'we're going to have a sieve, a screen, and at the bottom of the sieve would be the standards and the frameworks to improve student achievement in English language arts, math, social studies, and science.' Everything was going to have to filter through this sieve, and if it didn't impact those areas in some way, it wouldn't make it through."

School officials circulated an RFP to a host of local and regional cultural institutions, asking for a six- to eight-week series of presentations that would lead to a tangible product or performance that was closely connected to existing curricular goals. "You see, this was different from what we'd done in the past, where we'd brought an art museum in to do a program. Here, the classroom teacher and the cultural partner were presenting together. There's no partnership without real partners."

Principal Pat Gaudette chimed in. "They'd propose a program and Patty would say, 'This works; this doesn't. This is good, this isn't what we need; what we need is this.'" Patty picked up: "We got a proposal for quilting, and at that time, our fourth graders were working on national monuments. So I wanted to focus the quilting on national monuments. Big ideas are a better fit if you do it this way, cause it's so connected. That was our priority, not quilting for quilting's sake." They took us to the cafeteria, where a huge quilt now hangs with panels depicting the White House, Mt. Rushmore, the Lincoln Memorial, the Washington Monument, and more. Another new partner embedded into the curricular day was the Worcester Women's History project, which made classroom visits and performed a play about the Worcester-based nineteenth century anti-slavery and women's rights activist Abby Kelly

Foster. Hiatt even looked beyond Worcester to form partnerships, such as one with the Boston-based Paul Revere House.

Closing the "Opportunity Gap"

No matter where we went to visit new day schools, teachers and principals stressed the importance of having a full menu of enrichment activities. They know, from their professional experience with children, that some students thrive most when engaged in these pursuits, far more than they do in more traditional classroom instruction. Enrichment is more likely to tap into kids' artistic or musical or physical or athletic talents, by and large just plain ignored by the standards-based curriculum.

Former high school teacher Anita Shreve catches this phenomenon perfectly in her novel *Body Surfing*, whose protagonist has taken a job tutoring a somewhat "slow" high school junior in order to prepare her for the SATs. Quite by accident one day, working a jigsaw puzzle with her charge, she sees the girl assemble a section with uncommon speed. Following a hunch, she gives her a set of photographs to organize and display, and discovers that the girl has an exceptional talent for arranging colors and shapes—and quickly. When she buys her pencils and paints and an easel, the formerly balky, uncooperative student cannot wait to disappear into her bedroom for many hours at a time to draw and paint with great seriousness of purpose.

How would math or English or social studies class discover such facility, or the aptitude to play or compose music, or the ability to weave through a group of defenders on a soccer field or basketball court? As a society, we place great value on all these skills. (Some of their finest practitioners earn prizes and fame and wealth.) And yet we are moving further into an educational world in which children receive less and less instruction or even encouragement to consider them worthwhile forms of activity.

A mother of twin daughters at the ELT Edwards Middle School in Charlestown, Massachusetts, was describing the school's apprenticeship program. One twin, Bethany, "did both sessions being a lawyer during the mock trials. This will be Gabriella's first time. The other enrichment classes, Bethany's doing football with Mr. Thomas, and Gabriella is doing fixing bikes with—I don't remember the teacher's name—but she's also learning that. And she's basically learned how to put a bicycle together, which I feel like that's wonderful. I could never do that. I think the enrichment classes do help them both out very well."

Rodney, a self-described "band-geek" and "multi-musician artist," also at the Edwards Middle School, explains how his enrichment electives work: "We have A-Day and B-Day out of the week because there's five days—Monday and Wednesday is A-Day, Tuesday and Thursday is B-Day. A-Day is production class which basically, in our music room, we have computers that we are allowed to make beats and write songs on, and I do that, and I learn how to produce music and how to write it, and actually how to do everything that goes through the music process.

"On B-Day, I have band, which is the band ensemble, created by Mr. Rivera, and he gives us pieces of music and we learn how to read them and we learn how to play them."

Children, as parents and teachers and psychologists and coaches and cops and principals all know, are *different* from one another, learning different ways and at different rates and by different means. Enrichment allows children and their schools to gain from those very differences, rather than suffer from them. During enrichment activities, children interact with adults—oftentimes their teachers—differently than they do in the classroom. That's good for students and teachers. And sometimes kids get to interact with adults from local community organizations who come to lead enrichment. This kind of cooperation and intermingling only strengthens the ties between schools, children, and the larger communities.

Everyone involved in public education likes enrichment, it turns out, even if taxpayers and their representatives can't always pay for it. As we observed earlier, however, administrators stuck in a school schedule dominated by core academic instruction find it difficult to find the time for offerings—even those they *know* will improve students' well-being and perhaps even their academic performance.

Middle- and upper-middle-class parents address the problem of a six-and-a-half-hour day and paltry enrichment offerings head-on. They know their kids need, or would benefit from, different kinds of education to supplement the school curriculum—so they buy it. That's the meaning of the "overscheduled child" of current media hype, a surprisingly small sliver of the population in numerical terms, but one with enormous cultural influence. And however much critics may mock the overscheduling parents of these allegedly stressed-out children, they are responding to genuine problems: the narrowing of the public school curriculum due to high-stakes testing and suburban taxpayer revolts, increasing competition for admission to top colleges and universities, and the increased competitiveness of the educational and employment landscape as the United States has entered a truly global economy in the last decade—the precise challenges we propose to address through the new school day.

Many thousands of affluent families have chosen—often at great expense and psychic stress—to have mothers leave the full-time workforce and stay home with their children, at least partly to supplement their children's education as "soccer moms." Of course, *soccer mom* hardly catches the full measure of these mothers' days as they shuttle multiple children—their own as well as others in carpools—from lessons in music, dance, or art to SAT or ACT prep classes, or to soccer, baseball, softball, swimming, field hockey, lacrosse, volleyball, and basketball practice. But the principle remains clear, even if they have never thought about it in precisely these terms: They are voting with their own resources (money, minivans, and time) to fill the enormous gaps in their children's education.

It takes a certain amount of economic security, even affluence, to deploy family resources in such ways. A soccer-mom system assumes a two-parent family, the ability to live on one salary, and the means to purchase lessons that can cost thousands of dollars per year.

Children from low-income communities, the majority of whom go to school in urban areas (along with most children from middle-income suburban backgrounds as well), face no overscheduling problems when the dismissal bell rings. Across the nation, parents report less than half of all K–8 students participating in any sort of after-school program or activity. Most head for home—where they may have responsibilities to look after younger siblings, and a television will keep them company until their parents finish work—or worse: They find other children bored with home and homework, and they just hang out, all too often prey to the temptations of the street—gang activity, aggressive loitering, experimentation with drugs, alcohol, sex, or petty crime.

Figures from the U.S. Department of Education's National Center for Education Statistics testify to the stark socioeconomic after-school reality of children. In 2005, only 20 percent of the poorest children participated in any program or activity, while 27 percent of the "near-poor" did. By contrast, 63 percent of those from families with incomes over $75,000 participated in such activities. These patterns were mirrored when looking at education level of parents. Children whose parents had less than a high school education participated at the stunningly low rate of 8 percent, while two-thirds of those lucky enough to be born to parents with postgraduate degrees were likely to be active. And these outside-of-school opportunity gaps ran across the board. Highly educated parents had their children enrolled in academic activities and sports programs at ten times the rate of the least educated; their rates of participation in arts and community service differed by a factor of twenty!

Poor children have a variety of reasons for their low participation in such activities, ranging from their families' inability to afford fees or equipment (cleats, shin guards, instrument rentals) or provide transportation to the thinner offerings of their local community organizations and their public schools. And the most highly educated and most affluent parents see the need and have the opportunity to invest heavily in their children beyond the school day.

But no matter the source of the problem, no one suggests that its solution lies in sending poor kids home at 2 or 2:30 in the afternoon. Marilyn Luter has taught at Achievable Dream Academy in Newport News for fourteen years. She had reservations at first because "it was such a long day," from 8:15–4:45, when she had been used to 8:55–2:20. "I could see after being with these kids they needed to be here; otherwise they're on the street. I'd never been in a school where the children didn't look forward to Christmas vacation, or spring break. Vacations just put them on the street."

The key here is that the new school day promises to close what we call the "opportunity gap" between the enrichment offerings of affluent schools, communities, and parents and those of schools in low-income neighborhoods or cities. In upper-middle-class suburban middle and high school students' worlds, school plays, band, and orchestra continue to enrich the lives of children and their communities. In poorer school districts, especially in urban areas, much theater and arts instruction and many electives have simply been done away with, and families and communities have few alternative opportunities. As a result, almost no one objects to what the new school day can do for the poorest children.

What About Family Time?

The most affluent parents, however, wonder whether an expanded school schedule will cut into their family time or into such valued activities as sports or dance or other purchased extracurricular activities outside the school system entirely. These parents have not been in the forefront of efforts to expand the school day, at least partly because they've already solved the problem of their children's afternoon schedules and enrichment education. And since a new school schedule might compete with their established extracurricular patterns, they may very well object to expanding the school day.

Over time, however, these parents might very well come to prefer the convenience of in-school enrichment, as well as the much lower cost, since in many new day schools some of the same local cultural institutions charging affluent families for private lessons are offering similar programs built into the school schedule at no additional cost to parents. And for most families and children in the middle, the new school day provides enrichment opportunities that the data show their children aren't experiencing in any other way.

If we're honest about family life today and what children really like to do when they are left alone, we have to acknowledge that most discussion of these issues takes place in the realm of nostalgia and myth, driven by the fact that most of us only remember high school very well when we had the most activities after school. How many of us remember well what we did after school in third or seventh grade?

Even in two-parent families, very few parents are taking their kids fishing on Tuesday afternoons, or helping them build doll-houses or model rockets on Thursdays after school. The point is not to criticize today's parents, a group we belong to proudly. The point is to understand that the demands of modern economic life leave limited time for parents and kids to interact, and that an expanded school schedule is more or less irrelevant to this problem for the great majority of parents and children. The much more serious issue is that most children (including middle-income children) are on their own for large parts of the afternoon, choosing to watch TV or play video games or their online equivalent. If the average American child is spending three to four hours a day in front of a screen of some kind, in what most parents would consider at best "dead time," why not take two of these hours every day and replace them with educationally enriching activities? The new school schedule we're proposing in this book is not an assault on family time, or on parents' opportunity to be good parents, as critics sometimes object—it's an assault on the huge hole in most kids' lives, a hole that, left to their own devices, they fill with the fewest educational calories—and sometimes with the least nutritious ones as well.

By focusing in this book on the new school day, on an expanded, redesigned block of time for structured academic learning and newly added enrichment, we do not mean to imply that everything children need or want to learn can—or should—take place in school under a teacher's instruction. Far from it. But the school day we are advocating does have implications for a whole range of activities that have traditionally occurred in out-of-school time.

What about classic extracurricular activities like sports (which we take up in Chapter Seven), clubs, band, orchestra, choir, and theater? We realize that any substantial change in the size of the school day needs also to address the part of children's education and development that now takes place outside formal academic classroom instruction. Here's another way to look at this question. With the new school schedule, things schools are supposed to do (like teach core academic subjects), they can do better. Things schools aren't obliged to do but could do (like enrichment), they now can do. Finally, kids still can do the things that they and their parents might like to do outside school.

The experience of new day schools makes it very clear that even with an expanded school day, kids still have plenty of time for extracurricular activities. When Roxbury Prep's enrichment period finishes at 4:15, students meet in weekly clubs such as the Science Club, math Peer Tutoring, and Reading Groups. Last year the Science Club students conducted experiments, went on field trips, participated in the statewide Science Olympiad Competitions, and met with medical professionals about their careers. In the tutoring clubs, eighth graders met twice weekly with sixth and seventh graders to help them with math and study skills. The Boys' and Girls' Reading Groups both focus on improving reading skills and providing a "safe space for open and constructive discussion about the issues they face in and out of school"—the school's delicate way of describing pressures around alcohol, drugs, sex, and petty (and not so petty) crime in its annual report.

The reporting of Massachusetts parents who have experienced the before-and-after of the new school day offers persuasive evidence on the subject of extracurricular activities: Fully 74 percent of the 247 respondents at three expanded day schools in 2006–2007 said that the new day does not prevent their children from engaging in any outside activities. While the new schedule does leave a modest number of parents having to make adjustments for their children, few (if any) see it as sufficiently problematic to leave the new day schools.

Millions of schoolchildren attend religious classes in the afternoons. According to the National Center for Education Statistics, 20 percent of all U.S. K–8 students participate in religious activities (the second most frequent form of activity after sports) after school. Many Roman Catholic children have CCD, while Jewish kids often go to Hebrew School and (in middle school) Bar and Bat Mitzvah training. CCD typically runs weekend mornings, but occasionally on Wednesday afternoons or evenings. Some CCD programs start as early as 3:45 (though most don't). Protestant religious education typically takes place on weekends, mostly Sundays. Weekday religious school for most Jews usually begins at 4–4:30, on Tuesdays, Wednesdays, or Thursdays, running until

5:30 or 6:00. How big a problem would religious education pose for a new school schedule?

We don't want to dismiss the potential for some disruption. But since schools with large Catholic populations (as well as families and the churches) already work around this issue when their students have play or band or athletic practice, the problem seems easily surmountable. Nor would it be a major issue if synagogues and churches ended up changing the time of their classes by half an hour one direction or the other.

FORMAL AFTER-SCHOOL PROGRAMS

Partly to deal with the many familial and social problems posed by the current school dismissal time, and partly to improve the overall education of children, school districts; city, state, and federal agencies; faith-based organizations; and community-based nonprofit groups have developed or funded literally thousands of after-school programs for children, mainly in grades K–8. These offer an extraordinary range of activities for children, ranging from homework assistance to sports, and enrichment programs in such areas as science, writing, music, art, photography, martial arts, and dance. Organizations like the Partnership for After School Education have helped raise the level of after-school programs, providing staff development opportunities, roundtables on best practices in the field, and advocacy for increased public funding for after school. Gabrieli began his career in education reform by serving as Boston Mayor Thomas Menino's appointed chairman of the city's Task Force on After-School Time. Later, Gabrieli was a founding partner and chairman of Boston's After-School for All Partnership, which raised $25 million for after-school programs.

As committed as we both have been, and still are, to such programs, we have also been forced by several interacting realities—public underfunding of after-school programs, the short-term nature of philanthropic support, the ultimately scattershot approach to educational need—to search for an answer to the problems besetting American public education that is both deeper and further reaching. For one thing, by their very nature, after-school programs run by independent nonprofits include kids from different grade levels and often from different schools, so they rarely coordinate their educational activities with the schools' curricular objectives. Even in the fairly common "homework assistance" components in after-school programs, after-school staff know little about the way the academic subjects are being taught in school, though they can certainly still help with some math and reading homework.

But even if after-school programs were thoroughly aligned with schools' curricular objectives, the hard truth is that just 11 percent—roughly one in ten—of American schoolchildren attend a daily after-school program. Only 6 percent of kids in grades 6–8 (that's *fewer than one in sixteen* middle schoolers) attend. From the standpoint of national or even statewide educational policy, these are stunning numbers, suggesting that two decades of thoughtful, civic-minded, educationally sound, deeply committed efforts—as well as billions of dollars—on behalf of after-school programs have failed to make a significant dent in the problems giving rise to the programs in the first place. Many of the needs after-school programs are designed to meet would be addressed by the new school day, and all students at each new day school would benefit. New school days take much of the worthy models of the best after-school programs to a universal scale in a sustainable way, often inviting the current providers to move their efforts inside the school day, making the change a potential win for all concerned.

Safe, Engaged, Well-Rounded Kids

A central goal of the new school day is to ensure enough time to provide a well-rounded education that goes beyond the core academic subjects to embrace arts, music, drama, sports, and other worthy forms of learning and enrichment. By expanding these kinds of offerings, connecting them when possible to the school curriculum, and actively engaging children until most parents finish a normal workday, new day schools add different, high-quality, engaging experiences for children.

At the same time, the new school schedule helps parents worry less about their unsupervised children and helps surrounding communities by providing active supervision for children in the afternoons. For parents who are currently stretching family budgets—and their own ability to be in many places at once—to purchase programs in theater, dance, music, art, and sports, the new school day offers a true alternative: publicly funded activities, no longer extracurricular, during school, embedded alongside academic instruction, requiring no transportation at all. The wonder is that the parents of the "overscheduled generation" haven't risen up and demanded a new school day long before now.

6

TIME TO FOCUS

Making Space for Social and Emotional Learning

I must learn to earn. I can go to college if I work hard. Be cool, stay in school. Reading is the foundation of wisdom. Hard work is the price of success.

—BANNERS AT ACHIEVABLE DREAM ACADEMY

Satisfying the social and emotional needs of students does more than prepare them to learn. It actually increases their capacity to learn.

—COLLABORATIVE FOR ACADEMIC, SOCIAL, AND EMOTIONAL LEARNING

MANY OF THE NATION'S MOST elite private schools have required uniforms and character education for most of the last century. Many require the children of America's wealthiest families to work in school dining halls, or shovel manure in the school farm, or perform other sorts of school service activities. Families who expect their children to inherit or succeed to the leadership of corporations, universities, law firms, hospitals, cultural institutions, and governments have always had a deep understanding of the need for the education of their children as whole human beings.

<hr>

Teaching Focus

"Parents ask me, 'What is the first thing I want to teach?'" says Ann McPartland, a pre-Kindergarten teacher at the Jacob Hiatt School in Worcester.

"It's simple. I teach children how to learn and to focus: to sit, cross their legs, and look at me; to wait their turn; some perseverance and readiness skills. If I can't get them to focus on me, I can't get them to learn. So that's the first thing I teach. Once you get that, you can go to an unbelievable extent."

<hr>

Roxbury Preparatory Charter School, serving mostly low-income African American and Latino students, devotes a page on its Web site to "Character." It strictly enforces a dress code and code of conduct, and it employs an "Advisory Curriculum," in which "students read, write about, and discuss short stories, poems, and current-event articles." According to school officials, the curriculum, to which a Friday morning class is devoted, "helps students develop good character, creates community among students and teachers, improves literacy skills, and teaches students how to be positive participants in their own and their peers' education." The school also has what it calls "community meetings," awards for good behavior and leadership, and a variety of ways of singling out particularly helpful, successful, or spirited students. So focused are the school's leaders on creating a supportive environment for all their students that when students return from taking the state standardized test, the MCAS, they walk down a specially laid red carpet, while their fellow students applaud.

Over the past couple of decades, schools have been increasingly turning to programs designed to strengthen students' social, emotional, and character development (which often includes a consistent, effective disciplinary component), aiming to improve the overall climate for learning in their schools and to build character and interpersonal strengths in their students. While the specifics of these programs differ, they generally teach conflict resolution, ways to make good and healthy choices in a variety of areas (nutrition, drugs, risky behavior), fair and ethical behavior, self-respect and respect for others, and tolerance.

Schools have come to these efforts partly because of the growing body of research and evidence that happy and successful human beings employ skills and intelligences other than those addressed by an exclusively academic curriculum. The key research includes renowned psychologist Howard Gardner's work on "multiple intelligences," including the capacity for social interaction as well as the capacity for self-reflection, and Daniel Goleman's books on the importance of "emotional intelligence." Others, such as the economists Richard Murnane of Harvard and Frank Levy of MIT, offer an economic rationale for social and emotional development. In *Teaching the New Basic Skills: Principles for Educating Children to Thrive in a Changing Economy,* Murnane and Levy argue persuasively that in order to be successful in high-wage businesses, students need to learn what they term "twenty-first-century skills," including how to work well with others and how to communicate effectively.

Schools have two principal reasons for promoting "social and economic learning"—known increasingly as SEL—and character education: to remove barriers to success in school and in life while also building personal aptitudes beyond baseline survival skills. Private schools may focus more on the former, while schools for low-income children aspire to the latter.

After all, many of the students we write about in this book, those living in low-income urban neighborhoods, have lives outside school in a world suffused with the threat and the reality of violence. Children learn to cope with the most difficult of circumstances, but their coping mechanisms may involve high degrees of self-protectiveness and a readiness to return violence tit for tat. In other words, no real barrier separates the school and the outside world. Just about every issue in the world outside the school walls—family matters, economic recession, addiction, neighborhood crime, gang activity, landlord-tenant disputes—spills into the school and classroom, disrupting the educational process, at the very least distracting students and teachers. No matter how well-educated they are or how professional their training or attitude, when teachers fear their own students, they face crippling barriers to helping those students learn much in the classroom.

The extraordinary good news in the midst of this admittedly dismal picture is that all over the country, committed, principled, idealistic teachers and principals are attacking this problem—and having real success. In fact, the realization that social and emotional issues play a huge role in a school's overall learning climate, as well as the safety of everyone in the building, has helped create a true growth industry of books, consultants, and curricula focused on addressing these needs.

SEL AND CHARACTER EDUCATION

Many schools use a curriculum designed to help students recognize the potential sources of conflict and disruptive behavior in school, and to teach them conflict resolution skills they can use to reduce the possibility of violence and other risky behavior. The Collaborative for Academic, Social, and Emotional Learning (CASEL) has published a guide to the issues of social and emotional learning, describing literally dozens of curricula in use around the country and rating them according to a multifaceted scale. Titled *Safe and Sound: An Educational Leader's Guide to Evidence-Based Social and Emotional Learning (SEL) Programs,* the booklet highlights twenty-two of these programs as especially thorough and/or successful.

One of the biggest surprises we've had in researching this book has been discovering just how much SEL or "character education" (these overlap a good deal in the literature) schools choose to employ when they have the time to do it. Fletcher-Maynard Academy, a K–8 new day school in Cambridge, Massachusetts, for example, promises that part of its school improvement plan is to "encourage students in their roles as peacemakers, and engender an atmosphere free of bullying, harassment, or intimidation." The school works with a small nonprofit called Peace Games, which has developed a seventeen-week curriculum for K–8 that involves parents and school staff in providing support for nonviolent approaches to recess, discipline, and after-school care. At the Dr. Martin Luther King, Jr. School, another new day school in Cambridge, the principal wrote all the parents about the new programs that a full eight-hour school day would allow, including the "Responsive Classroom" curriculum (one of the CASEL-highlighted programs), which "offers daily lessons on solving conflicts peacefully." The Responsive Classroom approach, founded on the ideas that social learning is as important as academic learning (since without the former students don't learn anything else very well) and that how children learn goes hand in hand with what children learn, employs such strategies as these:

- *Morning meeting:* A daily routine that builds community, creates a positive climate for learning, and reinforces academic and social skills.
- *Rules and logical consequences:* A clear and consistent approach to discipline that fosters responsibility and self-control.
- *Guided discovery:* A format for introducing materials that encourages inquiry, heightens interest, and teaches care of the school environment.
- *Academic choice:* An approach to giving children choices in their learning that helps them become invested, self-motivated learners.
- *Classroom organization:* Strategies for arranging materials, furniture, and displays to encourage independence, promote caring, and maximize learning.
- *Working with families:* Ideas for involving families as true partners in their children's education.

These curricula stress that schools are concerned both with reducing the amount of disruptive behavior and violence—a goal that necessarily involves an approach to discipline—and, on the other side of the equation, equipping children with the social and emotional tools to help them learn and succeed in school and life. Both, after all, are simply essential—both for the success of the school and for the success of individual children.

Nearly all of New York City's charter middle and high schools (described in the 2007 NYC Charter Schools Report online)—about half of which employ an expanded day of eight hours or more—use an "Advisory" system in which each teacher is assigned a group of students for the entire year, meeting daily or weekly with them to discuss issues outside the academic subject matter, and to make sure they do not, as one report puts it, "fall through the cracks." Web sites and e-mail lists devoted to middle school education commonly discuss and debate the advantages of Advisory. These discussions reveal that when teachers feel pressed for time to teach academic subjects, which is common in the traditional schedule, Advisory can be felt as an interruption, competing for scarce resources. Other teachers insist that it is essential both for them and their students, as a way to build relationships and deal with the real-life issues faced by young adolescents. In any event, when the Kuss Middle School in Fall River joined the ELT—new school day—Initiative in Massachusetts, the principal added Advisory to the schedule.

A significant number of schools we describe in this book require uniforms of their students as well, for a variety of reasons. Especially in middle and high school, uniform, modest clothing limits the influence of the outside world (whether in terms of overt sexuality or gangs or musical styles), and emphasizes that school is a different place, devoted to a different set of activities and values from those of the street or the neighborhood.

We've seen no nationwide statistics on the effectiveness of SEL programs, but the CASEL booklet *Safe and Sound* tells some terrific stories about the turnaround in Hudson, Massachusetts, where a school system transformed its climate, its test scores, and its reputation dramatically through the use of the Responsive Classroom and Second Step SEL curricula. "Families are now moving to Hudson 'for the schools,'" the authors argue, and "even real estate values have been positively affected." They tell a similar story about an elementary school in Monroe, Louisiana, and describe the Social Development Project in New Haven (Connecticut) public schools, which launched an "Extended Day Academy," including "after-school clubs, health-center services, and an outdoor adventure class."

SEL IN ACTION: ACHIEVABLE DREAM ACADEMY

"We really try to focus on preparing the kids for the day," says Achievable Dream Academy's principal, Catina Bullard-Clark. "We know time is important so they're ready mentally to start their day. As soon as kids come in, we start working with them: What happened this morning? In urban environments, there might have been violence the night before right outside their door or even in their own home. We get to prepare them for the day. We let them know, 'No matter what has happened, you're in a safe place.'

We do the same thing every day; the routine doesn't change. For kids in an urban environment, it's great to have a routine. They may stay at different places during the evening if their mom works, or if there's no mom. In our safe place, they recite banners, and the routine of the day is very important. We don't lose time, because they know what to expect. We really appreciate that."

Achievable Dream Academy is in the process of converting from K–8 to K–12, adding a grade a year from 2007 onward. It's located across the street and around the corner from very poor, often crime-ridden housing projects in Newport News, Virginia, and its mantra is social, academic, and moral education (SAME). Students memorize "banners": a series of slogans including the ones quoted at the beginning of the chapter, which run the gamut from self-esteem (I *am* somebody) to school principles (Proper business English spoken here), and attend a morning assembly—a pep rally, really—in which they reaffirm the value of the banners. The day we visited, Principal Clark introduced a new banner at the morning assembly, and asked students to repeat it several times: "Academically I will learn, and morally I will make the right decision."

Character development at Achievable Dream focuses on developing such basic virtues as self-discipline, honesty, integrity, respect for elders, respect for others' property, punctuality, loyalty, making the right decision, peaceful conflict resolution, and responsibility. "At the beginning our extended day wasn't about instruction," said Director Richard Coleman. "This was before NCLB and before VSOL [Virginia Standards of Learning] tests—it was all about character development."

Coleman and three colleagues, Thelma Spencer, Harvey Perkins, and John Hodge, have published *Standing in the Gap: A Guide to Using the SAME Framework to Create Excellent Schools,* a terrific guide to creating the school and school day (including excellent advice on the expanded school schedule) that elaborates on all these ideas.

At Achievable Dream Academy, where the challenges resemble those at Roxbury Prep, children learn to speak "proper business English"—the only acceptable language in the school. Why? Because the school's leadership and teachers are committed to preparing students to succeed in the mainstream world, the world where proper manners and standard English usage matter. We attended a class in which African American elementary students learned, sometimes laboriously but clearly thoroughly, to raise their hands and say, "May I *ask* you a question?"—as opposed to their much more common locution "aks." We could watch them visibly unlearning what they had brought to school. They call it "speaking green," not for environmentalism but for the color of money, of business. Richard Coleman explains. "We teach only proper business English. They need to be able to speak green to go for a job interview. They have to be able to navigate through the English language."

And the language they come to school with? "We call it 'speaking slang,'" says Coleman. "We don't tell them there's anything wrong with it. They can speak two languages: With friends, it's OK. In this world, they need to speak green." Do families get offended? "No," he says. "We don't get in their faces. We've been teaching them, and our staff, too, to self-correct."

Achievable Dream even teaches etiquette—table manners, table setting, and the like—beginning in kindergarten. We asked

---

Speaking Green Under Pressure

Disgraced NFL quarterback Michael Vick was from the Achievable Dream neighborhood, and the news media descended on Newport News.

"I'm watching the news," Director Coleman told us, "and there's Billy Anderson, a seventh grader, one of ours, speaking green to the media. Expressing himself in a well-mannered way, speaking green, no one there telling him to do it; he just did it. We all saw him on TV. I was in the paper, he was on TV. No one but us knows he's an Achievable Dream kid. We in the African American community are always afraid they'll find the most illiterate person and put a mike in his face. Instead, they found Billy Anderson!"

At the morning assembly, Coleman praised Billy's excellent English to the entire school, even though he disagreed with his student's defense of Vick.

if there was push-back from the parents, but it hasn't been a problem. "One father told me," Coleman said, "his daughter taught him how to set the table at home!" The community can be more difficult, as Achievable Dream kids occasionally face teasing from kids in the surrounding community. "It was much tougher last year," explained Coleman, "before we had our own building, when we were in Huntington Middle School, which has never been fully accredited and had a lot of behavioral problems. One day our principal, Tim Sweeney, was taking something out to his car as they were dismissing school. Huntington kids were teasing, making comments to Sweeney, to the point that even as an adult, he felt like he wanted to fight. And one of our kids says, 'Mr. Sweeney, we're just passing through this place; we're going to college, and they're probably not,' and calmed him down."

We ask about data on the character education. Achievable Dream staff don't have hard numbers, but the stories they tell are remarkable. They take the kids on field trips—to Thomas Jefferson's home at Monticello, to the opera in Norfolk, and to fancy restaurants. "Imagine forty-five African American kids going into a swanky restaurant. When we left, the owner said, 'You can come any time, your kids were wonderful.'"

Teacher Marilyn Luter described the trip to Monticello. "I know the character stuff works," she said. "In fourth grade I organized the field trip to Charlottesville, and then to Mickey Tavern: Four teachers took a hundred kids. I will never forget. The guide rolls his eyes when he saw us. We're waiting outside, watching these high school kids act horribly with the guide, and our kids are looking at me, thinking I'd say something. 'Did you see how they were acting?' they said to me. 'They weren't listening to their teachers and they were being disrespectful.' As we left the guide said, 'You all can come back anytime, you're the best-behaved group I've ever had.'"

She continues, "Then the tavern—can you imagine? Four teachers with a hundred African American kids, sitting in tables of eight and ten. I didn't even have to remind them of their manners. Gentlemen need to seat the ladies, even if it's somebody you don't like. It was a buffet, but they waited for each table to get its turn. When we left, the staff practically followed us out. We went to a tennis tournament once, and a woman gave us a wad of one-dollar bills to give them spending money. 'Their manners,' she said to us."

Achievable Dream Academy has an unusual schedule, calling itself a year-round school. It has about thirty more days than a standard school, and the sessions are staggered throughout the year, so that the most time the school is closed is five weeks in the summer. Since many people suggest lengthening the school year to meet some of the same concerns we're trying to address with the expanded school day, we asked principal Bullard-Clark if she had to choose between the expanded school day and the expanded year, which she would choose. She didn't hesitate. "Oh, if I had to choose, I'd go with the extended day. It really helps you prepare. We have so much going on; kids have so much baggage, they're thinking about 'Where am I going to sleep tonight?'—not multiplication. We just can't gloss over the fact that with things going on in certain neighborhoods, our character-education piece is even more important."

THE PAYOFF

Achievable Dream's approach to character education throws light on the fact that behavioral distractions and disciplinary problems often go hand in hand with the lowest-performing schools in low-income neighborhoods, where the achieve-ment gap is the largest. "Dreamers," as students at Achievable Dream call themselves, have been closing the achievement gap for years (though they had a hard time in the 2006–2007 school year, with a difficult principal, since departed). In the words of *Standing in the Gap,* Dreamers, who are 96 percent African American and all from low-income families, have pass-ing rates on statewide tests "within a few points of those for white students citywide. This is remarkable in a city and state in which the pass rate for black students on state tests trails that of white students by about 24 percentage points."

Boxed in by the old school day, most schools with these demo-graphics face a common dilemma: Should they devote more time to core academic subjects or more time to social and emotional learning or character education to improve student behavior, engagement, and school climate? There is so little time to work with that neither choice feels right. The alacrity with which the Expanded Learning Time schools in Massachusetts instituted SEL programs as soon as they expanded their school day speaks volumes. To meet the demands of NCLB, school leaders and teachers felt they had had to focus on academics at the expense of the kind of education that would allow their students to fully concentrate on their academic work—and as soon as they had the chance, they moved immediately to right the balance.

These schools often make SEL programs a part of their broader efforts to improve school climate and the learning environment, including student uniforms, contracts with parents, and clear, forceful discipline. These initiatives interact more than we realize. Take "peer education," a growing trend in education at all levels, in which teachers help students themselves to be teachers of their fellow students. (Often students pay closer attention to what their peers say than to what their teachers do.) An SEL curriculum that teaches respectful modes of interaction makes peer learning more practical in the classroom. But without the time to teach or use peer education, many schools take a pass on it. In Expanded Learning Time schools, it's more common because time allows teachers to include it.

From the lowest-achieving schools in the United States, principally urban schools in low-income neighborhoods, to the most storied private schools in America, the development of children's social and emotional skills plays an enormous role in what they are able to learn. The new school day, whether it's been in use for a century or just begun last year, has enabled schools to combine the skills and insights of these curricula with their academic offerings—improving student achievement and discipline and creating the climate all teachers and children need for real learning.

7

NO MORE COUCH POTATOES

Recess, Physical Education, and Sports in the New School Day

The message I get from teachers is that the kids are doing more work than they ever did before, they are more engaged in their classes than they ever were before. They're really excited about being here. Their attendance has improved. They look forward to the football aspect of the day so much that they don't want to jeopardize it. They are doing everything that is asked of them.

—TEACHER AND FOOTBALL COACH,
EDWARDS MIDDLE SCHOOL, BOSTON

NOWHERE ARE THE CHALLENGES OR dilemmas of balancing academics and children's other developmental needs clearer than in the question of how to give kids enough time for exercise and just plain play. One of the oldest educational injunctions we have, the Roman poet Juvenal's *"mens sana in corpore sano"*—a healthy mind in a healthy body—is engraved over Horace Mann Hall at Teachers College of Columbia University, and our own common sense tells us that children ought to have time for what we think of as childhood: some unstructured time to run around, play, and otherwise discharge their often astonishing energy. Very young children's play, as child psychologists have been demonstrating for decades, is one of the key ways they learn and develop as human beings.

Why Play Matters

Older children may not need to play in the same way as babies, but here again, educational researchers who have carefully observed schoolchildren have confirmed our own common sense. One widely cited study looked at urban fourth-grade children's behavior when they had a twenty-minute recess and when they didn't, and found that recess reduced kids' fidgeting in class and increased the amount of time they spent on task. Recess seemed especially helpful to children with Attention Deficit Hyperactivity Disorder, who were able to focus much better after a recess period. For such children, argues one ADHD expert, "Recess isn't an extra activity; it's an essential one. Physical activity is healthy and relaxing, and provides focus and clarity of mind. But the benefits of recess go beyond reducing the fidget factor: Kids learn social skills on the playground, and teachers can learn a lot about their students by watching them play, by noticing who is being isolated, teased, or bullied."

Other researchers argue that physical activity actually stimulates brain activity, and that extensive evidence supports the notion that the brain works in cycles—and cannot sustain high levels of focus for a very long time. Children, argue child psychologists and experts in early childhood education, need breaks or their attention begins to wander. That's why effective classroom teachers, especially in long blocks of time, move children around from one activity—even one place (in elementary school)—to another. This is hardly rocket science: How often can most adults concentrate on a single task or subject without needing to move around, stretch, or change focus?

Receding Recess

The school-based answer to this need for balance has classically been recess, a period during the day in which kids can play and socialize, preferably outside (weather permitting) in a schoolyard or on a playground. Most of us recall recess as a fundamental part of school life, one of the places in which we could make up our own activities, hang out with our friends, share stories and crack jokes, and do physical things.

We're not making the argument that recess is or ever was all happy activity. It's hard to picture a playground that never includes aggression, teasing, or bullying. And even setting aside such overt aggression, children argue a lot over the rules of their games and whether things are fair or not. If adults cannot genuinely supervise, teach conflict resolution skills, and intervene when necessary, recess can become an intimidating psychological and physical experience for many children. Even so, parents and educators almost unanimously agree that recess gives far more than it takes.

Which makes it all the more stunning and distressing that school districts across the country are cutting back on recess time or eliminating it outright! As of 2000, two years before NCLB, only a little more than seven in ten schools—nationwide— offered recess, and many of those had cut back the amount of time devoted to it, while many more were considering major cutbacks. As early as June 1999, a *Chicago Reporter* survey found that 80 percent of the city's public elementary schools had no recess at all, and a *Chicago Tribune* reporter found that in suburban districts as well, recess was increasingly rare after second grade. "For administrators faced with a growing list of priorities," she wrote, "from foreign language classes to creative writing programs, the challenge remains how to shoehorn it all into the school day."

"It's really not about recess," one suburban principal from an affluent, overwhelmingly white school district was quoted as saying in the *Tribune* article. "It's about time management." Commentators across the country ridiculed the quotation, thinking he was talking about the children. They misunderstood. In reality, he was lamenting the lack of time in the school day to do everything he felt obliged to provide for children. "We keep adding and adding and we don't take anything away.... We're trying to be all things to all people, and it's an impossible task." Another school official, this one in the low-income city neighborhood called "Back of the Yards," argued that if "you take away [from class time] that extra 45 minutes" for recess, "you lose a lot of instructional time." Given this state of affairs *before* NCLB, it will come as no surprise that when *Catalyst Chicago* surveyed nearly five hundred schools four years later, in 2005, it discovered that "fewer than one in five schools—18 percent—provide daily scheduled recess for all kids, and *only about one in 16—6 percent*—provide for a recess of at least twenty minutes" (emphasis added).

What's going on here? Well, as one Florida official explained to the *St. Petersburg Times*, "The impetus for getting rid of recess really started with the liability. Kids were getting hurt on blacktops, injured on playgrounds. As society got increasingly litigious through the 1980s, schools started eliminating the possibility of recess accidents." And older playground equipment doesn't meet Americans with Disabilities Act accessibility guidelines, so districts are electing not to buy expensive new equipment that passes ADA muster.

A decade ago the Atlanta superintendent flatly eliminated traditional outdoor recess from the city's public schools. "We are intent on improving academic performance," Benjamin O. Canada told the *New York Times*, "You don't do that by having kids hanging on the monkey bars." Atlanta's new schools began being built without playgrounds. "Many parents still don't quite get it," the superintendent said. "They'll ask, 'So when are we getting a new playground?' And I'll say, 'There's not going to be a new playground.'"

Parents, who have a visceral understanding of the importance of play for their children, face a different set of pressures than the ones school districts are dealing with. As a result, many are up in arms on the issue. PTAs have organized to pressure schools to reinstate recess, and a number of Web sites offer advice to parents on how to bring pressure to bear on their local schools. There is even a group calling itself the "American Association for the Child's Right to Play," an affiliate of an international organization based around the United Nations 1959 Declaration of the Rights of the Child, which states, "The child shall have full opportunity for play and recreation which should be directed to the same purposes as education; society and the public authorities shall endeavor to promote the enjoyment of this right."

When the *New York Times* reporter asked a child he described as "a 5-year-old with a smart vocabulary and a zesty sense of wonder" about recess, the 1998 story continued, she could only respond, "What's recess?" Written years before passage of the No Child Left Behind Act, the story continued (in language that sounds as though it could have been published in today's paper), "The elimination of recess often causes an uproar among parents. But school administrators, who say they face growing pressures to increase academic performance, are being put in a box. Not only are they being required to teach children reading, writing and arithmetic, but they are also expected to prepare children for a whole set of worldly issues, from drugs to sex to safety. On top of that, many elementary schools are responding to increasing demands for fine arts education, like dance and drama, especially in more affluent areas." The only thing missing from this litany of competing pressures is the question of publicly accountable high-stakes testing, which is now prompting principals, superintendents, and school boards to cut back on many subjects and activities including recess and physical education. Seven years after the *Times* story, a reporter was helping his son's first-grade class create a newspaper. One of the boys had written a sports story about "open-court" Fridays, when "You can dig. Sometimes you can shoot baskets. And sometimes you can play soccer. . . . Everybody likes open court." Making conversation, the reporter said, "It sounds just like recess." But, "the boy looked up and asked a question that scared me," he wrote: "What's recess?"

Despite the initial fears of some parents that the new school day has an "anti-play" or "anti-sports" agenda, the reality is that the current school day is what's severely limiting recess and physical play. How much clearer can it be that the old school day is forcing dreadful choices on the largely well-meaning, committed, and caring men and women responsible for American public education?

When these educators have more time to work with, they put recess back into the schedule. More time lets schools reset the balance between academic instruction and physical play. When they never lost the time, as in private schools or charter schools, they naturally include recess and free time in the school schedule.

THE LOSS OF PE

It's not only recess, of course, that has suffered in recent years. Physical education, known popularly for decades as PE, has also taken a hit. According to the American Association and the National Association for Sport and Physical Education, in a 2006 report titled "The Shape of the Nation," while 42 percent of students attended a daily physical education class in 1991, only 28 percent did so in 2003. In Massachusetts, the *Boston Globe* reports, just 14 percent of public and private high school students attended daily PE; while by 2005, 59 percent of high school students had gym class at least once weekly, down from 80 percent a decade earlier. The National Association for Sport and Physical Education estimates that less than one in a dozen schools meet its recommendations of 150 minutes a week, 30 minutes a day, of elementary school PE instruction, and 220 minutes a week, an average of one 44-minute period per day, for secondary schools.

This decline has real consequences. Americans used to engage in considerably higher levels of physical activity. Much of this was painful and taxing, to be sure, such as carrying water long distances, but much else, such as walking, was generally less so. We have become more sedentary, which means that we sit more (whether at desks or in cars), and physical activity has become *exercise*, a hobby or a sport that is learned, paid for, prescribed, and at times even a luxury (downhill skiing, winter tennis). When one of the few institutions mandating physical education gives up the ghost on PE, children both lose an important dimension of a well-balanced life, and gain a set of health problems so serious that some in the public health community predict that this could be the first generation of Americans to have a shorter life expectancy than its parents' generation.

It is hardly news that American children are getting fatter. According to the Centers for Disease Control and Prevention, the percentage of children between the ages of two and nineteen who are overweight has tripled in the past three decades, from 5–6.5 percent (for different age groups) to 14–19 percent for these same groups. Nearly a fifth of children from six to eleven years old are overweight, something that comes as no surprise to any regular visitor to school classrooms. In fact, the acceleration of obesity rates in recent years has genuinely frightened some public health advocates, who also point out the increasing prevalence of obesity the lower the income group. Obesity is roughly half as common among college graduates as among those lacking a high school education.

Given the recent national alarm over childhood obesity and the increased risk of cardiovascular disease and diabetes that it brings to children and adults, it seems little short of astonishing that during the one pursuit involving every American child every

day of the week—attending school—we would be cutting back
on one of the few activities proven to reduce the chance of obesity: physical education and exercise. And if sports and physical
education really do encompass learned activities, why wouldn't
children learn them in school, which is organized for the teaching and learning of all kinds of different activities? (One study of
recess and PE even concludes that kids spend more time in vigorous physical activity in recess time than in PE!) But that is the
truth of today's schools. According to the CDC, only 6–8 percent
of the nation's schools provide daily PE for the entire school
year. RAND Corporation economist Roland Sturm concludes,
"Like arts education, PE is added, deleted, added, and deleted,
and teachers are hired and fired based on what is happening to a
budget at a particular time."

Even worse, perhaps, is that we have inadvertently reduced physical education for those families who cannot afford purchased alternatives, and pushed more affluent families to find other forms of
physical activity for their children. Data from the National Center
for Education Statistics shows a direct relationship between family
income and participation in sports. In other words, only 11 percent of children from the poorest families (incomes under $15,000
per year) play sports, while more than one-third of children from
families whose annual income is $50,000 to $75,000 per year do so.
More than half of those in the top bracket (over $75,000) partici-
pate in organized sports outside school. "I think one interpretation
is that we've privatized PE—not intentionally—but by cutting back
on physical education in the schools," Russell Pate, a professor of
exercise science at the University of South Carolina, told CNN.
"We've put parents in the position of finding these services elsewhere, and families with resources can get their kids into classes
and sports leagues, but transportation issues and safety issues can
be greater barriers for less advantaged families."

PHYSICAL ACTIVITY LEVELS IN THE NEW SCHOOL DAY

The desire to recover recess and PE are among the reasons low-
income parents get their children on charter school waiting
lists. They know that their kids need physical activity, and they'd

prefer it be supervised in safe places, rather than haphazard and in vacant lots or parking lots or the street. When we visited KIPP Academy, Houston, we saw first graders learning soccer in the gym at 8:30 in the morning. The message sent by this class, as well as the reality it represented, was clear: physical education, education in sports, belongs in the school day—not as a voluntary or accidental part of a student's daily life. More time in the day allows schools to build PE and recess back into their day— and it's a choice they make with great consistency.

When the Dr. Martin Luther King, Jr. K–8 School in Cambridge, Massachusetts, converted to the new school day, it added the opportunity for students to pick sports and physical activities as midday electives. One mother we met there spoke of how much her son enjoyed it and how much she felt he needed it to "blow off steam" before returning to class. At the Matthew Kuss Middle School in Fall River, not only do students have some pure physical activity electives, the staff have imaginatively created a math enrichment class called Fit Math where students combine physical training with quantitative analysis such as statistics. At the new day Greenfield Middle School, also in Massachusetts, students pick from a series of elective courses termed "encore" classes. In early September, students had the chance to listen to teachers' pitches. Competing for student attention with other choices including band, computer technology, woodshop, and theater, two teachers laid out their plans for a physical education encore class that would range from cooperative play to the opportunity to compete in tournaments.

Elite private schools *require* students to engage in athletics and set aside enormous amounts of time and resources for this purpose, on the theory that playing sports provides physical and psychological education of enormous value. We agree. Well-taught and supervised, sports help build and strengthen both individual self-reliance and group teamwork; they also develop physical coordination and mental discipline, perseverance and risk-taking, calmness in the face of pressure, and humility and grace in victory and defeat. They're also fun. And these qualities apply in dance just as much as they do in volleyball or lacrosse, ice skating as much as ice hockey, karate, or football. Between us we have played sports (and still do), coached sports, rooted for our children on fields and courts and tracks, written about sports history and issues, and followed favorite teams passionately.

So when parents worry that the new school day might cut into their children's time to learn and play sports, we empathize with the concern but disagree with the assumption. And we know of extremely few instances of a child no longer being able to play sports because of the new school day. We did interview a boy at Roxbury Prep who found that he was getting out of school too late for football practice, so he gave it up. But take KIPP Academy, Houston, where we asked Mike Feinberg how kids could play in city leagues requiring after-school practice. He was unfazed. "They can be in weekend and evening leagues."

Sports as a Lure

"I had one boy, an elite soccer player, who was on the city's elite soccer team," Mike Feinberg told us. "I worked out a deal with his mom and his coach. As long as things were going very well with us during the week he could miss Saturday school. He's now playing for Dallas in Major League Soccer. And there were times he wasn't doing what he was supposed to during the week, and I said, 'You can't go.'"

Jean Teal is the principal of a high school in football-crazy Florida, so she's had to think about how to combine the Zone with her school's sports teams. "I had a conversation with the football coach," she told us, "because a lot of his team members were in those intensive classes, and in mandatory tutoring all week long, and on Saturdays too. We've worked it out; they have to come to tutoring first, then football." In a sense, it's obvious—as long as the emphasis is in the right place, sports can be a genuine incentive.

But there are times that parents and students either want to make choices, or have to do so. At a community meeting in one Massachusetts town to talk about whether the local schools should think about adopting the new school day, parents hammered away on the town sports teams, and how bad it could be if children stayed in school for another couple of hours and missed some of the teams' scheduled practices. Finally, one parent rose and said to the room, "You know, I like football too. But I care a lot more about whether my kid can read and write well, whether he learns math and science." This struck a chord; the truth about most American public education is that our children's football teams are terrific, while their preparation for higher education and work in the twenty-first century has been mediocre. In school after school in the most highly educated state in the country, hundreds of thousands of children are failing or barely passing exams they ought to be able to ace. Why would Americans be satisfied with their children barely achieving minimum standards? Being satisfied with meeting minimum requirements means that the great majority of our children, even those in the top 10 percent or 20 percent of schools in the county, never get to the challenging and sophisticated levels of geography, physics, engineering, or foreign languages—the levels that create lifelong learners and give kids the kind of head start that prepares them for leadership as adults.

College teachers routinely observe that a shocking number of their first-year students—even those from highly rated affluent suburban high schools, cannot reliably write a paragraph of grammatical prose, or understand Abraham Lincoln's Second Inaugural Address, and approach their required elementary mathematics course as a horrible trial that they might well fail. We believe there's overwhelming evidence that the American educational system falls short for our children, their parents, and the larger society, and that an expanded, redesigned school day offers the best hope for far-reaching reform and results. And at most new day schools, *kids play sports.*

TIME FOR A WHOLE EDUCATION

We believe that the new school day should encompass more time for both deeper core academics *and* a more well-rounded education. That well-rounded education should include significant amounts of physical activity for every child. The new day schools we have visited agree—and accomplish this—and have thereby reversed what we consider a dangerous trend. As parents and as participants ourselves, we also believe in the value and importance of competitive sports for those talented, determined, and eager enough to play them. We've seen plenty of evidence that the new school day can be organized to leave enough time for such organized sports teams, whether run by the schools after the school day or run by towns and cities beyond the school day. And we realize that accommodating both might mean having to make adjustments in the sports schedule.

We will say this, too: If the price of children learning to read and write more fluently is having to move town sports times around, or even a little less time on the playing field, that's the kind of mature choice a town, school board, PTA, or society could gladly make. Even the Roxbury Prep student who told us he gave up football understood the stakes. "It was one of the best decisions to go here," he told us, "because sometimes you've got to do stuff for your future."

8

INSIDE JOB

Redefining Homework into the New School Day

*Take the stressor out of the family situation. Parents
say, "Boy, I'm so happy he gets homework time." There
are no fights over homework. It's a good thing.*
—TONY CAPUTO, FORMER PRINCIPAL, JACOB HIATT
MAGNET SCHOOL, WORCESTER, MASSACHUSETTS

*They have a lot of homework after but the majority of
the homework, the hard stuff, is done at school and the
easy stuff is done at home, which is good. And I think
that's a good thing for them.*
—PARENT, EDWARDS MIDDLE SCHOOL,
CHARLESTOWN, MASSACHUSETTS

JUST AS EVERY STUDENT KNOWS homework comes at the
end of the day, our chapter on homework follows our description of the new school day. The impact of the new school day
on homework is important for at least a couple of reasons.
Homework exists in significant part to allow for more learning
to happen after school dismissal, so we need to ask if the same
amount of homework is really needed in an expanded school
schedule. At the same time, parents frequently raise the question of how their children will have time to complete homework
if they're going to school more. Here we'll probe these issues by
looking at the experience of kids in new day schools.

Why Homework?

Homework is, in theory, supposed to address three educational needs. First, through homework students practice certain skills acquired during the school day: skills such as long division, multiplying decimals, conjugating verbs, or finding the subject of a sentence. Practice is required to develop these skills and render them nearly automatic. Second, homework should allow students to absorb or engage larger quantities of material than the length of the school day allows. A child might read two additional chapters in a novel, say, or take a first crack at reading Abraham Lincoln's Gettysburg Address before the class takes it up the next day. And third, by working out of school, particularly on a larger project like a research paper, students learn independence, the ability to organize their own time and effort, and a form of self-discipline and organization.

But like almost everything else in American education, homework has become a controversial topic in various education and culture wars. In reality, homework has been an on-and-off hot-button issue in the United States since the late nineteenth and early twentieth centuries, according to an authoritative study by Brian Gill and Steven Schlossman (of the RAND Corporation and Carnegie Mellon University, respectively). Around the turn of the last century, the Progressive education movement began to argue that assigning rote drills at home (the bulk of homework at the time) both placed alienating, undue burdens on children and failed to pay off in academic achievement. This critique of homework only gathered more steam until the watershed decade of the 1950s, when rivalry with the Soviet Union, particularly the Sputnik launch in 1957, galvanized a new national conversation about education as a weapon in the Cold War, in effect rehabilitating homework.

The late 1960s and 1970s again found homework on the defensive (along with much in the way of cultural authority), after which the new "excellence" movement, sparked by publication of *A Nation at Risk* in 1983, reinvigorated homework yet again. In 1986, the U.S. Department of Education, then under the leadership of William Bennett, published an extremely popular pamphlet called "What Works," arguing (among other things), "Student achievement rises significantly when teachers regularly assign homework and students conscientiously do it." A majority of educators, school districts, and parents appeared to have reached a rare consensus in favor of homework.

The National Center for Education Statistics asks high school sophomores how much time they spend on homework in the average week. The shift between 1980 and 2002 was dramatic. Whereas one in six in 1980 said they did less than an hour a week, by 2002 only two in a hundred reported such low homework levels. In 1980, 71 percent had reported less than five hours of homework for the whole week, but by 2002 that had fallen to 37 percent. By contrast, while only 7 percent of sophomores in 1980 reported more than ten hours per week of homework—that is, two hours or more a night—that had mushroomed to 37 percent of those asked in 2002. As a result of the shift toward more homework, children's backpacks seemed to grow—and grow—in the 1980s and 1990s, reaching the size and design of small suitcases in recent years. As a result, the early years of this century have witnessed something of a backlash, in such rousing titles as *The End of Homework: How Homework Disrupts Families, Overburdens Children, and Limits Learning* and *The Case Against Homework: How Homework Is Hurting Our Children and What We Can Do About It.*

Educators, social critics, parents—everyone's got an opinion. On one side, some argue that children and families struggle under an enormous burden of mind-numbing homework. Others fear that huge homework assignments further reduce the amount of unscheduled time children have, and that homework takes away from childhood freedom and creative play. No parents take pleasure in tussling with children over homework after a long workday or late into the evening—when they'd rather be enjoying family time. For all the rhetoric about parent involvement in children's education, even well-educated, English-speaking parents often struggle to understand their children's homework assignments (especially in math or science, but potentially in English and history as well). By the same token, even the most conscientious parents with limited English feel utterly incapable of helping their children with most homework.

A significant number of homework critics go further and base their concerns not on the argument that homework is unproductive but on the argument that it is inequitable. Evidence shows that college-educated, higher-income parents are more likely to enforce homework requirements, better able to supply a good environment (a quiet, well-lit desk area, for example), and both more likely and better able to offer homework help. One study even demonstrated that the type of homework help varies by education level, with highly educated parents pursuing Socratic methods to make their children think about the problems, while less educated parents tended to give their children concrete answers.

This equity-based objection is that more affluent children find homework easier to complete and easier to do well, than do their lower-income counterparts. In other words, homework assignments tend to widen the well-established achievement gap. Data from the National Center for Education Statistics support this concern. Among high school sophomores asked how often they came to school unprepared, half again as many low-income children as high-income children said they often or usually came to school without their homework completed. And while a portion of higher-income and high-achieving students fell into this "often-unprepared" category, less than 20 percent of the highest-scoring students fell into this category, while 40 percent of the lowest-scoring students did.

While we agree with the argument that homework tends to widen rather than narrow the achievement gap, we do not agree with many critics' conclusion that homework should be reduced or eliminated to level the playing field. It's not that homework doesn't help students learn, some argue, but since it's unfair to disadvantaged children we ought to get rid of it. We, on the other hand, think that the solution to the homework wars lies not in handicapping all students but in helping all students, regardless of their families' income level, to gain the learning benefits of homework. New day schools do exactly that, by increasing the percentage of "homework" done at school and by ensuring that all children complete their assignments.

On the pro-homework side of the debate, many parents and educators argue that homework assignments flow naturally from a rigorous curriculum, and that to succeed in today's globally competitive world, children need to supplement the school day with a substantial amount of homework. After all, for students to truly master new skills in subjects as different as math and English, they need to practice what they learn in the course of classroom instruction. It's not that "practice makes perfect," but that without genuine practice, students never truly master new ways of thinking, calculating, or expressing themselves. As University of Virginia cognitive scientist Daniel T. Willingham argues, "It is difficult to overstate the value of practice. For a new skill to become automatic or for new knowledge to become long-lasting, sustained practice, beyond the point of mastery, is necessary."

Despite the changing opinions of education professionals, surveys have shown parents to be consistently in favor of *some* homework for their children for better than a century. As measured in the 2006 Annual Phi Delta Kappa/Gallup Poll, 73 percent of adults felt that high school students are not given enough homework while only 15 percent thought there is too much.

Some homework advocates object to what they call "coddling" children. Either the "homework crisis" is utterly exaggerated, they claim, or the alarm is wrongheaded. If they are to be genuinely prepared for the tough global environment of the future, American schoolchildren need to take some lessons from their Asian counterparts and learn how to buckle down. As for parents, they need to recognize that they're not doing their children any favors by shielding them from the very real demands of a serious education.

HOMEWORK: STRATEGIES FOR GETTING IT DONE

New day schools vary considerably on how they manage homework. Some resolve the tension by taking some to most of the "home" out of "homework," moving the activity into the school day. There, children do a good bit of their assigned work in classrooms with their teachers. These are not passive study halls; they're active opportunities for students to get help and even tutoring as needed while they hone their skills. According to Tony Caputo, Hiatt School teachers assign very little homework. Why? "As the curriculum got more complex, one thing we heard from parents clearly was 'We can't help kids with homework; we don't understand it.'" They didn't understand science or the new reading curriculum, which had new terminology. "They told us, 'We don't know how to help our kids.'" These parents, including those with limited English skills, much preferred their children to do homework—maybe we should call it "out-of-class" work, or use math teacher Scott Miller's term, "home learning"—at school, where they could get the help they needed from teachers who understood the curriculum.

Homework issues ripple through much of school life. "In a lot of instances," Caputo continued, "a major cause of discipline issues in middle schools is kids who come back to school with no homework done, because they have no support at home. That gets them in trouble at school, and sometimes even gets them thrown out of school. Take the stressor out of the family situation. Parents say, 'Boy, I'm so happy he gets homework time.' There are no fights over homework. It's a good thing."

He continues, with characteristic bluntness. "You've got to look at why you're giving homework. If it's work that should have been accomplished in school and there wasn't enough time, then I understand. If it's just drill, but the child already gets it, maybe it's just taking up time. If the kid doesn't get how to do it at all, then it's a waste of time. If they get time during the day to get the work done, you've eliminated two of these situations, and in the third the kids shouldn't be doing it at all. If they get enough time and enough supervision, why send it home?"

One group of Massachusetts new day schools—those participating in the Expanded Learning Time Initiative—offers an interesting test case of how homework is handled, as they convert from the old day to the new, longer schedule. We have found that many parents and students have expressed considerable concern that a longer day capped by a large amount of homework would be too much for students and could take away from evening family time. Experience has shown that schools are getting it—half of parents surveyed from three of the first-year conversion middle schools reported that their children had less homework each evening. Listen to this ELT parent, from Charlestown, Massachusetts:

"I find that it's good for them because they get help with the homework. Some of the math I can say is different from when I grow up. So when they say, 'I need help with the math,' and it's algebra or it's trigonometry, or something different, I can say, 'If you stay after school, they can help you learn that, figure it out, because I didn't take that in school.' So it makes me feel better that they can finish their homework at that time, which they are still with their friends and they're all learning the same thing so they feel good."

But not all new day schools reduce homework sent home. Others embrace the value of the extra work but find ways to ensure that students can and do really get it done. At Roxbury Prep, where teachers assign substantial homework most nights, the school has strict, schoolwide homework policies: for full credit, homework must be submitted on time; students can earn partial credit if homework is turned in by the beginning of class the next day. A recorded, telephone "homework hotline" lists the day's assignments after 5 PM. But perhaps most important, the school says deftly in its annual report, it "has learned through experience that not every student has a home environment that is conducive to Roxbury Prep's rigorous and strict homework standards." School officials understand that students who "repeatedly fail to complete homework satisfactorily . . . would fall behind, receive poor grades, lose confidence, and fail to fulfill their potential." As a result, the school Homework Center "provides the quiet space, supervision, and academic support needed to make sure that struggling students complete their homework to the best of their ability every night." So even though the school culture pushes homework—lots of it, to be honest—school leaders take responsibility for making sure students can complete it. In fact, the Homework Center program "produces a near-perfect homework completion rate and thereby improves students' academic skills and grades."

A group of eighth graders told us that while sixth grade was easiest, during seventh grade they did homework during their computer classes, and eighth grade was tough. "I get home at 5, 5:30," says Kalina, "then eat, and finish about 8 or 8:30. My curfew is 9, and then I read every night."

Making a Trade-Off

Terence says, "You can finish your homework here [at school, but then] when I got out it was just too late [for football practice]."

"Do you regret coming here?" we ask.

"No, I'd rather come here. I was supposed to go to one of the worst middle schools. Even though you can't do stuff here, like pranks or Halloween, this place is really strict. But I think it was the best decision to go here because sometimes you've got to do stuff for your future."

"Did you lose friends?"

"Yes, but I made new ones, a whole bunch of new ones."

Before ending the chapter, we should point out that families whose children attend the most competitive schools in the nation generally have a very different take on the homework problem. They live in a world where homework levels and difficulty have grown considerably over the past ten to twenty years as their schools have raised the workload and intensity to improve SAT scores, college placement success, and other goals of more affluent parents. For those schools and students, a conversion to a new day schedule would have to be accompanied by a thorough review of homework practices, with a significant reduction in the amount sent home each evening. We believe that these students, these schools, and these families would all be better off by moving most essential practice work into the expanded school day, leaving only a more modest amount of independent reading, research, and writing to go home with students. Such a trade-off would help students and families, we believe, reach a healthier balance while ensuring students had the time—and where needed, the help—to reach their academic goals.

Bringing the new school day to thousands of additional American schools won't do away with the century-old debate over homework. It should, however, make it far easier for students to complete the homework they get, mostly on their own or with their teachers' help; reduce the amount of friction between parents and children; level the playing field for all children to be able to use the tasks of homework effectively to build their skills and knowledge; and ease the burden on all parents and the distress of less well educated parents and those uncomfortable with speaking and reading in English. Helping students practice what they've learned in school—a decision made possible by the new school day—can solve far more problems than it causes.

PART THREE

WHO BENEFITS FROM MORE LEARNING TIME?

9

THE GIFT OF MORE TIME

Teachers and Teaching in the New School Day

Adding some time to our school and having the opportunity to be creative with this program was a godsend for our school. . . . There's a lot more buy-in with our students and our staff . . . and I can only see it getting better.
—ELT DIRECTOR AND TEACHER,
EDWARDS MIDDLE SCHOOL, BOSTON

BEYOND ITS EFFECT ON INDIVIDUAL aspects of school life—reading, math, homework, enrichment, and the like—the expanded school day has a huge overall impact on schools. It gives students more time to learn and practice what they learn, and it gives teachers more time to teach, collaborate, and prepare. This chapter looks broadly at how the new school day helps teachers and teaching.

TEACHERS

Almost without exception teachers in new day schools appreciate the value and effectiveness of having more time. Many are also challenged by the added energy of the expanded day.

One group of new day schools—charters and experimental district schools—have had the expanded schedule since inception, and have recruited all their teachers on that basis. KIPP co-founder Mike Feinberg and Roxbury Prep co-director Josh Phillips both described the large numbers of applicants they receive for every open position, which they credit to their schools' national reputations for high-performance results. Since they want to keep the ones they do hire, they make very sure applicants understand that working longer hours with an intense sense of mission is demanding; any candidate who had concerns on this score, they felt, helped everyone by not coming to work there.

KIPP Schools have the longest hours—60 percent more time for students each year—and the most controversial reputation regarding whether teachers can work there over the long term. If you look up "KIPP" and "teachers" on Google, you will find scores of entries and the occasional blog firefight between partisans. KIPP is the iconic charter school network and receives the benefits—huge levels of support from foundations, close interest from leading thinkers, strong brand name appeal. It also gets the liabilities—strong criticism from those who feel KIPP's successes are overblown or come at too high a price. In this debate, supporters, including current teachers, emphasize the extraordinary gains and the time and attitude that they feel make this progress happen. Critics attack what they see as the schools' rigidity and describe the hours as unsustainable for mature adults.

While KIPP's rugged schedule may not be sustainable for some, we've been impressed by the quality and enthusiasm of the teachers we've met, many of whom had worked for KIPP for some time. An intense sense of collective mission, after all, sustains many of the most successful organizations, no matter the field. They vividly described the benefits of more time. Take Sam Lopez, a mature man who had taught in a standard public school before joining KIPP. "I like the way we structure the schedule, with PE and art, morning and afternoon. I have an hour-and-fifteen-minute class, which allows me to reinforce a lot of reading and writing. We have that time. You also have time to pull kids aside and talk to them. Lots of our kids are trying to figure out who they are, trying to make the right choices. Often parents can't help, and we get to talk to them. We can pull them aside and talk to them one on one, and say, 'You haven't been yourself—what's happening?'"

He told us about the enthusiasm students had for what has become a classic learning undertaking at the KIPP Houston

Middle School. Sixth-grade students of ancient Egypt may forget some dynastic facts, but very few forget science teacher Dena Garcia's annual project, in which they mummify and then bury a dead chicken following ancient Egyptian rituals. "The hours are mentally draining sometimes," she admitted in an interview, illustrating her hours by explaining how she used to drive by an auto detailing shop on her way to and from school—and it either hadn't opened yet in the morning or had already closed in the evening. On the other hand, she has stayed for nine years. She loves it when former students come back to visit, invariably asking, "When are we going to dig up those chickens?"

Roxbury Prep teachers work fewer hours than KIPP teachers do, but not by much—and have managed to build a strong team of teachers that stay for a while. Still, the school needed to replace six teachers for the 2006–2007 school year. (Three had moved away—to New York City, London, and Afghanistan—while two went on to full-time graduate study, and one decided to go into teaching the arts. The school received more than a thousand applications for these six slots. The problem lay not in recruitment but in selection—the most persuasive evidence that the model is working to attract teachers. Many of the applicants to pioneering charter schools such as Roxbury Prep and KIPP are new graduates, second-career teachers, or former teachers at standard public schools, which argues not only for the model's sustainability over the long term but for the changing nature of the professional workplace, in which many qualified people will work in many different specialties over the course of their working lifetimes.

The other types of new day schools—turnarounds and conversions—pose very different challenges for teachers, since in both cases schools and faculties that have long followed the traditional day are faced with the prospect of change to the expanded schedule.

When Miami-Dade decided to create its thirty-nine-school Improvement Zone by adding one hour per day, the district negotiated with the teachers' union for a window of opportunity and voluntary change for teachers at these schools. The negotiated language provided for "the transfer of teaching staff into and out of the Zone schools in a way that incorporates teacher choice, seniority and the instructional needs of the Zone schools." The net result was that as many as half of the teachers at schools elected out despite the higher pay and the new energy. Fortunately, the district easily replenished those ranks with willing replacements. So despite some musical chairs, Zone schools ended up, like pioneering charter and experimental schools, with teachers who understood the difference and consciously chose the new schedule, mission, professional development, and pay scale.

The Massachusetts Expanded Learning Time (ELT) Initiative is fundamentally different because local teachers are involved from the outset in the decision to switch to the expanded schedule. While superintendents and principals typically initiate the effort, they recruit teachers to the redesign committee that does the planning work; in most cases, faculty have to vote as to whether they want to proceed with conversion. Most votes have been strongly in favor, and in those schools where teachers voted a second time after the initial year, the margins stayed the same or expanded considerably. Further, since these schools have generally made participation by individual teachers voluntary, there has been no need for teachers less interested or personally not able to work the extra hours (because, say, of family obligations to young children or aging parents) to move to another school.

We have heard from many teachers in Massachusetts ELT schools who express the same kind of enhanced job satisfaction based on having more time to help their students succeed. Stephanie Baker of the Kuss Middle School in Fall River, a family and consumer science teacher for twenty-two years, told the *Boston Globe*, "this has been one of my most rewarding teaching years in all my life. I feel good about this year. There's something absolutely right about this." Grace Farias, a kindergarten teacher at the N.B. Borden Elementary School in Fall River, commented, "With the old schedule, there was never enough time for everything. Now I say to myself, 'How did I fit in the things that I'm doing now?' Everything was always a rush. 'I've got to get this done. I've got to get that done.' Now, there's time for science, for social studies, for nutrition. There's more time for reading and writing. There's more time to spend with the kids." Anne Wass, president of the Massachusetts Teachers Association (the state chapter of the National Education Association, the largest teachers' union in the country) monitored teacher satisfaction closely in the first year and told the *Christian Science Monitor* that the teachers were "shocked" at how satisfying it was to teach to the new schedule.

Teachers also appreciate the higher pay. Many teachers in schools with the conventional schedule have taken on second jobs. Estimates vary, but it seems that at least one-third of all teachers work at other jobs either after hours during the year or in the summer; many others earn stipends to tutor or coach. While a few say they do it for variety, most say they need the money. The Malden, Massachusetts superintendent reported that several teachers told her that they were looking forward to the extra pay from expanded learning time and the chance to stop moonlighting—a clear benefit to them, the school, and the students.

Some teachers worried about the impact of the extra work. Reading specialist Erin Pavao of the N.B. Borden Elementary School in Fall River spoke for many teachers when she said, "Teachers were saying, 'We're already tired at 2:30, so can you imagine how we'll feel at 3:30?' It went through all of our minds." Even though Stephanie Baker said she was having the best year of her teaching career, she also said, "I'm absolutely exhausted." Back at Borden Elementary, fifth-grade teacher Richard Borges says he actually trained for the new year by changing his diet and workout regime. By the end of the first year, however, the anticipated fatigue didn't seem to amount to much. Very few teachers felt they couldn't or didn't want to keep the new school day for the second year. At Borden, the teachers' union survey showed that 87 percent of the staff favored continuing with the new day schedule and two-thirds said it was either "never" or "rarely" the case that the day was too long for teachers.

While the anecdotal evidence is encouraging, there is also more extensive survey data for Massachusetts. Responses from 239 teachers across nine of the first ten ELT schools show that teachers endorsed the instructional advantages of the new school day schedule. Fully 70 percent thought the expanded schedule improved student academic performance (only 7 percent thought it was worse). Overwhelming majorities observed that the new school day allowed them to cover more material, incorporate experiential learning, make use of small group learning, and individualize instruction by students' skill levels. Of course teachers believe the new day works academically! Teachers we know went into their profession to help young people grow and develop; especially at schools with challenging students, teachers find it personally and professionally compelling to see an important reform—the new school day—translate into immediate and substantial student gains.

So what can we conclude? That new day schools can easily recruit and retain committed, talented, and experienced teachers. Some teachers who have been accustomed to the old school day and perhaps some new teachers will prefer the old schedule. But most appreciate the chance to earn more in their chosen profession instead of at a retail store or on a construction site. And most teachers who experience the new school day feel its educational power and report impressive increases in job satisfaction.

Teaching

Although Woody Allen claims that 90 percent of life is just showing up, teachers taking on the new day schedule are confronted with a good bit more, including new teaching challenges and opportunities. While simply putting more "time on task" and allowing a more reasonable pace provides considerable academic benefit, expanded time offers the opportunity to go far beyond the constraints of the traditional day. Although this book is not intended to be a textbook for teachers, it is worth quickly surveying some of these key teaching opportunities (and even a challenge or two).

Block Scheduling and Experiential Learning

One of the most common uses of expanded learning time is for schools to move at least some classes from the longstanding forty- or fifty-minute period to blocks as long as ninety minutes or even two hours. Advocates of so-called block scheduling have long urged this change, even within the constraints of the traditional day. In such a rearrangement, since no more time is added to the day, certain classes meet less frequently but for longer periods of time when they do meet. In new day schools, class periods can become longer and continue to meet daily.

Block scheduling advocates stress the advantages of spending less of the day on such overhead as moving from class to class, taking attendance, review, and the like. They argue that with more time teachers can dig more deeply into a given topic and can draw on a broader palette of techniques. At the same time, they acknowledge that teachers need help on figuring out how to make the best use of the added time.

Most teachers ache to pursue learning that engages students by drawing them into the ideas being taught. Projects and other forms of experiential learning allow students to actively participate and explore ideas and information rather than passively receive them as lecture notes. Consider the mummified chicken project at KIPP Houston—the combination of chemistry, biology, and history brought together in a complex, multistage process. Projects, as this example suggests, take time—too precious a commodity in the traditional schedule to risk using on a more involved activity. Having more time allows teachers to combine conventional teaching with other, more exciting ways for students to learn.

"People initially panicked at the ninety-minutes," admitted Sandra Carreiro, a teacher at the new day K–8 Salemwood School in Malden, Massachusetts. But she explained to a visiting *Christian Science Monitor* reporter that teachers quickly learned to break the time into pieces, leavening lessons with experiences that drive concepts home. While she chatted with the reporter, students in her fifth-grade math class were outside flying paper airplanes and measuring distances flown, analyzing which design elements made a difference, and competing for the class distance record. And students feel that difference. As ten-year-old fifth-grader Janae at the N.B. Borden Elementary School in Fall River explained, "We get to learn more. It's fun, and we think more schools should try it. We learn things to play, like in math we learned a math fractions game, so we can play that at home if we want to."

With some training or coaching, teachers can use longer blocks of teaching time to create learning environments that allow for far greater flexibility and creativity, that use multiple instructional strategies on any given topic, and that make students far more active in the work of learning than they ever are in taking notes on a lecture.

DIFFERENTIATED INSTRUCTION

Differentiated instruction is a fancy term meaning simply that it is better to teach different students in different ways. Not all students are at the same skill level and not all learn the same way. A conventional "stand and deliver" lecture by a teacher offers the same content in the same way to all students. Some will get it; others will not. Teachers with enough time and the expertise to use it can allow different students in the same classroom at the same time to take different paths at different paces. To do this, teachers must have accurate assessments of where students stand and how they learn best, as well as the time to launch students down these different learning paths and to coach them along the way. A great deal of professional development training for teachers focuses on these techniques because, to put it crudely, while we once were content to have teachers "teach to the middle" and let the students above and below that level either idle or fall behind, we now expect (and NCLB demands) that teachers bring every student in the classroom along to success.

Effective techniques for differentiating instruction include asking different level questions to different students during discussion, giving students different assignments, flexibly grouping students into small groups working at different levels, and supervising independent study. Only with generous helpings of time can a teacher pursue these approaches in parallel to match all the students to work that is both challenging and appropriate for their personal skill level and learning style.

SMALL-GROUP AND PEER LEARNING

One hallmark of a modern classroom is the presence—in the middle of a class period—of five to ten separate small groups of students working cooperatively but separately from the other groups of students. The main reason teachers break up classes this way is to form groups by skill level. Teachers can then move around among the groups helping each one in turn. Good teachers periodically rearrange the groups based on evolving patterns of student gains. Beyond making differentiated instruction possible, peer learning draws out higher activity and attention as students compare ideas and answers and explain their work to their peers. It also teaches children to work cooperatively and in teams—a key skill of immense value in and of itself.

TUTORING

Time and again as we visited new day schools, we discovered that they all concentrated on identifying and tutoring students as needed. Surely, one-to-one tutoring must be the most ancient of teaching techniques—in fact, before schools existed, the privileged few received their whole education from tutors. Yet a standard school schedule allows precious little opportunity for students to work with teachers on the specific, personal academic challenge they are currently facing. With just enough time to get through each day's new lesson, most teachers in conventional schools can offer tutoring only sporadically, if at all. By contrast, new day schools often build in far more time with teachers available and also build in processes to identify—and take the stigma away from—students in need of tutoring.

Some of that tutoring occurs in the longer block period. While small groups of students are working on level-appropriate materials, teachers can pull out an individual student for at least a few minutes of direct help. More powerfully, many new day schools provide several fifteen- to thirty-minute periods per teacher per day where students who need tutoring can get it.

The value of tutoring is hardly news to middle-income parents. Americans today spend an estimated $4.5 billion on tutoring away from schools. Some of that is for tutors coming to families' homes; a great deal of it goes to a growing number of site-based providers such as Sylvan and Kumon for younger students and Kaplan and Princeton Review for older students. In any case, all that spending, growing at an estimated 15 percent per year, is aimed at augmenting what schools offer. It is just this kind of purchasing that leads us to argue that many families have already shrugged off the bonds of the traditional school schedule by purchasing and manufacturing a "new school day" for their children. By contrast, the new day schedule allows for significant amounts of tutoring built into the regular school day.

Classroom Management

Many of the techniques we've described require sophisticated classroom management abilities. We were consistently amazed to see a single teacher managing a classroom of twenty-plus students pursuing several different parallel learning paths. Teachers need to learn how to plan out such parallel activity and then how to functionally be several places at once, simultaneously providing direct instruction to one student or small group, managing workflow for several others, and keeping behavior under control. Most new day schools have adopted some form of SEL or classroom management program that helps them with this general issue. Hiatt Magnet School, for instance, uses "Assertive Discipline," which its Web site describes as "a structured, systematic approach designed to assist educators in running an organized, teacher-in-charge classroom environment." As parents who have struggled to handle three or four kids at once, we are in awe of their ability to pull this off.

Using Technology

For a while in the 1990s, it seemed many schools were in an arms race to have the largest number of computers and Internet hook-ups possible. What teachers and students would do with all that computing power was entirely unclear—but surely the more computers, the better, right? Well, while many parents and community members may have been impressed at the bells and whistles, research showed remarkably little impact on education. But that is now changing quickly.

Software developers have been hard at work at turning computers into smart tutors for students. For example, Scholastic offers a reading intervention program for struggling readers called Read 180. We described it in action in the Miami Improvement Zone, where all the lowest-scoring readers in certain grades get a daily Read 180 period as a second literacy class. While parts of Read 180 look like conventional classroom literacy techniques—such as teacher-guided small reading groups—the hallmark of the program may be the computer-based instruction. Each day, the students all spend twenty minutes on a computer that supports their individual literacy development customized exactly to their current reading level and adapting to their own learning pace. Besides providing what amounts to an automated tutor, even pronouncing words for the student on request, the computer allows some unique features such as capturing the student's recording of the word.

At two schools we visited, we saw students using software that allows them to practice their math facts. More advanced math cannot effectively be pursued until students master fundamental math facts (such as the multiplication tables), which have been students' chores for generations. Lagging students are often far behind on these essentials, and there is no substitute for practice. Students can sit at a PC and use software that tests them, that automatically adapts to them as they gain skill, and that provides teachers with data on how students are progressing.

Beyond these relatively simple uses of technology to augment traditional classroom teaching, far more opportunities are on the horizon. The Internet, though noisy, full of junk, and not entirely safe, holds out the opportunity for students to conduct unprecedented research projects and to participate in active learning with others around the globe. For example, students we visited at one school can pursue astronomy by watching live feeds from one of the world's most advanced telescopes. There are also emerging attempts to harness the incredible engagement power of video games and advanced computer graphics to the task of education rather than shooting or blowing up imaginary characters and vehicles, as with Immune Attack, recently released by the Federation of American Scientists. According to the FAS, Immune Attack is a "first person strategy game where immune cells face off against bacterial and viral infections," in which a "teenaged prodigy with a unique immunodeficiency must teach his immune system how to function properly, or die trying. Using a nanobot and aided by a helpful professor, the teenager explores biologically accurate and visually detailed settings in pursuit of this goal."

As these new technological approaches to learning proliferate, the expanded time of the new day allows them to find their proper place in teaching and learning. Some will no doubt help strugglers; others will challenge the most advanced students. Some will turn out to hold no great benefit while others may offer unique new ways for students to learn and excel.

James Hayden: Walking the Walk

It's August in Newport News, Virginia, and no one is back at school except the "Dreamers"—students at Achievable Dream Academy—who have been in school for a month. We're sitting in James Hayden's new ninth-grade math classroom. Hayden is an impressive teacher. The test scores say so. He has been teaching Algebra I and Geometry to eighth graders for the last four years. Not a single one of his students has failed the Virginia Standards of Learning Tests, known locally as the VSOLs. Not one. That's leaving no child behind.

Hayden empathizes with his students. He's African American—like virtually every student in the class. He grew up in Youngstown, Ohio, and got his education degree from Youngstown State. His dad worked in the steel mills that have mostly closed. There's not a lot of opportunity in Youngstown these days, so when the Newport News schools recruited him, he came. He started off teaching for several years at the Hines Middle School, with a conventional schedule. He worked hard, and about 70 percent of his students passed the VSOLs.

"So, how do you teach differently?" we ask.

"I use all the extra time I have," he says. "I have about twice as much time because we meet for ninety minutes every day here; there it was ninety minutes every other day."

We press a bit: "Yes, but what do you do differently?"

He grinned. "I get them hooked with these Texas Instruments Navigator calculator-computers. This is a generation of text-messagers so they love this. I don't give homework only on it but they wish I did. First day of the year, I had them playing around with absolute value function tracing a V on their graphing calculators. I asked them to change the function to move the V around. Lonnie got it. His results were displayed electronically on the board. What did he do? It was a whole lot better that he explained as opposed to me telling them the formula."

Students ambled in for class. They all wore Achievable Dream's uniform and were well behaved, but we wouldn't have pegged them for math nerds. Wrong. They started pulling out their large handheld graphic calculators and hooking them up to a local area network so they could communicate with the teacher's desktop PC and their answers could be projected onto the screen.

Hayden gives them a Do Now—a problem they can work on with their calculators. They start clicking away—and on the board you can see, as if it were election results, how many have answered the question. Hayden clicks a few keys on his PC, looks at their answers and then has the computer project the range of answers the kids gave, along with how many kids chose each answer, onto the whiteboard at the front of the classroom. Some of the answers had several advocates; some looked lonelier. Hayden gets the students defending their answers without embarrassing anyone. Kids try hard to make the case for their answer until they find a problem with their reasoning and rush to change their answer and join a more popular, better answer.

Hayden says he never lectures on the new topic for the day for more than thirty minutes. He then uses the next forty-five minutes to have them do a group activity. At his previous school, he felt he had to do too much of the work himself. He barely had time for more than the daily lecture. "Here, I can have the kids do the work and I am just the facilitator—it's much better."

He breaks the class up into groups of two and wanders among them. He tells us that he did research on Asian math instruction—"because they do the best on the international tests"—and learned about how effective such peer instruction can be. "They don't teach as much as us but they go deep," he says. He adds that he likes to research one new teaching technique in depth each summer to keep himself fresh. The new school day has been a gift to James Hayden and his students.

TEACHER COLLABORATION AND PROFESSIONAL DEVELOPMENT

We have learned through our visits to schools that teachers need time and support to adapt to the new school day, but that they're perfectly capable of doing so, and they like the results.

Parents and others not professionally involved in education generally don't realize just how important it is for teachers to have planning time together—and how little time they have for planning in most schools under the current schedule. A few years ago Goldstein worked with a group of Connecticut high school history teachers, and was shocked to learn that the teachers almost never got together to discuss their curriculum, teaching strategies, syllabi, or the like. And parents often object to "teacher planning days" when school lets out even earlier than usual.

Teachers also recognize that too often professional development takes place in name only. The following description appeared in *American Educator,* the magazine of the American Federation of Teachers, in 2002: "Across the United States, professional development is typically delivered in isolated sessions offered after school or on weekends to large, heterogeneous groups of teachers. Inevitably, these sessions offer generic strategies, little time to absorb the ideas behind the strategies, and even less time to understand just what the strategies will look like in the classroom. For too many teachers these sessions are simply a periodic ritual to be endured."

But the opportunity for teachers to develop common approaches, talk about their students, and think about what really works in their curriculum (and what needs to be changed) is absolutely essential for *student* success, which is the most important yardstick for parents, administrators, and the general public to be using. Listen to former principal Helenann Civian, who now works with the Massachusetts ELT Initiative, talking about what she likes the most about the new school day: "Oh, gosh— giving teachers an opportunity to talk to each other about good instruction or about student work and saying to each other, 'Johnny's not doing so great, I'm talking to his math teacher.' Teachers have never had the opportunity to talk to each other about individual students; they've never had the time. It takes *time* to do that, providing opportunity during the school day, instead of asking them to stay after school, instead of making them do it after school. This is treating teachers as professionals."

Principal Catina Bullard-Clark of Achievable Dream Academy explains what goes on in her expanded school day: "Teachers are constantly involved in rigorous planning, grade-level planning, time for administrators to meet with teachers about planning. Without planning, the extra time would be wasted. When kids are in morning program, teachers can have a quick grade-level meeting. Our teachers don't eat with the kids, so they can have time to get together to do additional planning. We don't assign teachers hall, cafeteria, or bus duty. For that we use resource teachers and instructional assistants. But they know, when they have this time, that they're not just sitting around discussing who won on *American Idol* last night."

These observations mesh with the practice at other successful new day schools like Roxbury Prep, where teachers start school well before the children come, and where every teacher knows every student's name. At Roxbury Prep, every student gets two math classes a day, taught by two different teachers taking somewhat different tacks—an act of cooperative teaching that requires careful synchronization and communication. "Five of us are in the same office," explained seventh-grade math teacher Kathryn McCurdy. "We spend a lot of time in conversation making sure there as few inconsistencies between our classes as possible. There's a very common structure through all math classes. Kids know what's going to come next." And in August, "we have three and a half weeks every summer, regardless of whether you're new or in your fifth or seventh year. Very valuable conversations take place then. We sit down and realign the curriculum. Jen and I talk about the year: perhaps this should become a pre-algebra standard. Or we find a missing item in a problem dealing with a mean: should it go in pre-algebra or problem-solving? Last year it fit nicely into mine, into my equation developing. This year she's doing more data analysis, so maybe she should have it."

This kind of time also allows teachers to overcome what nearly all of them refer to as the isolation of their profession. Now they get to meet and plan and talk to each other about what's going on in their classrooms. Massachusetts new day schools use their redesign to provide significant new time for teacher meetings, sometimes at grade level, other times within subjects. Good teachers hunger for collaborative time, which increases their effectiveness and professional satisfaction. In strong charter schools built around the new day, teachers take planning time for granted. At Roxbury Prep teachers thrive on it. Common teacher planning time is simply essential for student success at any school. Because the new school day opens up so many new opportunities, this planning is probably even more essential and even more productive.

CONCLUSION: FIRST AMONG EQUALS

All the theory and logic in the world demonstrating the value of the new school day wouldn't be worth the ink used to print this book if it weren't for real teachers in real schools eager to use the additional time in the expanded schedule to help their students learn more and better. Of all the elements making the new school day a reality and a success—and there are many—teachers are far and away the most important. They have shown their willingness to experiment with new techniques and strategies, to retrain themselves in new curricula, to work even harder than they thought they could, and to intensify their commitment to children's growth and development. Because of them, the new school day is changing many thousands of lives across the country—and will, we think, change millions more.

$$\boxed{10}$$

MORE SCHOOL?

Why Kids—Yes, Kids!—and Their
Parents Like the New School Day

> *When I first heard that we were going to have
> a longer school day, I decided that I wanted to
> transfer schools. . . . My mom said to just try it
> out . . . if I don't like it, we'll make another plan.
> But, hey, I tried it and I liked it—something
> new . . . and it got me into a great high school.*
> —STUDENT, EDWARDS MIDDLE SCHOOL, BOSTON

> *The reading groups—we felt they were extremely
> helpful because, for Tyler, his strength is math.
> He doesn't necessarily run to pick up a book.
> They really do spend a lot more quality time on
> reading. He's learned a great deal more. He
> comes home and teaches us things that we didn't
> even know."*
> —PARENT, JACOB HIATT MAGNET SCHOOL,
> WORCESTER, MASSACHUSETTS

IN THIS CHAPTER, WE LOOK first at students and how they receive the expanded school schedule. No reform can work without their willing participation and engagement. Then we turn our attention to parents and benefits they derive from the new school day. We also contrast the anxiety some parents have in anticipating the change with the enthusiasm most parents report once they experience it.

STUDENTS

We have to be honest about this. We have virtually never met or heard of a kid who likes the idea of more school. Even children who excel at school and receive terrific positive reinforcement for their performance in the classroom crave weekends and vacations and snow days. For most of us, including adults, school feels more like going to work or eating your vegetables or doing exercise. You know you have to do it, that it's good for you, and at times you may even enjoy it, but mostly, you define freedom by the time you get away from it. In fact, Gabrieli once ran for office using a television ad in which he extolled the virtues of expanding learning time to a room full of skeptics asking probing, doubting questions—his own children. The ad ended with his cute five-year-old son telling the world, "Dad, lucky for you kids can't vote!" The ad was a big hit.

Having said that, visitors to new day schools and journalists examining these schools almost always come away surprised by how accepting and often even enthusiastic students are. The *Boston Globe Sunday Magazine* ran a cover story on the Massachusetts Expanded Learning Time schools, titled "Saved by the (Later) Bell." Its subtitle was telling—"Ten schools in Massachusetts are testing a first-in-the-nation initiative to extend learning time. *Believe it or not, the students (after initial grumbling) seem to like it,* and so do their parents. Shouldn't every school rethink its schedule?" (italics added).

WHEN KIDS HAVE MORE TIME IN SCHOOL, THEY DO BETTER

The primary reason students like the new school day is the added enrichment. Most of the charter and experimental district schools with the new schedule carve out meaningful time for students to pursue elective opportunities in arts, music, drama, sports, and other engaging areas. All the Massachusetts ELT schools do so—it is part of the "balanced model" the initiative encourages them to pursue. Even inside the Miami Improvement Zone, where additional time is just an hour and the focus is highly academic, the district also allocates enrichment time for students whose past performance is strong enough to allow them to forgo a second, remedial literacy or math period.

This is not an accident. Leaders of most new day schools believe their goals are twofold: to improve the depth and strength of the core academic skills of their students—and to provide a more well-rounded education. Enrichment opportunities aim squarely at both goals. They are an integral part of the second goal—a well-rounded education for the whole child—but they also matter for the first goal. Students who are more engaged with school are more likely to want to attend and to participate actively in the academic portion of the day.

But students also recognize and appreciate other key aspects of the new day. They see themselves doing better in school and express their satisfaction at that. Most of the new day schools we visited serve children whose past educational experience has been terrible—ranging from low performance to much worse—and who live in communities where academic achievement tends not to be the norm. They notice that in new day schools the teaching is different. They comment on the fact that learning is more fun when they do projects. They notice that teachers now have the time to answer their questions and to engage in dialogue with them. And many of them acknowledge that if they were not in school for that expanded time, they could just be getting into trouble.

Sixth-grader Tyler of the Hiatt Magnet School in Worcester, Massachusetts, gave us a clear before-and-after comparison. "At first, I was like, 'Come on! Two more hours in school!'" But he gave it a chance. And now he says, "Last year, we just, like, hurried to get something done and this year, we would just, like, take our time and do it right. We have a lot more time for reading and math and science and you get more time at recess, more time in gym. Everything you can imagine!"

A reporter visiting the N.B. Borden Elementary School in Fall River asked students what they liked best about the new school day. Ten-year-old Chuelsia replied, "Yeah, it's fun. You get to hang out with your friends and you get to learn more. Kids' College [the name of the elective enrichment series at the school] is my favorite part. I'm taking cake decorating." Note the blend there—more time with friends, loves cake decorating, but also says, "you get to learn more." Not a bad combination.

Chuelsia's friend Janae agreed. "A longer day is better. We get to learn more. It's fun, and we think more schools should try it. In science, we used to just have one period, but now we get to have two. It's really fun. Right now, we're learning about electricity." Chuelsia piped up, "Janae is the electricity queen." Janae explained, "We have to connect wires to build a light. I'm always the first to build my light."

According to the *Christian Science Monitor,* Yaritza, a fifthgrader at the Salemwood K–8 School in Malden, Massachusetts (which was in its first year following conversion to the new day schedule), is well aware of the benefits: "She likes having extra time for gym, computer class and homework help. 'My grades are getting way better . . . and my mom's really proud of me because I pay attention in class more.'"

We discussed the new day with Rodney, an eighth grader at the Edwards Middle School in Boston. The conversation took place in the fall of his second year under the new day schedule. Rodney was honest about his first reaction: "Well, I actually initially thought what every teenage kid thought. I was like oh, great, now I can barely stand six and a half hours. Who'd want to go for nine?" Once he got into it, his opinion changed: "But as I kind of went on through the school year, I realized that it was more fun, like it gave school a purpose for me. I know every teenager out there hates going to school. They hate it. They hate waking up. But for some reason, when you get to choose what you want to do and actually have fun, it makes the day go faster. It makes everything more fun. It makes it more interesting to kids."

WHEN KIDS HAVE LESS TIME TO "HANG OUT," THEY'RE SAFER

While the new school day's most significant benefits are its contributions to academic achievement and the development of well-rounded young people, it also keeps kids safer, both physically and morally.

The Kuss Middle School in Fall River holds the dubious distinction of being the first school in Massachusetts partially taken over by the state for "chronic underperformance." It is in the midst of an exciting transformation under new leadership and has added the new day schedule to its arsenal. It is also in the middle of a very poor city and its children face great adversity. Fifteen-year-old Jennifer had gotten D's in math and English in 2005–2006. Since discipline issues often go along with poor academic performance, it doesn't come as a surprise to learn, as the *Boston Globe* put it, she "was often in trouble (once for bringing a knife to school)." The following year, in the expanded and redesigned school day, she found classes less "boring" (the young person's kiss of death) and was getting B's in both subjects and considering a nursing career. As Jennifer reported, the math teacher "won't give you ordinary math problems. It's more hands-on stuff." Eighth-grader Markus turned himself around too, steering clear of the principal's office and landing leading roles in the new theatrical productions of *Macbeth* and *You're a Good Man, Charlie Brown*. He said, "We're learning more than we usually do from teachers. And it keeps me out of trouble."

Back at the Edwards Middle School in Boston, we asked Rodney what he would be doing if he went home early, as in the traditional school day. "If I went home at two, I'd probably be sitting on the couch with a Mountain Dew watching TV or I'd be out skateboarding. . . . I'd be doing nothing. That's it. . . . You could go out with your friends as much as you want; you'd probably go out and get in trouble." Instead, having seen and lived the new day, he concludes that considering what he has at Edwards, "I'd give up skateboarding and Mountain Dew any day of the week. . . . Nothing that you would do out there at two o'clock will ever amount to what people are doing here at 4:30."

And when we ask Rodney what's important about the new schedule, he quickly brings home the stark reality of life in the city: "This kind of gives kids like an escape so you don't have to worry about 'Am I going to get into a fight on the way from school.' . . . You'll feel safe in this school knowing that you're not going to get into a fight or get shot hopefully." Lest you find this too dramatic, last year two students who attended Edwards Middle School were killed in separate incidents in their neighborhoods in off hours.

Kids don't generally ask for more time to learn or to be at school, and they are generally apprehensive about converting to a new day schedule. It's hard to imagine that ever changing.

Younger kids barely notice, of course, but middle school children are old enough to notice and comment. Even so, the experience of new day schools is that students accept the new schedule and in many cases come to genuinely appreciate it. Attendance, for instance, has actually improved in Miami's School Improvement Zone. Kids living in low-income, frequently dangerous neighborhoods know what they would be doing if they were on their own, and they can be honest enough to admit that it would be useless and in some cases risky. They genuinely enjoy electives and enrichment added to every school day. But they also perceive the difference educationally. More time translates into higher achievement and satisfaction. And it changes, when well done, the very way they are taught, the process of teaching and learning, toward a better-paced, more interactive, more engaging approach. When it comes together like that, it's a bit of educational magic.

PARENTS

"Will it be too long for a third-grader?" some parents wonder at first. "Won't my ten-year-old be exhausted? What about special needs kids? What if my kids are bored?"

Parents are a critical constituency for schools and the new day schedule affects them directly. They are sometimes anxious about change, especially when it is in the hands of a system, a bureaucracy they don't wholly trust. But the verdict is in—once parents experience the new day schedule, most are enthusiastic about its benefits.

Generally speaking, the new school day affects parents two ways. Its effects on their children are of paramount concern. Will they gain educationally? Will they enjoy it? Will they thrive? But it also has an impact on their own lives. The most obvious change is quite attractive to most parents: their children will be in a safe, constructive, supervised place until a time far closer to when most adults get off work. On the other hand, many families have worked to fill at least some of that void with extracurricular and enrichment activities they value, and they worry about losing these activities as well as about losing what precious little "quality family time" remains for them.

WHEN KIDS DO BETTER, PARENTS ARE HAPPIER

The easiest way to measure parental attitudes is to look at how they vote with their feet. Pioneering new day charter and district schools are usually "schools of choice"—meaning parents have to elect to have their children attend them. These schools would go out of business if there were no demand. Far from that fate, KIPP Academies and Roxbury Prep, two charter schools we visit in this book, have huge waiting lists of parents eager for the opportunity. The Timilty School, an experimental district middle school in Boston (not a charter), converted to the new school day more than twenty years ago and quickly became—and has remained—one of the most in-demand schools in the city. While some predicted a mass exodus from Massachusetts ELT schools when they converted to the new day, very few parents actually left; in fact, the schools are now attracting increasing numbers of parents.

At Kuss Middle School in Fall River, mother Dawn Oliver opposed the new school day—"I was the one most against it at the start," she told the *Boston Globe*—because Brittany, her learning-disabled sixth grader had always found school a "constant struggle." She worried that 30 percent more of an already rough road would discourage Brittany even more. But it turned out differently, and now Oliver calls herself "one of the program's biggest boosters." Brittany was really getting it for the first time. The difference? "I used to sit with her and go problem by problem on her math homework," says Oliver. "Not anymore—I ask her if she needs help, and she says, 'No, no. I got it.'" The *Globe* reports that Brittany has made the honor roll two terms running and has a career goal—to be a forensic anthropologist.

Oliver has plenty of company at Kuss, where 72 percent of the parents approved of the new schedule last year; 91 percent were satisfied with their children's performance; and 70 percent saw improvement in their children. Parents are excited to see their children doing well at school. And they understand the differences. At the beginning of this chapter we gave you Tyler's view. He's the sixth grader at the Hiatt School in Worcester. Here's what his mother sees: "The reading groups—we felt they were extremely helpful because, for Tyler, his strength is math. He doesn't necessarily run to pick up a book. They really do spend a lot more quality time on reading. He's learned a great deal more. He comes home and teaches us things that we didn't even know." And his father appreciates not just the gains but the shift in homework strategy in which more of the necessary work can be done at school with teacher help available: "What I like about the extended learning day is that Tyler gets an opportunity to do his homework independently, but if he has any questions or any issues he can work with his teachers to make sure his homework is done right the first time."

New immigrants—from Asia, Latin America, the Caribbean, Eastern Europe, Africa—have become a fact of life in modern American cities (as well as in many rural communities). In a reprise of the early twentieth century, when large numbers of immigrants (then too, known as "new immigrants")—from Italy, Poland, Hungary, Czechoslovakia, and Russia, among others—flooded into American cities, today's urban schools have become international.

The Malden superintendent held an informational meeting for non-English-speaking parents, providing interpreters in Chinese, Vietnamese, Portuguese, and Haitian Creole—and discovered that *all* of the parents supported expanding the school day. Many said they would transfer their children to one of the schools considering the change. Listen to a Haitian immigrant mother active in the PTO at the Forestdale K–8 School: "A lot of parents will be very grateful to have the help, and to have the extended program, because it will challenge the children more. Remember, we are parents, but we are not teachers. Some of us don't have the skills to help our kids with certain homework projects. I can help my kids a little bit, but not all parents have the training." When, under heavy pressure from a small group of vocal parents, the school board voted to keep Forestdale on the old schedule, she said, "I'm sad. If my kids don't succeed, *I* don't succeed."

Malden did bring another K–8 school, Salemwood, into the ELT Initiative, and here's what parent Mary Shank told a *Christian Science Monitor* reporter: "It gives us extra time to get home from work. My son is developmentally delayed, and he's doing awesome now. He's willing to do homework when you ask him, and he's not having as many troubles." It doesn't seem surprising that Malden converted an additional school the following year.

John Chaves, father of a seventh-grader, Mindy, at Kuss, described to the *New York Times* a similar blend of satisfaction with the better hours and pleasure at academic gains. "Today, she came home saying that men have a bigger forehead than women. She never used to do that. I ask, 'Where are you learning this stuff?' 'Forensics class,' she tells me. 'I love it.'"

WHEN KIDS ARE SAFER, PARENTS ARE HAPPIER

While we would support a new day schedule on its educational merits alone, we are also happy to highlight the considerable advantage to parents of having schools constructively use so much more of the time when most children would otherwise be unsupervised because their parents are still at work. If the sole benefit of expanding learning time were better child-care coverage, we're not sure it would justify the cost; taxpayers have agreed over the years. Nonetheless, we see these consequences of the new school day providing terrific extra value for everyone—including parents.

Kids who do better in school are also safer, posing fewer risks to themselves and their fellow students and larger community. The lure of a part in a school play can prompt a more organized form of thinking and making choices. "Everybody's more involved with what they're doing," is how one young thespian put it, giving unknowing support to the educational theory that engagement itself is one of the keys to children learning.

And given what we know about parents' concerns for their children, particularly in poor neighborhoods, their overwhelming endorsement of the new school day may owe a good deal to this reality: three-fifths of Kuss parents felt their children were safer under the new schedule. As one Kuss father told the *New York Times*, "We're never home at the time" they used to come home, "so at least [now] we know where our kids are."

Pushing the school dismissal time back to 4:30 or 5:00 PM (often with activities going later) brings immediate benefit to parents—in their wallets and in their peace of mind. All working parents of school-age children know the problem, particularly those working full time. They get out of work sometime between 4:30 and 7. But most schools let out between 2 and 3—or sometimes an hour later, if there's an after-school activity. In middle school and high school, sports or play practice might go late as well. But for most kids a 2:30 dismissal time creates a weekly after-school gap of fifteen to twenty-five hours per week, posing a real dilemma for working parents. Because they need to work—and not get fired for taking time off in the middle of the afternoon—parents come up with solutions as varied as the contents of their bank accounts, the size and location of their families, the safety of their neighborhoods, and the age and personalities of their children. Think about the arrangements your parents made for you, or those you have made for your own (or your family members' or your neighbors' children).

Some few arrange for after-school programs at school; others pay for programs that bus children to a different site. Some rely on members of their extended family, some on stay-at-home neighbors who pick up their children at the same time, or who meet the school bus. Others pay baby-sitters to pick up children or meet the bus. And still others, who cannot arrange for family or other adults or programs or transportation, train their children to come home, let themselves in, make sure their home is as safe as possible, get a snack, and start household chores or homework. These parents rely on telephones, cell phones, and now e-mail to monitor their children from work as best they can, hoping their supervisors and coworkers are either extremely understanding or not paying close attention. More often than they acknowledge—and they acknowledge plenty!—their children spend the afternoons watching television or playing video games or computer games. At least they're not on the street. Except for those relative few so defeated by their own histories, immaturity, or addictions that they give up entirely, parents try to figure out some way to watch over their children.

But the very variety of these measures suggests just how fragile they can be at any given moment: easily disrupted by illness, traffic jams, car trouble, bad weather, or emergencies. Parents describe these shifting, overlapping, less-than-reliable arrangements as houses of cards, ready to collapse in a moment. And way too often, as young people enter their teens, they rebel against their parents' plans and instructions and pursue their own ideas about how to use their unsupervised time.

IMPACT ON SOCIETY

The larger social context helps explain the scale of the problem. "Using the most generous calculations," and not even considering the possibility of a long commute to and from work, a U.S. Department of Labor report titled *After-School Worries* concluded in 1999, "only about 64 percent of a full-time worker's standard work schedule is covered by the hours children are typically in school." As of a couple of years ago, respected research and policy think-tank Catalyst reports, more than a third of the American labor force—nearly 50 million people—were parents of minor children, three-quarters of whom were school-aged. Two-thirds of the parents of minor children—some 33 million employees—were employed full time.

According to Catalyst,

> Parental concern about after-school time [referred to as PCAST] can affect productivity both directly and indirectly. Our analyses show that high levels of PCAST lead to increased job disruption, including missed work, distractions on the job, not meeting expectations, and poor quality of work. High PCAST also leads to lower satisfaction with one's job overall as well as with advancement opportunities and pay. And what happens when employees are unhappy with their job? Low job satisfaction is related to lower organizational commitment and decreased personal well-being.

Catalyst sampled some 1,700 parents at three Fortune 100 companies across the country, across racial and ethnic lines. Most of these findings come as no surprise—the older the child, the greater the parental concern, especially if the child has had behavioral or social difficulties—though the fact that many parents whose children attend formal after-school programs still experience high levels of concern raises eyebrows. "So few after-school programs exist," speculate the Catalyst authors, "that parents may be forced to put their children in whatever program is available regardless of whether it meets their or their children's needs in terms of quality and content." The most reliable predictors of low concern among working parents are a part-time schedule, allowing them to be home after school; flexible work schedules; a partner or spouse who stays at home, works part-time, or works a different shift; or having a thoroughly trustworthy older child.

It's clear from this study—and from the parents you know or work alongside—that single parents and dual-earner, full-time working couples are anxious about their children's after-school lives, and inevitably bring that concern to work. But the Catalyst investigators were willing to go a step further and put a price tag on the loss to American business, in health care costs and productivity: *$50 billion to $300 billion* per year.

Now imagine that instead of worrying about how to occupy their children for fifteen to twenty-five hours every week, parents could rely on the school system to assume responsibility for most or all of that time, in a newly designed and revitalized school day and curriculum that engages their children and increases their chances of academic success. That's why parents of students at new day schools don't worry about their children between school dismissal and the end of the workday. It's why the parent survey results in Massachusetts were so overwhelmingly positive about the new school day, after just seven or eight months.

Let's go a step further ourselves. If the Massachusetts pilot program were a clinical drug trial, and results were to be based solely on the experience and conclusions of the Massachusetts parents in the ten new day schools in the 2006–2007 school year, researchers would have called a halt to the trial in the spring of 2007 and given every school the new school day.

Consider, as an example, single mother Dorcas Chavez, whose autistic twelve-year-old son Kenan gets on a 6:10 AM bus bound for Mario Umana Middle School. Even though he won't be returning until nearly twelve hours later, at 5:30 PM, Chavez told the *Boston Globe,*"you should see how happy he is when he sees that bus coming." The boy, it turns out, has improved markedly in such skills as feeding himself, which his mother chalks up to "a full day's attention in a class with five other autistic boys." For her part, Chavez used the extra time to take on a full-day shift at work, instead of working part time so she could spend afternoons with Kenan at home.

As another parent from an ELT school explained, "It works well because if you work say an eight-hour day and you start at eight o'clock and then you've got to be home and your daughter gets home at say two o'clock, you can't do that because you're still at work. With the extended day, they are there until about four o'clock so about the time they get home, you'll be on your way home so they're not home alone; it's a lot shorter time."

At the Dr. Martin Luther King, Jr. K–8 School in Cambridge, Massachusetts, teachers and parents organized a presentation to the governor's special adviser for education in late February, arguing that the new school day, in the words of Principal Carole H. Learned-Miller, allows them to

- *Fully implement the Literacy Collaborative program K–8*
- *Fully implement the TERC Investigations/CMP math programs K–8*
- *Fully implement the science curriculum K–8*
- *Fully implement the Responsive Classroom curriculum K–8*
- *Fully implement electives, wherein every child K–8 is able to choose an enrichment class*
- *Have a school day that is calmer and allows time for reflection, collaboration, and discussion*

Don't be misled by the King School's location in Cambridge, where the wealth and reputation of Harvard University renders much of the city invisible to outside eyes. Low-income students make up 56 percent of the school's population (well over the district percentage and twice the state's), while about a third speak English as a second language. Parent surveys at King, nevertheless, were even more enthusiastic than the others. Fully 77 percent "felt the expanded day had a positive impact on their families' lives," while 71 percent "felt that their children were not too tired as a result" of the new school day. Equally telling, "17 percent of families work more this year, as a result of the new school hours."

The state's investment of $1,300 per child will pay off many times over if working parents can earn more and pay more taxes. And if Chavez's son Kenan—and kids like him—can learn skills to make them (the 21 percent of King's students classified as special needs, for example) less dependent on caregivers, the new school day could produce long-term savings for the state in unspent social services money. As Chavez told the *Globe*,"I'm wondering, why aren't they doing this extended day at more schools?"

Good question.

11

"I DON'T HAVE KIDS IN SCHOOL—WHY SHOULD I CARE?"

Beyond the Classroom—Public Health, Neighborhood Safety, and the New School Day

We don't have as many fights after school; we don't have as many house parties. The kids don't have time to meet up and get a party going before the parents are home.
—EAST BOSTON JUVENILE GANG OFFICER, COMMENTING ON THE EFFECTS OF EXPANDED LEARNING TIME IN MASSACHUSETTS

To be honest, I'd rather have the 500-plus kids at Kuss Middle School here under our supervision than sort of at home unsupervised or walking the streets or whatever it might be. . . . The benefits of expanded learning time here at Kuss Middle School have ranged from individual student success to overall school success.
—MATH TEACHER AND MARTIAL ARTS INSTRUCTOR, KUSS MIDDLE SCHOOL, FALL RIVER, MASSACHUSETTS

NOWHERE DOES THE CONVENTIONAL PUBLIC school day seem sillier, more archaic, or more poorly adapted to the needs of modern society than in the fact that it dismisses children between three and five hours before most of their parents get home from work. As a result, most schoolchildren spend between fifteen and twenty-five hours per week out of school when their parents are not home. As we said in Chapter Ten, parents go through a whole range of contortions to minimize the impact of this absurdly early dismissal time.

In this chapter, we'll look at the public health and public safety consequences of the antiquated school day and how the new school day offers advantages for both. In this case, the gains for children and families translate directly into gains to neighborhoods and society at large. When young people, who have extraordinary amounts of energy, are supervised, engaged, and safe, they and their families benefit.

So, to be blunt about it, do those to whom they're not related, some of whom don't even have kids. All of us are right to worry about all those hours when the kids are out of school and unsupervised, because the kinds of things young people do when they have too much time on their hands often have consequences far beyond their own families.

Police chiefs strongly favor keeping teens busy and supervised, because they believe such programs will both reduce juvenile crime and hinder the development of young criminals. Public health advocates favor keeping young people engaged and supervised because they know that prevention (rather than treatment) of obesity, substance abuse, unwanted pregnancy, early smoking, and sexually transmitted diseases requires early intervention. We all benefit when we have to pay less for the social and economic costs of these ills.

There is, in other words, a thoroughly hard-headed economic reason to endorse the new school day even if you don't have children or grandchildren, don't care much about international competitiveness or the future of the American workforce, and couldn't care less about No Child Left Behind. You may not even care about the juvenile delinquents walking across the street from you, but you probably do care when they key your car or steal the CD player to buy drugs. On public safety and public health grounds alone, the new school day ought to have your support.

The new school day makes a profound and far-reaching contribution to the health and safety of American schoolchildren and their neighborhoods, well beyond the classroom. When schools adopt an expanded schedule, it is immediately evident that a large block of time in which many young people are unsupervised by adults simply disappears, replaced by structured time in which they are supervised, protected, and constructively engaged. It is difficult to overstate the significance of this issue: for parents, for children, for neighborhoods and communities, and for American society as a whole.

Where Are the Kids?

The great majority of schoolchildren have nothing constructive to do for stretches of time making up as much as a quarter of their entire day. Of course some children attend after-school programs until a family member (or another adult) picks them up, but relatively few children do so. The numbers, often surprising even to those in the field, bear repeating: nine in ten children (89 percent) participate in *no daily after-school program at all.* For middle schoolers, the proportion is nineteen out of twenty (94 percent). However crucial for some millions of children and families, after-school programs are all but irrelevant for the vast majority.

Some children are cared for by a combination of neighbors, other adult family members, and older siblings. Estimates vary and hard numbers are difficult to come by, but parents themselves report (and we can reasonably suppose they underestimate) that one-third of their own children in grades 6 through 8—roughly *four million middle schoolers*—are in "self-care," expected to take care of themselves, sometimes with parents supervising by telephone or computer, more often not. In other words, record numbers of children spend record amounts of time unsupervised, as latchkey children.

Under the best of circumstances, these children are spending an enormous amount of time watching television or playing video games. A Kaiser Foundation study back in 1999—ancient history as far as Internet access is concerned—found that, on average, children spent 5.5 hours per day on these activities, 38.5 hours per week. From ages eight through eighteen, these same children averaged 6.75 hours per day—more time than they spent in school. A number of studies have pointed to the fact that a significant proportion of African American children watch upwards of six hours of television per day.

But we have already discussed the sheer educational, moral, and physical waste experienced by children with little to do after school. In this chapter we broaden the focus to the neighborhoods outside the school, where risks and temptations for children have never been greater, ranging from tobacco and alcohol to drugs, gangs, sexual activity, and outright crime. Here we address public health and public safety—that is, respectively, the public consequences of the health choices children make when they spend so much unsupervised time, coupled with the safety of the children themselves as well as that of the surrounding society.

PUBLIC HEALTH AND KIDS ON THEIR OWN

The question of public health is not ordinarily associated with the school day. Too many of us have the impression—*myth* would be more accurate; *fantasy* might even be closer to the truth—that when children have time to themselves they play ball or dolls, or jump rope, or visit the local library or read while listening to the radio, or talk with their friends on the phone. In fact, when they are at home they watch television, play video games, or play online—and eat. The poorer the household, the more television the kids are likely to watch. And is it any wonder that between the high-fat, high-calorie prepared or fast food (pizza, McDonald's, Burger King, Taco Bell) hawked in television commercials, children's own tendency to snack on junk food and sodas, and the more sedentary habits that come with spending huge numbers of hours per week in front of a TV or computer screen—that American children are fatter than ever before?

Obesity rates have simply skyrocketed in the last twenty years. In 1988 roughly 6 percent of six-to-eleven-year-olds were obese. By 1994, the rate had nearly doubled, to well over 11 percent; by 2000 it had jumped to 15.1 percent, and to 18.8 percent in 2004. Nearly one in five elementary school students is obese—not just overweight, but obese. Children exercise less than they did ten or fifteen years ago, and recess is being squeezed out of the current school day. Why does this matter to a society as a whole? Because obese children have more health problems as children and as adults—and the cost of dealing with these problems ripples through the entire health care system.

Just look at Type II diabetes. There is truly a national epidemic of this disease—even a sober outfit like the Centers for Disease Control (CDC) says so. It blames overweight and sedentary lifestyles for *300,000* premature deaths a year, second only to tobacco in causing such unnecessary loss of life. Type II diabetes has been accelerating in incidence and emerging earlier and earlier in life, and it now affects growing numbers of teens and young adults. The primary risk factor for Type II diabetes is obesity. While many medications are available to help mitigate the disease, the truth is it tends to cause increases in cardiovascular disease, kidney disease, and blindness, and it ultimately reduces lifespan.

While the cost to individuals is tragic enough, the cost to society is enormous. The United States spent an estimated $132 billion in 2002 on diabetes and its complications. A 2005 study showed that the average diabetic patient incurs $13,243 a year in medical expense—compared to $2,560 for a nondiabetic. Some diabetes comes from genetic and other factors, but the obesity that is driving the current growth in diabetes incidence appears most often in low-income populations, producing a genuine health care and financial crisis for the victims of the disease and the publicly funded program—Medicaid—that is paying for their health care.

If unsupervised children aren't watching television or playing video games or surfing the Internet, they tend to get into trouble, either in their own homes or in other places where they are unsupervised—a public park, a friend's home, a vacant lot, an abandoned building, the woods. They experiment with or use tobacco, alcohol, and drugs, all of which they can obtain relatively easily, sometimes, of course, without even leaving their homes. There is no lack of studies indicating that the more time children have on their own, the more likely they are to use these. One study of five thousand eighth graders found that kids home alone at least two days a week were *four times* more likely to have used alcohol than children supervised by adults. And 39 percent of teenagers report seeing people their age using drugs or alcohol every day or almost every day.

Eighth graders who are drinking or using drugs not only aren't doing their homework, they may very well be impairing their ability to learn during the few hours they do attend school. And by experimenting with addictive substances, they place themselves squarely in the way of multiple risks that could affect them the rest of their lives. These risks are not limited to teens and their families: the rest of us pay for the social services, the health care costs when uninsured young people show up in hospital emergency rooms, and the remediation classes in public schools and colleges.

We now know that cigarette companies have marketed their products specifically to teenagers, because they know that most adult smokers got hooked when they were young. Many teenagers consider smoking to be a mark of "cool," even though nicotine is an extremely addictive drug. This is not the place to rehearse the well-known health dangers of cigarette smoking for smokers, for their children, and for those who share their physical space. Smoking also has highly public consequences that the entire society pays for: the Surgeon General has called it "the leading preventable cause of disease and deaths in the United States." Cigarette smoking makes people far more likely to suffer from cardiovascular diseases and a whole range of cancers, which helps explain why it has been banned in so many public places, and why minors aren't allowed to buy tobacco products. We all know this, and the public health community is united around the need to combat teen smoking. Why, then, do we turn teenagers out of a structured, nonsmoking environment at 2 or 2:30 in the afternoon, when they could be in new day schools engaged in healthy activities?

Tobacco is only one of the public health risks children find tempting. The dangers of alcoholism or heavy drinking need no recital here. Nor do the perils of using drugs such as ecstasy, methamphetamine, or crack cocaine—or even marijuana. But children and teenagers, most of whom are still developing physically, face even more damage from using drugs and alcohol than their elders—yet another public health problem. What's more, they have even less ability than adults to judge the effect of alcohol or drugs on their physical coordination, mental acuity, or moral reasoning—which can lead them into behavior dangerous not only to themselves but to many others as well, including sober, law-abiding residents going about their daily business, especially if the kids have access to automobiles or guns.

The point here is not to wring our hands about "today's kids"—a perennial lament rather than the foundation of good social policy. The point is to see that, by and large with our consent, one of the key institutions in American society—the public school system—is, however unintentionally, abandoning our children every afternoon and expecting them, on their own, to "just say no" to tobacco, alcohol, and drugs, and then complaining about "kids these days." Children deserve better from their elders and their entire society, but we also appear to be shooting ourselves in the collective foot. No wonder parents with the resources to do so enroll their children in a welter of activities, or send them to private schools—or that low-income parents fill the waiting lists of charter schools offering an expanded school day!

We know that half of all high school students are sexually active (65 percent of seniors), but no matter our beliefs about the morality of teen sexual activity, we ought to pay close attention to the fact that a great many teen pregnancies—favored by few of us—appear to begin between three and six PM. Today's teenagers did not invent premarital sex, or even unprotected sex, which appears to be far more common than the widespread availability of contraception would predict. The hormonal acceleration of puberty has been exciting and derailing young people's judgment for centuries, if not millennia. Some 40 percent of brides in Hingham, Massachusetts, were pregnant at the time of their weddings—in 1730!

But a generation or two ago, when today's parents and grandparents were engaging in their own sexual experimentation, there were fewer sexually transmitted diseases (STDs), and none were as lethal as the HIV virus. Some STDs have reached epidemic proportions, as an estimated 3 to 4 million teenagers contract them every year, more than eight thousand per day.

Thirty years ago the religious or social sanctions against single motherhood were stronger, so fewer young unmarried women and girls kept their babies. Teenagers who keep their babies tend not to obtain good prenatal care, so their babies have lower birth weights and consequent health problems, which frequently lead to learning difficulties; these mothers simply don't have the resources or preparation to provide good health care and decent nutrition to their babies. As a society, we have choices about which behavior we encourage and which we discourage; why on earth would we, in effect, give teenagers—by definition an age group with sex on the brain—massive amounts of unstructured, unsupervised time? Simply as public health policy, the current school day makes no sense at all. The new school day would provide immediate, large-scale, and far-reaching public health benefits for our entire society.

Public Safety and Kids on Their Own

The traditional school schedule has serious consequences for public safety. Within the law enforcement community it is well known that the juvenile crime rate triples on weekdays between two and six PM, the hours between school dismissal and parents' returning home—not, tellingly, on weekends, when more parents' work schedules allow them to supervise their children. (Weekend juvenile crime follows adult patterns, peaking between eight and midnight.) Within these afternoon hours juvenile crime spikes between three and four PM, when children are also most likely to commit an assault with a weapon, a sexual assault, or an assault inflicting serious bodily injury. Kids themselves are most apt to be victims of a crime in the hour after school lets out. (By contrast, adults' most vulnerable time is between nine PM and midnight.) Fatal automobile crashes, the leading cause of death among teenagers, take place most often between three and six PM. Accidental deaths from injuries, the second leading cause of death among young children, occur most often at home, after school, among unsupervised children.

With little to do and no safe, structured place to go in the afternoon, too many children are attracted by the streets, by peer groups (or older kids) out for thrills, and inevitably by vandalism and petty crime. By padlocking school doors most afternoons, the current school day literally pushes children toward this sort of activity, on their own or in organized gangs. Kids know this themselves. At the Kuss elementary school in Fall River, for example, one student explained what he liked about the expanded school day: "I know who I would be hanging out with if I wasn't here and they are gangs and I would be in trouble." Or as a student at Edwards Middle School in Charlestown, just outside of Boston, explained, "Half the kids here that I've seen, I know would be on the street doing something else. They could be the nicest kids in school to you but they'll be totally different on the street."

We have already described how the new school day finds its most vigorous support in low-income neighborhoods and school districts—and among the wealthiest parents. Middle-income and more affluent areas have more ambivalence regarding the idea, since either their schools and towns provide more afternoon activities for children, or the parents have organized themselves to ferry their children to and from different after school lessons, sports, or other pursuits. Should these more affluent neighborhoods and towns have fewer concerns about what their young people are up to in the afternoons? Not necessarily.

A good bit of data suggests that suburban teenagers engage in plenty of risky behavior involving tobacco, alcohol, drugs, and sex, often involving cars (unlike most urban children), though they may be a little less likely to run into trouble with the police. Teenagers with independent transportation may actually face more temptations in these areas than children more or less confined to their neighborhoods. Most groups of teens have at least one member whose home is less likely to have adult supervision, and the kids congregate there. Some research on the sources of juvenile crime argues that merely living in a single-parent family (especially if the father is absent) helps predict higher rates of criminal behavior among children—not least because parental supervision is so much more difficult—and the hard fact is that even the most affluent American suburbs have no shortage of single-parent families. So should middle-income neighborhoods be concerned about the consequences of their children's school letting out at 2 or 2:30 PM? Absolutely.

Well short of having to confront organized gang activity, how many residents of any town—how many people you know?—enjoy approaching a local drugstore or mall entrance surrounded by a group of teenagers? One Public Agenda poll, with the terrific title "Kids These Days '99: What Americans Really Think About the Next Generation," found that some 71 percent of Americans held negative views of teenagers. Even though we are both male (and one of us is pretty tall), neither of us takes any pleasure walking through a clutch of teenage boys to go into a convenience store or coffee shop. Many shopping malls, responding to complaints from other customers, whether elderly or parents with young children (who also find teen behavior threatening), have simply barred unescorted teenagers from one of the few places they used to be able to congregate for free.

Teenage loitering frightens women more than men, and seniors most of all. A minister of our acquaintance explains that her elderly parishioners all make appointments or lunch dates designed to conclude by early afternoon. "I have to get home before the kids get out of school," they tell her. She says that clergy have this experience in every town or city she's ever worked. Seniors find shopping when the "kids are out of school" too threatening.

In groups, teenagers tend to be loud, aggressive, and wrapped up in their own worlds, and they also tend to use a good deal of foul language. Teenage boys in particular engage in frequent public roughhousing, often paying little attention to the things and people they might bump into. Generally frailer than in middle age, men and women in their seventies and eighties walk more slowly, sometimes with assistance of walkers and canes, and dread falling for very good reasons. Simply being on the same sidewalk, or boarding a public bus, with a group of boisterous teenagers can give seniors anxiety bordering on genuine fear. At the same time, the elderly tend to drive more slowly and tentatively than the young, and when the high school parking lot empties, streets and shopping mall parking lots fill up with younger, more aggressive drivers with energy to burn.

Juvenile crime is expensive for any society, requiring tax dollars to support courts and court personnel, probation officers, social workers, drug and alcohol programs, security personnel at schools, emergency medical services, extra maintenance costs for repairing vandalized property, remedial education for kids missing lots of school, and lost income on the part of parents attending court sessions. According to a 2002 report, "[One] high-risk juvenile prevented from adopting a life of crime can save the country between $1.7 million and $2.3 million."

As significant as these costs are, the deeper price exacted by juvenile crime lies in the alienation of young people from a path that could gain them education, achievement, and long-term success. Once children and teenagers adopt the short-term values of the street—instant gratification, lack of respect for the law or society's rules, deriding the "straight" or "square" world of studying, school, and jobs, using violence to settle disagreements—the road back is considerably longer and more difficult to navigate.

Even a prison term—far more likely to be imposed now than a generation ago, even for minor offenses—produces more determined criminals than rehabilitated young people ready to go straight. In fact, for too many young people in low-income neighborhoods, prison itself has lost its deterrent power. A teacher at Achievable Dream Academy in Newport News, Virginia, told us about taking her third-graders on a preventive field trip to the local jail, intending to reinforce the school's emphasis on character education. Instead, she said (exaggerating only slightly), "they knew everybody in the jail. 'Hey, how you doin?' 'Hey, how *you* doin?' It was like old home week. So I went to the principal and said, 'I don't think we should do this any more. They don't need to go to the jail to understand what it's like.'" The real job—and burden—for schools in low-income areas is to reorient children toward a path of learning and achievement in the straight world.

The shocking downfall of famed Atlanta Falcons quarterback Michael Vick illustrates how deep these problems go. A Newport News native, Vick grew up in the housing projects in the part of town known locally as "Bad News," which makes it all the more telling that he named his dog operation—the site of the truly bad news that ended his NFL career—"Bad Newz Kennels," recalling his old neighborhood, the way of life he ever entirely escaped, and the place where he'll always be a hero, no matter how long his prison term.

SOLUTIONS

Americans know, deep down, that no social good is served by turning kids loose at 2 or 2:30. Research so clearly confirms that after-school programs help reduce juvenile crime that a national organization of more than three thousand police chiefs, sheriffs, prosecutors, and other law enforcement leaders—Fight Crime: Invest in Kids—has organized to make the case publicly. They cite a 2002 poll of police chiefs in which 71 percent of respondents picked "more programs to engage kids in after-school hours" as the best way to fight juvenile crime, ahead of "more police officers"!

That's one reason we already spend millions on "youth programming" and "youth centers" and "teen programs" after school. Some of these work wonders. One recent study followed a group of high school freshman who were randomly assigned to either "no intervention" or to a four-year after-school program. Six years later, the boys who had had no after-school program had six times more criminal convictions than those in the program. Boys and girls outside the programs were four times more likely to lack a high school degree, and 50 percent more likely to have had a child during their high school years. Another study tracked the effect of Boys and Girls Clubs established in housing projects. Researchers looked at the levels of vandalism and drug activity in projects with Boys and Girls Clubs, and those without, and compared these levels in five projects that established new clubs to those in five that did not. The projects without clubs had 50 percent more vandalized housing units and 30 percent more drug activity than those where young people could attend Boys and Girls Clubs after school.

An East Boston juvenile gang officer loves the new school day, according to the *Boston Globe,* and says there's been a decrease in "that latchkey effect." And one parent of a Kuss Middle School child commented to the visiting Massachusetts governor that she liked the expanded day for her child for many reasons, including the fact that she lives up the block from the school and since the beginning of the new schedule, there haven't been any group fist fights on her lawn. Parent surveys, not surprisingly, indicate that nearly 80 percent of new school day parents in Massachusetts think more schools should adopt the new schedule; fewer than one in five disagree.

Similar concerns help lead affluent parents to send their children to private schools (despite their occasional disciplinary and drug problems), where it is taken for granted that a top-flight education, which includes enrichment, extracurricular activities, and athletics, requires far more time than the public schools' six-and-a-half hours. All the relevant education takes place either on-site or under the supervision of the school. Parents don't pay extra for "after-school programs." Their children's days are scheduled—with breaks—from early morning until evening, and they are supervised by adults the great majority of that time.

THE SIMPLEST SOLUTION: THE NEW SCHOOL DAY

So why do we depend solely on after-school programs, worthy as they are, that have to be created from scratch, that have to rely on uncertain public or private funding and haphazard connection to in-school programs, and that cannot require all students to attend? We could be expanding the school day, providing teenagers with a structured educational experience—including enrichment and extracurricular activities—involving no additional transportation, and at far less expense than we are now paying as a society for not supervising these children.

The new school day offers children and their families a powerful alternative to the dangerous stretch of unsupervised time rung in by the final school bell. Instead of abandoning millions of children to their own devices—TV, video games, and online stuff at best; smoking, alcohol, drugs, risky sex, or gangs at worst— the new school day offers a far better alternative: a constructive, engaging, supervised set of educational and enrichment activities only ending as parents are returning home from work.

But the new school day also provides powerful incentives to neighborhoods and to our society as a whole. Preventing obesity and smoking will lead to healthier, happier lives for young people while reducing the spiraling costs of Medicaid and health insurance increasingly consumed by diabetes treatment and cardiovascular disease. Preventing crime helps keep kids on the right path but also helps keep the rest of us safer. Preventing addiction helps teens stay clean but also reduces crime and saves money. In this case, what's good for kids and families is great for neighborhoods and society. You don't have to be a student or a parent to benefit from the new day for schools.

PART FOUR

TRANSFORMING THE SCHOOL DAY

12

ALTERNATE ROUTES?
Other Ways to Make the Most
of School Time

THE CORE PREMISE OF THIS book is that to achieve its goals, America needs to focus on how much time is scheduled in schools for children to learn. Throughout the book, we chiefly focus on one approach to that—expanding the school day to approximate the work day of eight hours. We argue that schools that expand and redesign the existing schedule demonstrate benefits to students of stronger core academics and a more well-rounded education; the benefits to parents of reducing or eliminating the high-risk hours in which children are now left unsupervised while their parents work; and the benefits to neighborhoods of keeping teens occupied and supervised.

However, expanding the school day is not the only way to expand or improve learning time. The most obvious idea is simply to improve the way schools use existing time today. It's also possible to modify the time when schools start—could a later start time in the morning increase learning effectiveness, especially for "sleepyhead" teens? And finally, the school calendar may offer some potential improvements: What is the cost in "learning loss" of the traditional long summer vacation? Should students attend more than the now-commonplace 180 days a year?

MAKING BETTER USE OF THE TIME WE HAVE

Many people reasonably ask us, "Can't we do more with the time we already have?" Yes, we can and we should—but even when optimized, current learning time is insufficient for students, parents, and neighborhoods. Nonetheless, before looking to other ways to expand or adjust learning time, it is worth briefly reviewing what we know about how time is currently used.

Academic analyses divide the total time children spend in school into four nested boxes, each containing smaller boxes until one reaches the core. The outermost box is "allocated time"—the time students are supposed to be at school, which includes everything that happens throughout the day. One level deeper comes "instructional time"—the time available for teaching and learning as distinguished from time spent on lunch, recess, passing between classes, and so on. Within instructional time is "engaged time," defined as the classroom time when students and teachers are engaged on the core task of learning as opposed to time in class spent on such activities as taking attendance, finding books, setting up equipment, and the like. Finally, within engaged time comes the core sustenance school aims to provide—"academic learning time," also known as ALT. Joy Zimmerman of WestEd defines it as "the precise period when an instructional activity is perfectly aligned with a student's readiness, and learning occurs." Note the need for the teacher to be teaching and for the students to be learning, either with the teacher or on their own.

The point of this hierarchical analysis is to focus attention on the value-creating part of the day—academic-learning time—and to highlight how much of the day is, by necessity and by habit, not devoted to it. Some of this diverted resource cannot be avoided: Students must eat and walk between classes, and teachers must take roll or make announcements. Still, critics of how schools operate today claim that as little as a quarter of the school day may be devoted to the core function of academic learning time, and often not more than half.

To improve the efficiency of schools' use of time, experts suggest focusing on three areas: classroom management, instruction and curriculum, and student motivation. Poorly managed classrooms waste a great deal of time on administration, disciplinary issues, and inefficient lesson plans. Teachers need appropriate professional development on these tasks. A curriculum that engages students across a spectrum of skill levels and instruction that draws students into learning must surely be the most important aspect of successful teaching. Student motivation is also crucial; alienated, tuned-out students won't learn even if instruction is brilliant.

Unquestionably, schools can and should focus energy on these improvement strategies. But we do not believe such improvements would obviate the need for more learning time in each school day. They would provide some more time, but we just cannot see how they would end up with sufficient time for students who simply need more time than others to learn things. It would not afford the time in an individual day or block class for teachers to group students by ability and have them work on different, appropriate levels, and for teachers to apportion their time where it is needed most. It would not give students more time to practice and perfect their skills—by doing math problems or by independent reading and writing during the school day, for example, instead of doing it at home if they get around to it and can remember how. If all concerned worked as hard as they could to reduce the amount of downtime in a school day, the schedule might come to resemble an even faster and more harried succession of necessary activities—which is the way we heard many teachers describe the conventional school day.

Nor would an optimized day add enough time for subjects that have been cut or eliminated, such as history, science, or social studies, or for subjects such as foreign languages and cultures or technology. It would not provide time for a well-rounded education to become the standard, where music, arts, drama, physical education, and health find their rightful place. It would not give teachers enough time to plan and share strategies, and it would not restore a sane pace to teachers and students. It would not address the dangerous incompatibility between the time students attend school and the time their parents are at work, which leaves too many children at risk for destructive behavior, and too many neighborhoods beset by loitering teens. So, while we do strongly favor taking best advantage of all available learning time, we do not think efficiency alone is enough. Students, teachers, schools, parents, and communities need both better and more learning time.

School Start Time

Everyone knows, and research confirms, how important it is for kids—or anyone, for that matter—to get a good night's sleep so they can perform well and be happy. Children generally meet their sleep needs until they reach middle school. At that point, surveys show that most students get too little sleep—typically around seven hours per night instead of a recommended nine or more. One reason is a shift in their circadian rhythm, which means things only get worse through high school. A growing body of evidence shows that this biological rhythm, which governs body temperature, wakefulness, and energy level over each day, shifts in adolescence to a pattern where most teens are at a low tide in the morning and reach a peak in the afternoon and evening. Thus, left to their own devices, they would (and do) go to sleep late in the evening and "sleep in" until later in the morning.

Unfortunately, for reasons chiefly based on tradition and school-transportation operations, most school districts set high schools' start time quite early in the morning. To maximize use of school buses and to keep younger children off the street in the dark, high school start times are often between 7 and 8 AM so that the buses can turn around and make a second run picking up younger children and delivering them to school for their later start time. Thus, at an age when what we know about the biology of circadian rhythms would argue for a later start to the day for teens, we actually do the opposite and start their school day even earlier than when they were younger.

Numerous studies have shown that the combination of shifting natural hours of teens with early start times for schools leads to chronic sleep deprivation for many students—with measurable results on many scales, including increases in irritability, sadness, and other emotions. Students who report the least sleep also report falling asleep in class frequently, struggling emotionally, and risking the consequences of driving while very drowsy.

As a result of this growing awareness of sleep needs in teenagers, some school districts and some policy leaders are taking action. U.S. Representative Zoe Lofgren has lobbied, so far unsuccessfully, for a law to provide financial incentives to districts to move high school start times to after 9 AM. Based on the argument that more sleep will help academic performance, this law has one of the cleverest names of any bill we know—"The Z's to A's Act"!

Even without federal funding, many districts are considering this change and some have acted. Ten years ago, Minneapolis shifted the start of its seven high schools from 7:15 AM to 8:40 AM. Independent studies done by the Center for Applied Research at the University of Minnesota, one the year following the switch and a second three years later, show that the schedule change led to a sustained sleep increase of an average of one hour per night among students at these schools. Since critics of the idea have argued that students will not sleep more but rather just stay up later, this is an important finding. Moreover, attendance has increased and stayed at a higher level, and student reports of falling asleep in class, of struggling to stay alert and concentrated, and of negative emotional states all show significant improvements compared both to the same schools before the change and to other schools in the state with earlier start times.

So why hasn't the later start time spread more widely? As with most things having to do with schools and their structures, any change faces enormous inertia in the status quo, and demands positive action and a good deal of will. Communities that have considered the change have found some parents opposed based on perceived or actual impacts on their current routines. Some sports programs feel squeezed, and some of the strongest opposition has come from coaches who want more time than they have now for youngsters in a handful of sports, not less.

Still, based on the powerful biological data and the overwhelming evidence that students are not getting enough sleep, shifting school start times later to better match students' natural cycles seems like a commonsense move. Districts that have done it have found it successful and stuck with it. It is probably about time for many other districts to look to these examples.

THE LENGTH OF THE SCHOOL YEAR AND "SUMMER LEARNING LOSS"

Extensive research on the history of school schedules shows that the current 180-day schedule emerged as a compromise between far shorter rural schedules and longer urban ones. Agrarian communities focused on the need for youngsters to take part in the family's farm work, developing schedules that initially operated school in the winter and the summer, with time off to work in the busiest farm seasons of spring and fall. Given that farm labor demanded only modest school-taught skills, attendance was low and the number of days in the school year relatively few. Urban schools in the late 1800s took on a different pattern. City schools often operated nearly every day of the year, and city leaders, increasingly faced with large numbers of new immigrants, believed that schooling was crucial both to impart skills needed for city jobs and to culturally assimilate millions of foreigners.

By the early 1900s, schools, driven by state policies aimed at improving education for all, were increasingly standardizing on or about a 180-day year, spread across three seasons and leaving summer for vacation. Medical claims that too much studying would cause harm, combined with an increasingly romanticized urban view of summers spent in nature, led to consensus on the long summer vacation.

As we attempt to review the time scheduled for learning in the fresh light of the twenty-first century's demands and realities, two issues about the school calendar deserve scrutiny—the total number of school days, and the apparently sacrosanct ten-week summer vacation. The number of days, aside from the summer issue, is chiefly a question of overall learning time, and the arguments for adding that learning time chiefly by means of an expanded day seem stronger to us.

Practically, the arguments for more time per day are persuasive. It is cost-efficient. Once the buses have already run, the buildings have been heated (or cooled), and the teachers and administrators have been assembled, adding on two hours a day is cost-effective. Many of the new day schools profiled in this book are able to add about 30 percent or even more time for only about 15 percent more cost, because they are not driving up any of these fixed costs. By contrast, for each day added to the year, the buses must run again, every teacher and administrator must add a full day, and all the utility and other overhead costs must be incurred.

There are also educational advantages unique to the expanded day, such as the opportunity to use significant blocks of time every day for literacy and math. More hours in the day affords the chance to leaven the academic content with time for engaging enrichment activities, for physical activity and sports, and for recess and lunch. These desirable changes remain difficult, if not impossible, to achieve by simply adding days to the year.

The advantages to parents of a longer day are the better match to their work schedules, along with the greatly reduced (or even eliminated) time when their children are left unsupervised and at risk. While a longer year also reduces the disparity between parental work calendars and children's school calendars—who has a job that requires only 180 days a year at work?—the elimination of the after-school mismatch is more crucial to most families. The same analysis applies to neighborhoods—the benefit of fewer unsupervised teens hanging out comes mostly by expanding the current daily schedule, not by making more of the same thing.

In sum, to get the most learning in the most cost-effective manner, while gaining the secondary benefits to parents and communities of reducing or eliminating afternoon-latchkey children, the strongest arguments support expanding learning time by adding to the day rather than (or before, in policy terms) adding to the year. The primary reason to consider changing the current calendar lies in the strong evidence of what researchers call "summer learning loss."

What happens to students' skills and knowledge between that craved-for final bell on the last day of school in June and the first bell of the first day of school in August or September? Many schools test students on their basic skills near the beginning and near the end of the school year, so quite straightforward answers to the question have emerged. In a recent review of thirteen well-designed studies over twenty years, Harris Cooper of the University of Missouri concluded that, on average, students' skills decline during summers by about one month's worth of schooling. This conclusion matches up well with teachers' experience that they must spend much of September on review. Spending about 10 percent of each school year just getting back to where the kids were at the end of the previous year is an extremely high cost for the current summer vacation.

Closer analysis of the data reveals findings of even greater concern. Not all students lose ground at the same pace or on the same subjects. Most analyses suggest that summer learning losses are considerably higher and more uniform in math. Those math losses average, according to one study, 2.6 months worth of school—more than a quarter of a school year! Many American schools are struggling more with math than with literacy. International comparisons—of such great importance for careers in science, engineering and technology—show American students scoring in the middle to lower half of tested countries. Perhaps we should focus more on the contribution of summer learning loss to the challenge—as a country—we face in math.

It is not surprising that socioeconomic status plays a far bigger role in literacy than in math. Few families of any income level do much "recreational math," whereas many studies have shown the huge differences in the culture of reading between affluent or highly educated families and those at the opposite end of the spectrum. Upper-middle-class children often *gain* reading skills over the summer, while low-income students lose about two months' worth of schooling. At a time when our country is focused on raising achievement for all and taking on the chronic and pernicious achievement gap between low-income and middle-income children, we must pay attention to the major role played by our long summer vacations.

Karl Alexander and Doris Entwisle, researchers at Johns Hopkins University, have made the case most elegantly and persuasively in their nearly twenty-year longitudinal study following the trajectory of 790 randomly selected Baltimore students as they progressed from first grade through their final interviews at age twenty-two. Their stunning finding is that in comparing the paths of children from the lowest socioeconomic backgrounds to those of the highest, school played little part. According to their calculations, one-third of the difference between these two groups was already evident in the first tests the children took in first grade, clearly based on different preschool experiences. Even more strikingly, the remaining two-thirds of the difference arose not from what they did during school years, but from how much ground they gained or lost over the summers. In fact, the poorer children actually gained a little more than the better-off children did during school years. The long-term effects of these differences, chiefly locked in place during elementary school, were striking. In their sample, over one-third of the lowest-income students had become long-term dropouts; just 7 percent were attending a four-year college. By contrast, among the more affluent group, only 3 percent had dropped out and nearly 60 percent were in college. Alexander and Entwisle conclude, reasonably, that we cannot address the achievement gap in America without addressing the learning gaps created outside the traditional school calendar.

In short, taking off ten weeks or so for summer vacation is a costly choice for student learning, with particularly high consequences in math and for more low-income children. Leading advocates in the summer learning field argue that a large portion of the achievement gap can be attributed to the differences between the lives of children when away from school for the summer. They point to data supporting this point. Their conclusion, again quite reasonable: School is a powerful pro-learning intervention that should be sustained longer into the summer, especially for children whose lower income level also puts them at greatest academic risk.

Innovative schools have taken two different approaches to changing school calendars to fight summer learning loss. The simplest is just adding more days to the calendar, which both expands time for learning and reduces time for forgetting. A different strategy is to use a balanced or year-round schedule, in which schools offer the same total of 180 days but spread them more evenly across the year, eliminating the long summer vacation. These are the two most relevant whole-school changes—though for a long time, many school systems have held remedial academic summer school for students who fell behind during the school year.

KIPP schools add three weeks to the normal school year in addition to running from 7:30 to 5 on weekdays and every other Saturday. KIPP uses the additional time in a very interesting way—those three weeks are the first three weeks of the next grade. That is, a sixth grader finishes sixth grade in June but then continues on and has three weeks of seventh grade *before* taking a six- or seven-week summer vacation. The idea is not only to add to students' opportunity to learn, but also to introduce the students to their next grade and give their new teachers a chance to get to know them before doing their summer planning, which can now be informed by direct experience with the class. Academics are not as intense at this time as they are during the regular year.

Achievable Dream Academy operates for 210 school days per year, using 180 expanded school days (each of which is about two hours longer than a conventional school day), to which it adds three ten-day "intersessions" between terms throughout the year. During intersession, students follow different curricula—those in greatest academic need receive intense remedial tutoring while those faring better have enrichment and project opportunities. After two weeks of intersession, all students get a one-week vacation before the next school block or term begins. Summer vacation lasts about five weeks, from late June until about August 1.

Nearly three thousand schools with more than 2 million students now operate on what they call a "balanced schedule" of 180 days spread across the year. That schedule typically features blocks of nine-week terms followed by three weeks of vacation, with a six-week summer vacation. The majority of these schools, however, have adopted this new calendar not to battle summer learning loss but to accommodate more students in school buildings. Parts of the country with high population growth rates have discovered that they can "rotate" more students through an existing building if they use the balanced schedule with different groups of students on different cycles.

Research on these schools shows high degrees of satisfaction among teachers, parents, and students, along with modest though statistically significant academic gains. These appear to be more impressive among the lowest-income students, as we might have predicted.

While the data on summer learning loss argues strongly for action, and experience with longer school years and balanced school schedules has generally been positive, we see little movement in this country toward this approach to modifying student learning time. For example, in Massachusetts, schools applying for the Expanded Learning Time Initiative are free to use whatever mix they desire of longer days or more days to reach the requirement of 25 percent more learning time for all students. While some schools have added a few days to the year, nearly all added time at all the schools applying for and receiving funding has come through the new school day strategy.

While we believe the expanded school day has some important advantages over the expanded school year, especially in cost-effectiveness and the curricular and pedagogical changes the new day uniquely allows, we suspect far more of the issue has to do with adult resistance to change. Polling data consistently show far less support for a longer year than for an expanded day. Organized summer-entertainment interests, such as amusement parks and movie theaters, actively campaign alongside nostalgic parents to preserve the full, classic summer vacation. We think more schools ought to try a longer year or a summer term that might feel quite different from the school year: less academic time (perhaps no homework) and more project-based and experiential learning and more enrichment. These approaches are particularly worth exploring among lower-income student populations, where research shows the summer lag to be most serious, and where families are less able to keep their children safe and constructively engaged throughout the summer.

13

FOR WHOM THE NEW BELL TOLLS

Why the New School Day Works for Many Different Children, Families, and Communities

I don't know of a single educator who wouldn't say this is a good idea.
—JOSE SALGADO, PRINCIPAL, MARIO UMANA
MIDDLE SCHOOL ACADEMY, EAST BOSTON

AFTER READING TWELVE CHAPTERS SINGING the praises of the new school day, you may find this one has an odd title, especially so near the end. But here we want to step back and look at the big picture. After all, we live in an exceptionally diverse country. We have urban, suburban, and rural schools. We have small, medium, and large public schools, and elementary, middle, K–8, and high schools. We have neighborhood, district, regional, magnet, and charter public schools. We have private religious and nonsectarian day and boarding schools.

We have wealthy children and poor children, and children from all levels in between. We have children who've grown up speaking English, and we have immigrant children, or children with immigrant parents, who speak one language at home and another in school; and we have some children who are learning English for the first time at school—known as English language learners. We have children who learned to read in preschool and children who are struggling with written language in the seventh grade. We have children with mild to severe learning disabilities, children with Attention Deficit Hyperactivity Disorder, children who are hungry in the morning, and children who were abused the night before. We have undernourished, malnourished, healthy, overweight, and obese children. We have children being raised by no parents, foster parents, older siblings, single parents, grandparents, and two parents. In short, we have an extraordinary range of children in our public schools—and we need to think about how to provide an education for all of them.

That's why we've been led to the new school day. We think it's the best way to help the most kids experience the most improvement in the most efficient *and* most politically feasible manner. So who would benefit most from the new schedule we've been describing in this book? Here we're going to be as candid as we know how.

WHO NEEDS THE NEW SCHOOL DAY MOST?

One way to answer the question of who needs the new school day most is to first ask another. Where are the neediest public schools in America—the ones with the crummiest buildings, the least qualified teachers and principals, the oldest equipment and books, the lowest morale, the most dangerous atmosphere, the hardest children to teach, and the lowest indicators of academic performance? The answer is all too simple, if deeply disturbing for anyone who believes in the American dream of equal opportunity for all: schools in urban neighborhoods, in which the students come overwhelmingly from low-income families and are disproportionately African American or Latino.

These are the children who are the subject of deep concern throughout the education world. Usually that worry takes the form of discussion of the "achievement gap," the predictable difference between the test performance of these children and that of their more affluent age-mates. And it has fueled any number of education reforms over the years: busing, small learning academies, efforts to reduce class sizes, and turnaround packages and state takeovers or interventions. The gap remains. So we propose that a new school day, not just new hours tacked on but a schedule expanded, redesigned, and backed by the commitment of principals, teachers, and families, will do the most good in these schools, with these students.

In fact, it is already transforming the educational experience and achievement of children in some of the lowest-income neighborhoods in America. Richard Coleman, founding principal of Achievable Dream Academy, a public lottery school smack in the middle of the toughest neighborhood in Newport News, Virginia, actively seeks children from the most challenging circumstances. Applicants go into a lottery. "We send out invitations to all kids in the downtown community on free or reduced lunch," he explains. "We specifically go after the poorest kids in the district. There's a point system that affects the lottery. They get additional points if the kid has a single parent. The kid gets more points if he's being raised by foster parents, or aunts and uncles. They get points for living in public housing, and for renting." Why does he do this? Because these are the kids who need education most. These are the children from "Bad News," the neighborhood where the kids are more likely to go to jail than college.

For these children, an expanded school day is a no-brainer. Who is going to make the argument that children in extremely low-performing urban schools with a history of failure are getting what they need? Presented with the possibility of a new school day, what parent of such a child is going to make an argument for less time in school and more time in front of the television or on the streets? Not one.

There's plenty of evidence on this score. In Massachusetts, which launched the most extensive new school day program in the country over the past couple of years, the ELT Initiative, nearly two hundred schools have applied for and received planning grants to consider changing over, and nearly twenty took the plunge in the first two years. More than a hundred are still in the planning pipeline. After the first year, of the schools that had changed over, none—that's right, *not one*—wanted out of the program. In fact, four of the five original districts added new schools from their districts in the second year. These are all urban schools. Many were in deep trouble with their NCLB-mandated Adequate Yearly Progress. One—the Kuss School in Fall River—had the dubious honor of being the first school to be taken over by the state for persistent failure. And in just one year of the new school day, parents, teachers, and tests all agree that the ELT schools demonstrate real gains—in some cases, phenomenal success.

For the five years before the ELT Initiative (2002–2006), the average difference between the percentage of students reaching Proficient or Advanced in English language arts in the state as a whole and the percentage among the schools that later joined the ELT Initiative was about 22.5 percent. In 2007, just the first year of the new school day, students in these schools narrowed the gap to 13.3 percent. In other words, in one year, the achievement gap closed *more than 40 percent*. Using the same comparisons, the number of students scoring Proficient or Advanced in math jumped from 20 percent in the new day schools to 30 percent; half again as many kids in ELT schools scored in the top two categories in a single year of the new school day.

In Fall River, the Osborn Street School achieved truly breathtaking gains. Not only did the school score better than the rest of its district in every tested category (third-, fourth-, and fifth-grade math and ELA, and fifth-grade science)—it also got close to or surpassed the statewide averages in every one of these areas. Students in the ELT schools made significant progress in closing the achievement gap.

What we now know is that the new school day promises to level the educational playing field for low-income kids in urban school districts, a field that despite decades of court cases and reform efforts has remained stubbornly rigged against the poorest children in America. After all, as Mike Feinberg of KIPP Academy, Houston, explained, "Beyond teaching the kids, we have to win the marketing war. Any ad agency knows that to win a marketing war, you need your message in front of people as much as possible. The messages in society aren't, 'work hard, be nice, study, and graduate'—that's why we're in a marketing war with the kids. 'Why education? Why college?'—That's what we're doing 7:30–5, all day long. *Vale la pena.*" (Which is Spanish for "it's worth the trouble.")

He continues, "We may be doing a great job with our kids, but then we send them home to the same environment they were in before they came here. You know, a lot of schools celebrate incremental gains; when scores go from 62 to 64 percent, they throw a party. But the emperor's wearing no clothes. That's not good enough. We need a whole new paradigm, and we can't do it in a disjointed way. Kids should be in one dedicated place, under one dedicated roof, with one dedicated faculty, in one dedicated culture that's in place for as many hours as possible every day, week, and year for the kids. If you look at our hours, we come close to tipping the balance when kids are spending more hours with us than with anyone else. It's not a coincidence."

Nor is Roxbury Prep's experience a coincidence. They don't have KIPP's "No Shortcuts" slogan, but the math teachers might as well. They commit to making sure their students learn what they need to move on, and what they are going to get tested on. And their scores keep going up. And although Roxbury Prep's directors worried a good bit about English language arts, that area also showed real improvement in grades 7 (86 percent Advanced or Proficient) and 8 (92 percent in the top two tiers).

So what can we conclude from the disparate experience of KIPP Academies, Roxbury Prep, Achievable Dream Academy, Miami-Dade's Zone, and the Massachusetts ELT schools? We don't say that expanding learning time automatically turns all schools into A+ educational institutions. Sometimes we may sound evangelical on the subject, but we've both been around education long enough to know that there are no magic bullets. On the other hand, there's no doubt that the first three are achieving something between real gains and phenomenal success. That also seems to be the case in Miami-Dade's Zone, but we worry that the three-year experiment may be ending far too soon, just when it has demonstrated its potential.

In Massachusetts, some schools, like Fall River's Osborn Street Elementary School, do turn a corner into truly exceptional territory. Others have more modest but still genuine positive gains worthy of noting widely. All gained significantly over the year before they converted—in aggregate, 44 percent higher in math, 39 percent in ELA, and 19 percent in science—and eight out of ten gained more than the state did—that is, they narrowed the achievement gap. And of the other two schools that improved but did not exceed statewide gains, what can we say? Change can take time, and the struggle goes on. (Even Achievable Dream

Academy has just emerged from a difficult patch with a principal who has now moved on.) But while there was real variation among the ten ELT schools, taken as a whole the schools outperformed the state in math, science, and English language arts and began closing the achievement gap—significantly in English, meaningfully in science, and modestly in math.

As we see it, then, the problem is large enough, and the data and early returns are strong enough, that as many urban, low-income school districts as possible ought to put the new school day into practice as quickly as humanly possible. Without saying it in quite these terms—although some do—parents are agreeing. After all, the charter and experimental district schools that take on the hardest cases have huge waiting lists: Roxbury Prep, the various KIPP schools, and Achievable Dream. And the parent surveys regarding the ELT Initiative in Massachusetts make the case just as strongly. By large proportions and for perfectly obvious reasons, parents of children in urban schools prefer the new school day. Their children get a better and more rounded education, and parents have to worry less about what their kids are doing—or is being done to them—after school.

We understand, as we explain in Chapter Fourteen, that, aside from schools taken over for chronic, unremitting failure, it makes no sense to impose the new school day on any group of schools, teachers, principals, or families. If these constituencies don't buy in to a redesign of the school day, it will become yet another failure in the long history of educational reform failures. Even top-down, district-initiated turnaround strategies need to build in a lot of choice for parents and teachers.

But here's what we can say with some level of confidence now. The new school day works for some of the most challenged and challenging kids in American public schools. It engages them more fully in learning. It gives them enough time to learn and practice the fundamental skills of literacy and numeracy that too many are—by all measures—failing to learn under the current school schedule. It gives teachers enough time to teach kids who learn at different rates, and it gives them enough time to provide individual tutoring and attention to the kids who need it the most. And it gives them and their schools the time to provide a balance between core academic instruction and instruction in the subjects that make people more fully human beings: the arts, history and social studies, geography, foreign languages. And finally, it gives schools the ability to offer an education that includes the body as well as the mind: recess, physical education, athletics, health, wellness, and the like.

Once the poorest schools make these kinds of changes, and once the kids themselves start to experience school as a realm of achievement and success rather than a dreary zone of obligation and failure, then students in urban schools can start thinking about going to college—something far too few of them consider seriously today. Without going to college, they are condemning themselves to relatively low-paying (or soon leveled out) jobs that will keep them and their families close to the poverty line their entire lives.

Without the new school day, most obvious educational principles and goals are impossible in practice.

That's right—simply, utterly, entirely impossible. There aren't enough hours in the day, and schools are demonstrating this fundamental fact from coast to coast, as reading, writing, and math classes have grown and grown, eating up time that used to be devoted to enrichment, art, music, recess and PE, social studies, and languages, and *still* not getting the results they expect, and certainly not closing the achievement gap.

And while we've said this before, it's worth saying again. More time is absolutely necessary—but it's just not sufficient in and of itself to bring about the transformation we want and need. That transformation requires all stakeholders to buy in; it requires money; it requires bold leadership in districts and individual schools; and it requires the good will, creativity, and persistence of America's public school teachers.

Without more time in the day, we remain convinced there's just no way to make the far-reaching revolution needed by our urban schools. You might find a successful school here and another there, as Karin Chenoweth, the author of *It's Being Done: Academic Success in Unexpected Schools* did, though a number of her schools also used a new school day. But you will not find the kinds of large-scale changes Massachusetts is already getting after a single year, where a group of historically low-performing schools are actually *closing the achievement gap*. That's why time is at the center of the admittedly knotty problem of "where do we start?"

English Language Learners

The new day makes a big difference to some other groups of public school students, too. How about English language learners, kids who are learning English as a second (or third or fourth) language while they're going to school? Raise your hand if you think these children (numbering in the millions nationally) would do better in school if they had more time to work with their teachers on their English language skills, and to practice English with their schoolmates. Keep your hand raised if you think that these children would be better off seeking homework help from their parents, many of whom are learning English themselves, and many of whom did not have advanced schooling in their home countries. Ah, you're such a good class!

Many native-born Americans complain that too many of our newest immigrants don't bother to learn English. Why then wouldn't we as a society want their children to learn English as quickly as possible, something that will happen in an active, engaging school day far faster than passively in front of a television? Immigrant parents, not coincidentally, overwhelmingly prefer the new school day when given the chance, even though many of them work in just the kind of small businesses that can make good use of the extra labor of children in the family. We saw this among immigrant parents in Malden, Massachusetts, and we saw it in Miami Edison High School.

"We have another group," said Principal Jean Teal, "that we call 'new beginnings,' who've had no formal schooling in their own country. They've never had instruction, fifteen- or sixteen-year-olds who've never gone to school, never had phonics, never held a pencil. They stay homogeneously in their own cohort; they travel together, and we start teaching them from kindergarten on up. A lot of our students are English language learners, because their primary language is Creole. [Miami Edison is in Little Haiti.] All together 240 of our 1150 students are taking English as a second language."

Special Needs Children

Then there are the children with learning disabilities, children with ADHD, and the entire category of "special needs" children. The whole point of identifying children with difficulties in learning is to be able to give them additional instruction tailored to their individual needs or disabilities. Special needs education takes patience and, above all, time. Remember Dorcas Chavez's autistic son Kenan in Boston, who rode a school bus more than an hour each way to his new day school? His mother was tremendously excited about his social and motor-skill progress in less than a year, and she has been able to move her hours to full time instead of staying part time to care for her son in the afternoons. Parents of special needs children worry all the more about what happens to their kids in unsupervised settings, and many make substantial financial sacrifices to be with them. Look at how this mother's experience of the new school day played out: not only did her son get excited about school, he was making important social progress—and she was able to increase the family income. Who knows? Maybe, working full time, her job started providing health benefits.

"We have inclusion math class," Mrs. Cohen of Jose de Diego Middle School in Miami's Zone told us, "special ed and regular kids together, doing math together. Because of the Zone, we are doing many more inclusion classes, and it's working better. Now we pair a special ed and math teacher. So kids do better. Special ed kids work better with other kids, sort of see them as role models and learn from them."

Here's another way to think about children and school. When school is a place of engagement, excitement, and felt success, children like it. When it's a nonstop struggle, a site for frequent failure, a place where slower kids get ignored by teachers in a hurry or routinely teased by quicker classmates, school for them becomes a dreary, unpleasant, depressing slog, and can't end too soon. When there's not enough time for learning-disabled children to learn in the ways they can learn best, we're giving them an alienating experience of school that actively discourages them from higher education—and works against vocational success in their future lives as well.

GIFTED AND TALENTED CHILDREN

For some of the very same reasons, the new school day makes just as much sense for gifted and talented kids as it does for kids who struggle in the classroom. When teachers have so little time to make sure the "great middle" of their classes learn the required material, how can they give good attention to the kids who get it right away? These children find themselves bored, drifting off into their own worlds just as much as the kids who are left behind as the lesson advances. For both, the question is engagement.

In Kim Langhill's second-grade class at the Jacob Hiatt School, there was a boy—let's call him Jared—who appeared to be off the charts with respect to his classmates. And yet he was fully engaged by the class. His teacher spent extra time with him, in the way she did with more traditional kids. And he worked along with the other kids when it was appropriate and on his own when he finished that. The point is that Jared got just as much out of the two-hour literacy block as his fellow students, because the teacher could use different teaching strategies with kids at different levels of comprehension and skill. His parents didn't have to think about buying him a special program for gifted and talented kids. His public school teacher could match him with a group of stronger students, and give them all extra projects. In a standard classroom period, that would have been nearly impossible, and Jared's parents would have had to engage in some soul-searching about how to engage and stimulate their exceptional child. The old phrase probably had it wrong: it's not idle hands that are the devil's plaything, it's the idle mind. Without an expanded schedule, Jared could be exercising his mind on the latest video game or the reruns of action movies on television—if he, his parents, and we were lucky. Far worse could easily await a bored, restless, intelligent boy. Thanks to the new school day at the Hiatt School, Jared has plenty to occupy his voracious and interesting intelligence.

CHILDREN OF AFFLUENT PARENTS

Let's shift focus a bit, to a different group of families, those for whom college has been assumed—and a reality—for generations: affluent professionals or successful businesspeople or men and women who work in the upper reaches of corporate America. Many of these never even consider sending their children to a school featuring the six-and-a-half-hour day, no matter how high their local school taxes. They pay a premium to get what a new school day could offer for free. They spend $10,000 to $30,000 a year to send their kids to the private schools that continue to produce a wildly disproportionate share of American business, professional, philanthropic, and political leaders. Why? Because they want their children to receive an education that is at once academically rigorous, broadly inclusive in terms of subject matter (visual and or performing arts are generally required, as are athletics), and committed to the education of the whole child. These schools put a real emphasis on individual attention, and make sure kids get tutoring if they need it.

That's the kind of education these parents believe to be essential for children on the path toward leadership in and of American society. In their minds, these schools are preparing children to step up as their parents' successors. And even if private schools and their students are not immune from drug and alcohol issues, by and large what the schools provide works. Their alumni populate the most storied and competitive colleges and universities in the country, in numbers entirely disproportionate to the size of their group, or to the very narrow socioeconomic level from which they come. Roughly 10 percent of American students attend private schools, yet private school graduates account for a third of the students at top American colleges and universities. Their parents don't need public schools to change to get a new day for their children and they probably won't come back to the public schools in their community even if they do convert to the new day. But our point is that the new school day—private school version—works for them.

So if the new school day makes sense for poor kids, English language learners, special needs kids, gifted and talented kids, and the children of the wealthy and influential, who isn't it for?

WHO'S NOT SO EAGER TO ADOPT THE NEW SCHOOL DAY?

This is an excellent question, and it's worth taking a look at who's not adopting the new school day, either by opposing it when it's brought up or by not paying any attention to it at all.

Broadly speaking, the answer seems to be schools in suburban districts, either middle-income communities or affluent upper-middle-class communities. These groups have some similarities, but differ in important ways as well. One important similarity is that the educational stagnation we described at the beginning of this book is just as true for their children as it is for the poorest and the most affluent. Children at all levels of society, whether stratified by income or parental education, have had flat reading scores on the long-term NAEP for thirty-plus years, and similar results in math (except for very modest overall gains at age thirteen that disappear by age seventeen).

Middle-Income Suburbanites

First is a group we might call suburban middle-middle-income folks: men and women working in the trades, manufacturing, or lower-level white-collar jobs. In such families men tend to be the main breadwinners, and when women work outside the home they often do so part-time. In many communities, they provide the backbone of the local PTA, civil organizations, and kids' sports leagues. Most have high school degrees, and many have attended at least some college; a few, teachers and nurses, for example, have master's degrees.

At meetings to discuss the new school day, these parents have expressed a menu of consistent objections, all across Massachusetts. They say, "if it's not broke, don't fix it"; occasionally they compare their children to the less fortunate ones, saying, "our kids aren't latchkey children. They don't need this." They often say a version of "if the current schedule was good enough for me, it's good enough for my kids." Oftentimes the mothers are staying home with young children and chauffeuring older children to lessons or sports practices after school, and they worry that the new school day will interfere with their children's activities and their family lives. As one mother put it, according to the local paper, she loved seeing her boys ask each other "What do you want to do?" when they came home after school. With a new school day, "where does that time go? I don't care whether it's cutting edge or not, but my children belong to me."

There's certainly no point to changing the school schedule if a significant number of residents, particularly parents, oppose it, but we feel compelled to answer the objections, both because this debate will continue for years as the new school day becomes an increasingly popular idea, and because we think they are based on deeply flawed assumptions. So, is public education in white middle-class suburbs "broken"—in need of fixing? Ask the question this way. Is it preparing students to attend college and gain the skills that will make them reliably employable and financially secure for the rest of their lives—in a world economy that is globalizing at breakneck speed, moving jobs rapidly from one continent to another, and changing technologically faster than ever before in human history?

The blue-collar factory jobs that high school graduates used to be able to count on for stable employment have evaporated all over the country. Consider the state of Michigan, home to the American automobile industry and one of the manufacturing giants of the twentieth century—now on economic life support because of the decline of the Big Three. It is true that Americans will always need auto mechanics and plumbers, electricians, house painters, and carpenters, tile installers and stonemasons— all honorable trades and professions. Most don't require a college education (though many are becoming increasingly complex technologically), but they quickly reach an upper limit in terms of income.

Do we really want to organize our public schools so that high school students don't think of a college education as the natural next step in their preparation for life, when just to maintain their parents' standard of living, much less advance beyond it, most young people will have to get a college degree? Or, if we do assume that most middle-income high school graduates will go on for higher education, do we want to prepare them just well enough to do mediocre work in college? That's what we do now.

Parents may be upset or even shocked to hear this, but college teachers know it intimately. Very few high school graduates in middle-income communities are prepared for what their professors consider college-level work—and we're not talking about MIT or Stanford. Most entering students at most colleges and universities are frightened of math, foreign languages, history, and all natural sciences—and cannot routinely write prose that is grammatical and even largely free from spelling errors. That's why as many as a third of today's college students end up in remediation classes in their first year of higher education.

And yet, for children to aspire to employment as teachers, physical therapists, software developers, TV production staff, accountants, financial planners, or graphic designers—without even mentioning doctors, lawyers, business executives, architects, engineers, or psychologists—they will need college *and* post-graduate degrees. Today's college degree is more of an essential ingredient for a decent job than a high school degree was a generation ago. So when we hear parents object to an expanded school day on the grounds that the current setup "isn't broken," we understand what they mean, and we respectfully—but vigorously—disagree. There's an important difference, after all, between "broken" and "not working very well." When would you rather repair your car? When it's stuck on the side of the highway, belching smoke—or when you start to hear weird noises under the hood?

But the new school day isn't only about future employment. It's also about children getting a genuinely well-rounded education, and gaining what they need to participate meaningfully in their society. When their school experience ends up focusing almost entirely on core academic subjects, we all become less interesting: schools, teachers, parents, and the objects of our concern—children themselves. If we know anything about what will be required of citizens and voters in this century, it's that they will need to be able to take in and evaluate a huge amount of information, and they will have to learn to be flexible in what they know how to do for a living. These skills require the broadest possible education, and the desire to continue learning throughout their lifetimes—not a narrow emphasis on a very few subjects.

When today's parents say, "It was good enough for me," we don't disagree at all. If they feel comfortable with the education they received and its contribution to their lives, so much the better. The only problem—and it's a big one—comes when they claim that because it was good enough for them, it will be good enough for their children. Because that argument assumes that the world hasn't changed fundamentally in the past generation or two, when in fact the world of work is in the process of an immense global computer- and telecommunications-aided transformation. Wherever we turn, we can barely glimpse the outlines of the future in media, biotechnology, energy, nanotechnology, or information technology. In all these fields the United States is losing ground to other countries, at least partly because so many American families appear to have dismissed math and science as irrelevant or painful fields of study—to be taken like bitter medicine but not to be enjoyed.

How, exactly, is an education good enough for stable middle-income jobs thirty years ago adequate for young people who may have as many as five different careers in their lifetimes? One of the meanings of the American dream is the way Americans plan for their children to move beyond them—in education, income, security, and the like. Do we really want to be the first generation of Americans to confront a future changing right before our eyes by saying, "Keep things the same—everything will be OK"? Or to say, in effect, "In a world demanding more, we want less for our children."? We sympathize with the mother who wanted her kids at home and distrusted the "outside experts" pushing a new idea. But there might be unintended consequences from her point of view. In her town, for example, where many of her fellow parents attending a public meeting on the issue all but hooted down the new school day, just 23 percent of the adult population has a college education—well below the state average of 33 percent.

Despite their feeling that the current school day "was good enough for them," it seems to us that many Americans must have had unpleasant, even alienating school experiences. Many adults respond, almost immediately, to the idea of "a longer school day"—and polling data bears this out—by saying, incredulously, "You want *more* school for my kids?" Well, yes, precisely. We do. Not a rushed and harried, "teaching to the standardized test," nose-to-the-grindstone, math-and-grammar, grammar-and-math kind of school, but school that opens up the day, makes use of teachers' skills and professionalism and creativity, and thinks long and hard about how to keep young people intellectually and emotionally engaged and successful in school. Interestingly, when we poll on that kind of new school day, parents respond far more positively.

Parents in these middle-income communities are justly proud that their kids aren't "latchkey children," because they have often made sacrifices to make sure the kids get more supervision than they would if both their parents worked full time outside the home. But we need at least to ask what these non-latchkey children are up to when they come home from school? Are they reading challenging novels or nonfiction books? Are they going on nature walks or carrying out science experiments? Playing with math problems? We doubt it. Too much evidence suggests that when their parents aren't shuttling them between sports practices and music lessons, and we've seen this in all of our own kids, the boys are playing video games and the girls are IM-ing or caring for "webkinz" or playing in virtual communities online—or just watching TV.

True latchkey children *do* need the new school day more than kids being supervised by their parents, mainly because unsupervised children watch even more TV and find it far easier to get into trouble. Which raises the question, we think, beyond all the academic reasons, of why not have athletics, sports, and music and dance lessons as part of the new school day, so kids get the supervision they need, without parents having to drive them about, while freeing parents to make other choices about how to use family resources?

But what about family time, the precious hours when children and parents are out of work, out of school, able to be together? We estimate that the new school day would mean that instead of children spending 20 percent of their waking hours in school, that number would rise to 25–26 percent. In other words, the parents and children will still have about 75 percent of the kids' waking hours not in school, available for family time and other activities. The time that would go toward the new schedule would come chiefly in the afternoon, when most parents are working; it does not usually cut into evenings and weekends. It is true that KIPP schools and some other public charter schools do use Saturday mornings, but the Massachusetts ELT schools add their 25 percent more time only to the weekday school hours.

Moreover, the evidence of people's real lives—as opposed to the mythical ones that seem to drive too much of the public policy debate—doesn't support the notion that there's much family time left at present. Plenty of studies show that under the current school schedule, in today's world, precious little genuine family time remains. Children and parents eat few dinners together as it is: take-out restaurants do a booming business, and many meals are eaten on the run. The reason there's so little family time is that real wages have stagnated in the past generation, so parents need to work more hours just to stay at the same economic level they had twenty-five years ago.

Another reason there's so little family time is the homework revolution of the past decade or so—kids are bringing home far more homework than they used to, and we think it's far too much. Such family time as exists is full of friction as parents push and monitor their children's homework progress all evening. And the quality of life is not helped by the inevitable moment—far more common among parents who did not attend college or who have limited English skills, but also experienced by the most educated among us—when parents simply cannot help their children complete certain assignments. Children feel caught between their teachers and their parents, while parents feel stupid and find themselves annoyed with the teachers or the homework itself. As a result, in most of the new day ELT schools in Massachusetts, kids are doing more of their homework at school, where they can get help from the teachers who assigned it, and bringing much less home. We saw this at KIPP Academy in Houston, too, where teachers are encouraging students to complete as much homework as possible while they're at school, where they can get help from their peers and teachers, as well as at Roxbury Prep, where the school's homework center plays a crucial part in getting kids to finish their homework.

So, on balance, would the new school day help these middle-income children and their parents? We think so, mainly by opening up the realm of possibility to children who otherwise will likely experience real limitations on their mobility in adult life, but also by improving the quality of their family life. But there's little point spending scarce resources trying to convince these parents that their children have much to gain, if they are going to dig in their heels. We're a little surprised that there sometimes seems to be more moral outrage directed at the folks proposing the new school day than at the fact that the schools are offering their children so limited an education, which looks to us like a tragedy in the making. Sadly, the economic devastation that is already haunting middle-income communities—disappearance or export of manufacturing jobs, export of many white-collar jobs, increasing automation, decreasing benefits in the remaining jobs, soaring health care costs, decreasing bankruptcy protection, corporate downsizing—may be further magnified in their children's lives by a stand-pat attitude toward public education.

AFFLUENT SUBURBANITES

Another group dominates most media coverage of college-bound high school students and their parents: the upper-middle-class families in affluent suburban school districts with high-performing schools where 95 percent of graduates attend college. Think Whitman High School in Bethesda, Maryland, Hall High School in West Hartford, Connecticut, New Trier High in Winnetka, Illinois, Wellesley High School, Massachusetts, or Oyster Bay High School, New York. Considering themselves and their children competitors in a fierce battle for the limited number of slots in America's top—read most famous, expensive, and selective—colleges and universities, these parents have become legendary for their overscheduled, super-pressured children and lives. Given how much they populate the front pages of major newspapers and the covers of newsmagazines, it may come as a surprise to realize just how small a sliver of American parents and schoolchildren they are: surely less than 10 percent.

Perhaps the hardest question confronting new school day advocates is, What does the new school day have to offer the most affluent and currently successful parents and children? It's an important question, too, because these parents tend to be active in public affairs, serve as opinion leaders in their communities, and want their children to succeed as intensely as any group of parents on earth. Here's what we think. These parents have already decided that the current school day is woefully inadequate for their children. Even though they have decided not to pay private school tuition, they are spending large sums on athletic instruction, equipment, and teams, as well as the transportation costs for their children to travel to meets, tournaments, matches, or games. They are renting musical instruments and paying top dollar for individual lessons. They are paying tuition at schools of dance, and voice, and art. And they are paying for SAT tutors ($150 per hour in Westchester County, New York), Kaplan SAT review classes, Kumon Math and Reading instruction. With their checkbooks, their minivans, and their time, they are purchasing high-end activities that make up a new school day—and they are doing so from elementary grades through high school.

What a new school day can offer them first of all is financial and psychological relief. An expanded school schedule brings back into the curriculum the very subjects and activities—music, art, dance, athletics—they are having to buy on the open market, all offered in one place, requiring no complicated transportation timetables, making use of the school building they already pay for with their taxes, and bringing their local school into the twenty-first century. The truth is that even in these schools, the six-and-a-half-hour day limits the education children receive, and much of what we have outlined in terms of narrowed curriculum, reduced recess and PE, and a harried in-school atmosphere applies to these schools as well.

In some cases, certainly, the quality of programs that these parents are buying is much higher than the programs schools would provide, so some of these parents would remain uncomfortable or dissatisfied with the generic SAT prep class offered by a public school, and might still choose to pay for a brand name program. But there would be many, we'd guess, who would be just as happy to send their kids to a school-based program—and advocate for making such programs very high quality.

IT'S REALLY FOR EVERYONE!

The core of our argument is this: a change is happening in the school day, and it offers results to low-performing schools as well as high-performing schools. Since low-income parents and parents of children in low-performing schools embrace the new school day, as do immigrant parents and parents of special needs children, school officials ought to focus on these constituencies as they begin to consider the idea and put it into practice. The case for change is far stronger at the bottom—that is, at the schools with the lowest-scoring students, the schools that keep superintendents up at night. These are the kids who need the new school day the most—tomorrow. These are the students our society both has responsibility for (a responsibility sometimes established by lawsuits, but no less real for that fact) and has, to put it mildly, not been doing a very good job of educating. Courts are ruling increasingly that just because students come from low-income communities where the tax base is low and property taxes can't support good schools, children still deserve a fully adequate education. And based on our experience with the Massachusetts ELT schools, Achievable Dream Academy, and charter schools such as the KIPP network and Roxbury Prep, but also that of the Zone schools in Miami-Dade, these are the schools that can show the most improvement the most quickly.

For schools in the middle, both in terms of performance and in terms of constituency, we probably need more data on how much change the new school day would bring about quickly. Moreover, given that parents are less enthusiastic, that the new school day does cost money, and that it's usually a mistake to try to force a change on a system controlled locally that the local folks don't much want—these schools shouldn't be a first priority. We see signs that some of these communities may soon take more of a chance on the ELT program in Massachusetts, and we suspect that success will breed greater interest and support. In any case, we would hope that some of these communities would look more closely at new data on incomes and education, take a chance on the new school day, see some real results, and get more enthusiastic—but there's no point in forcing it on them. On the other hand, we would want to insist that expanded educational opportunity not be limited to low-income students in low-performing schools.

For kids in the most affluent, highest-performing public schools, well, we think they and their parents could benefit from the new school day, but since they're already getting one version of it, it doesn't seem to be a good use of resources to try to expand their schools' schedules—unless the parents push for it first.

So you've just finished the long answer to the question, Who is the new school day for? But based on this chapter, there's a much shorter one, which we also like: Everyone!

14

GETTING DOWN TO BUSINESS
Do's and Don't's in Creating the
New School Day

BACK IN THE INTRODUCTION WE promised that if we managed to persuade you that the new school day was worth trying to bring to your neighborhood school or to a school district you care about, we wouldn't leave you high and dry. Well, since you're still reading you've at least given us the benefit of the doubt, so here's our part of the bargain. In this chapter we explain, based on our (and a few others') experience, how you can go about transforming the school schedule to help make kids smarter, parents happier, and neighborhoods safer. We'll try to answer these key questions:

- Who would have to agree?
- How can you convince them?
- Who are your key potential allies?
- What are the biggest obstacles you're likely to face, and how can you overcome them?

And if we haven't answered all your questions, feel free to e-mail us at the National Center on Time and Learning, at chrisandwarren@timeandlearning.org.

Depending on your level of involvement in public school issues, you may already know some of what follows. Feel free to skip ahead. Like the teachers we've visited, we're trying to reach many different audiences.

BACKGROUND: SCHOOL POLICY 101

To make change in public schools, we need a road map to the way school policy gets made. In most of the United States, public schools are locally controlled, meaning that a city or town runs its own schools, nearly always through an elected school board, though a handful of big-city mayors (New York, Chicago, Boston) appoint school board members. School boards set policy for their school districts. They also hire a superintendent both to make policy recommendations and to execute all school policy. In most school districts the board also has independent taxing power, usually through property taxes, to raise the money that pays for the local schools. These local school boards and the superintendents who report to them control or negotiate everything from teacher contracts to bus schedules—as well as the hours and days on which school will be held (above the state-mandated minimums).

States have rapidly grown as financial partners in public education in recent years. Since smaller and poorer districts have always struggled to afford schools funded by property taxes alone, states have long supplemented local education funding, the amount often determined by a complex formula. In the past few decades, as a result of parent lawsuits, states have increasingly been held accountable for equitable financing of poor schools and been forced by courts to ensure that every school is "adequately" funded. In the modern education-reform era, many states have become far more active in setting standards and in influencing school-level policy. For example, even before the passage of No Child Left Behind, many had adopted state standards of what students should learn at various grade levels and added state tests tied to those standards to try to ensure students reach adequate achievement levels.

The federal government has always been a modest partner, financially and in terms of policy, in K–12 education. In modern times, federal funding has not reached even 10 percent of total education spending and has generally been focused on support for poor students based on the civil-rights argument that the federal government should pursue a decent education for all of its citizens. The No Child Left Behind Act (NCLB in shorthand) represented a huge shift in this role, since it required states accepting federal money to test elementary and middle school students in English and math, and develop plans aimed at getting all students to "proficiency" by 2014.

The NCLB requirements on reporting and their strict timeline for progress have added to pressure that was already building for ways to break through on academic performance, especially among high-risk student populations. States have a good deal of flexibility under NCLB as to how they define proficiency but they all face two fundamental challenges: How they can drive improvement, and what to do about schools that continue to struggle.

WHAT DOES IT TAKE TO START OR CONVERT TO A NEW DAY SCHOOL?

As we've said, more than a thousand public schools have already adopted a version of the new school day: charter and experimental schools that have started from scratch, turnaround schools like those in the Miami Improvement Zone, and converted schools like those in the Massachusetts Expanded Learning Time (ELT) Initiative. Their experience illustrates much of what it takes to succeed in launching a new day school. Across these schools, four key elements are always in place:

- The will to make a major schedule change
- The support or at least approval of the school district
- The agreement of teachers (and, where applicable, their unions) on how to manage change fairly
- The new funding, or flexibility in using current funding, to pay for the newly expanded schedule

THE WILL TO CHANGE

To break from the norm of the old school day requires willpower. Designing and putting in place a new schedule requires a truly collective—and collaborative—will in the school itself.

In a newly launched school, as with most charter and experimental schools, the school's creators choose an expanded schedule and all the employees, parents, and students come to the school knowing of its different and longer hours. Mike Feinberg and Dave Levin, founders of KIPP, identified the need for considerably more time for their students from the very beginning. All KIPP teachers, parents, and students are forewarned about this far more extensive schedule.

Whereas the will to change in experimental schools typically comes from founders, school districts themselves are increasingly choosing large-scale change to reverse years of low performance— a process that takes vision, will, and bureaucratic skill. As chancellor of the New York City school system from 1995 to 2000, Rudy Crew fashioned a "Chancellor's District" consisting of schools plucked from their geographical district homes and run directly by the chancellor's staff in an effort to turnaround years of dismal underperformance. As part of the turnaround plan, these schools all received more time for their students.

It was a bold experiment, and the data showed that it began to work quickly. Even though they remained well below the city average, the new day schools showed significant gains in math and science scores; in fact, they improved faster than the system as a whole. In 2002, the Council of the Great City Schools cited the Chancellor's District as one of the "model turnaround" districts in the country. Crew's successor, Joel Klein, ended the Chancellor's District on behalf of a system-wide change using more time: Now a third of all New York City students (selected on need) get two-and-a-half hours more instruction per week.

Now superintendent of Florida's Miami-Dade School District, Crew has reprised this strategy, which he felt worked for him in New York, under the name of the School Improvement Zone, where the superintendent's office directly supervises thirty-nine chronically underperforming schools, including 3,600 teachers and 45,000 students. All Zone schools add one hour a day for students to focus on core academic needs in literacy and math. In 2004, the year before the Zone, thirty-two of the schools, received a D or an F in Florida's grading system. Two years later, the number of A or B schools had grown from zero to eight, and the number of D and F schools had dropped from thirty-two to nine.

This formula for turnaround schools—direct management by the superintendent's office plus changes in leadership, teacher corps, and curriculum, combined with (typically) one more hour per day for student learning—is being emulated in several other urban districts, including Pittsburgh and Boston.

Massachusetts has pioneered the third model of broad-scale change regarding the new school day, in which the state government empowers change by making funding available to those schools determined to pursue conversion to a new schedule. Converting an existing school requires more time and deliberation to reach consensus. It usually requires a highly motivated, visionary, and persuasive principal; and it often entails allowing teachers, parents, and students who do not like the idea to switch to a standard-schedule school.

For example, at all eighteen ELT schools in Massachusetts, conversion was preceded by at least one school year of public planning, led by a school-redesign committee usually including the principal, some teachers, and some parents, and sometimes skeptics or outright opponents. Our experience suggests that the principal and some teachers must be strong advocates for the change in order to stick through the whole process.

THE SUPPORT OF THE SCHOOL DISTRICT

Very few schools have the autonomy to make a large-scale schedule change without the approval of their district. In a typical district, several key components of the new day, such as changed busing schedules and negotiated compensation for teachers who work longer hours, require district action. In the Massachusetts ELT program, districts apply to the state with one or more of their schools; the district also generally leads the process of selecting schools for conversion.

In turnaround new day schools, the involvement of the district is intense, ongoing, and absolutely essential. "We have challenges beyond the ordinary" in the Zone, says Miami-Dade's associate superintendent, Dr. Geneva Woodard. She adds, "Our schools were selected because they had an ongoing history of low achievement. And the factors affecting them? Economics. They're located in areas where families are economically challenged; that means we don't have parental involvement. The mobility rate is very high. They may leave one school and end up at another a few blocks away. (That's one reason the Zone has a common curriculum.) They've had in the past a high percentage of serious incidents on a daily basis: fights, disruptions, neighborhood issues, a lack of order—all these things pulling at them.

"To overcome these challenges we have to be very focused; that's what we've done in the Zone." Her staff meets with principals at least monthly and visits the schools and classrooms constantly.

Many of the schools across the country that have converted to a new school day are from the relatively small pool of schools that have the freedom to do so with little or no district approval. Charter public schools generally have the right, under the state chartering law, to set their own rules. Some districts have been experimenting with giving greater autonomy to individual schools. In Boston, for example, the district and the teachers' union created a category of schools called "pilot schools"—schools with far greater autonomy. A new school must start out as a pilot school if it wants that flexibility, or an existing school must have the vote of a "supermajority"—two-thirds—of the faculty to become a pilot school. At least half of the Boston pilot schools choose the new school day once they are freed to consider what they believe will work best for their students.

The Support of Teachers and Their Unions

Sometimes, when we raise the idea of the expanded school day to a new group of people, be they parents, journalists, civic groups, family members, friends, acquaintances, or colleagues, the very first skeptical comment we hear is, "What about the teachers' unions? There's no way they'll go along!" Clearly, in the eyes of many, unionized teachers themselves make up one of the most powerful obstacles to any serious educational reform, regardless of the proposal's intrinsic merit. Our experience, however, suggests something quite different.

Like most people, teachers have mixed initial reactions to large-scale change. But in general, we've found most teachers agree that providing more time in the school day can help teaching and student learning. And like most people, they respond better to proposals for change when they are genuinely consulted on whether the changes make sense and how they might play out, and given real responsibility in helping bring the changes about. Most people want a real say about the processes that affect their work and lives—why should teachers be different?

That said, the most significant challenge in converting a standard-schedule school into a new day school is the need to contract with teachers to serve the expanded hours. The main issues are: which teachers are key to the change, which are willing to participate, and how they should be compensated. For example, math and English teachers tend to be most involved in the added learning time, while more specialized teachers may find little change in their hours.

Some of the needed staffing can be achieved by staggering start times for teachers. Many union contracts don't provide for staggered times, but it turned out that in Cambridge, Massachusetts, that provision had long been in the contract though rarely used. When two Cambridge schools elected to convert to the new school schedule, it proved useful. Some teachers start their days later in the morning and work later in the afternoon, which many teachers prefer—and that change costs the district nothing at all. Cambridge also pays many teachers more for their longer hours. And all the noncharter public schools we know that use the new schedule pay more overall for teachers.

The main issue in new teacher agreements has to do with whether the teachers are unionized. At charter public schools, which generally don't have unions, the process is simple. KIPP schools and many others do pay their teachers more—15 to 20 percent more than the comparable district salary at KIPP schools, for example—to compensate for the longer hours. But the amount isn't calculated by multiplying an hourly wage times the longer hours.

In Newport News, Virginia, the public Achievable Dream Academy pays all teachers a flat extra stipend of $4,500 per year for working longer hours than their counterparts in the rest of the Newport News system. Since Virginia is a "right-to-work" state in which teachers' unions have relatively little influence, the Newport News district could simply decide on this amount without negotiation; as long as enough teachers were willing to work for this amount, the district could proceed.

In the New York City Chancellor's District, the United Federation of Teachers (the American Federation of Teachers local) negotiated a 15 percent pay raise for all teachers working the new hours, but there was more: When a big-city district chooses some schools for conversion to a new school day, officials generally give teachers a chance to "transfer out" as well as to "transfer in." In both New York and Miami, as many as half the teachers opted out of the new schedule.

"Why?" we asked Miami District Supervisor Diana Taub. "Some for personal reasons," she said. "They had little kids, or elderly parents they were caring for, or second jobs. Others, because they had just come to work with us and got assigned to the neediest school, saw it as an opportunity to go to a 'better school.'" But the same number opted in, so staffing wasn't a problem.

"We had quite a few new principals, too," said Blanca Valle, assistant superintendent of the Zone, who took us around Miami one day in fall 2007. "I'm a strong believer that leadership is the most important part of the school. A strong leadership team has made all the difference. We started the Zone with twenty elementary schools—and five or six brand new principals. We also had a few new ones in high schools, and had some changes after the first year."

In Pittsburgh, where Superintendent Mark Roosevelt instituted Accelerated Learning Academies, expanding the school day by roughly forty-five minutes for elementary and middle school students in eight poorly performing schools, his agreement with the teachers' union included a $6,300 raise, five extra preparation and professional development days, and an additional forty-five minutes a week for professional development. The contract addition prohibited teachers selected for the Accelerated Learning Academies from transferring to another school for three years. Since students respond so well to stronger relationships with teachers, reducing transience is a simple way to help stabilize those relationships. As Marilyn Luter, who teaches third grade at Achievable Dream Academy in Newport News put it, it takes time for teachers to learn how to teach and learn the culture, so "if you're just here to put a notch in your résumé and move on, it's not worth it to us."

In a strongly unionized state like Massachusetts, union negotiations involve a lot of give-and-take. In most cases, ELT schools have allowed teachers to volunteer whether to teach more hours or to transfer to another school if they prefer. In fact, schools have seen very few departures, but the feeling of choice engendered by the offer has made it easier to reach consensus.

All eight of the districts where schools have converted to a new school day have worked out specific pay rates and other terms (such as making that extra pay subject to pension benefits). Generally teachers receive proportionately more money based on the additional hours they work. Both statewide unions in Massachusetts, the American Federation of Teachers–Massachusetts and the Massachusetts Teachers Association (the state NEA affiliate), officially endorse ELT and have facilitated its adoption. But actual negotiations are local, and in some instances—usually due to a difficult overall labor-management climate—the parties could not reach agreement and the process stalled.

THE MONEY

The time has come to talk about money. New day schools cost more, so in this budget-challenged world, how can we be seriously proposing to spend more money on public education, especially since more money has produced so little in the way of results over the past generation? The answer is that Americans don't object to increasing education funding in principle—they want to see their taxes used wisely and well, and we think the new school day makes excellent, efficient, targeted use of their money.

New costs come chiefly in the form of added compensation to teachers or others such as community-based organizations that provide enrichment. The incremental cost is relatively efficient— as noted in Chapter Twelve, in our experience, about 15 percent more spending buys about 30 percent more time. The efficiency arises from the fact that overhead increases very little. The costs of busing, central and school administration, maintenance, books, and much else remain more or less fixed. Still, the added costs amount to $1,300 per student per year in Massachusetts and about $1,200 per student in KIPP schools across the country. In Miami-Dade's School Improvement Zone, a more modest (compared to Massachusetts and KIPP) expansion of learning time appears to cost about $700 per student per year.

To finance a new school day, a school or district must either use its current money more flexibly or obtain significant new funding, or both. The schools with the greatest flexibility—charter public schools and autonomous district schools such as Boston's pilot schools—are able to choose how to use most or all of their funds. As a result, they often need surprisingly little new money. For example, the Roxbury Prep Charter School in Boston does not pay its teachers more than other city teachers even though it schedules its students for longer hours. The directors manage teachers' schedules carefully to avoid overburdening them; they also hire more teachers and fewer administrators, and teachers consider the overall climate and approach of the school sufficiently compelling to be satisfied with the pay. At Roxbury Prep, expanded learning time costs essentially no more than the old school day. One Boston pilot school managed to use schedule and hiring flexibility to keep costs low by using staggered starting times, more paraprofessionals, and some part-time teachers to cover the longer day.

However, the overwhelming majority of public schools do not have the flexibility to stretch their existing resources very much and must pay teachers proportionately more for more time at school, and therefore must receive additional funding for nearly all of the added time. At present, three kinds of extra revenue are possible: private and public grants, district funding above the normal level, and state funding above the normal level. Each of these has advantages and drawbacks—both for the schools themselves and for any large-scale program to bring the new school day to many more schools. Since we find that many schools would adopt the new school schedule if money allowed, it's useful to take a careful look at these financing possibilities.

Beyond Bake Sales

Many new day schools simply raise private money to cover some or all of the extra costs. For example, the Achievable Dream Academy raises all of the costs—about $2 million per year—of its expanded time and programming through private fundraising. Started by Walter S. Segaloff, a successful local businessman who wanted to help poor, inner-city Newport News students succeed academically and socially, the Achievable Dream Academy Foundation now runs an annual fundraising campaign, the centerpiece of which is a gala Tennis Ball that in 2007 included ninety-two corporate, non-profit, and individual sponsors, ranging from nationally known corporations such as Verizon to local leadership groups such as Towne Bank to three local elected officials. Even if not on such a grand scale, charter schools often raise money for overall operations, some of which is devoted to costs associated with longer days, longer years, summer programs, and extra tutoring. When Boston decided it could no longer afford $600,000 to subsidize the new school day at the Timilty Middle School (a pioneer new day school dating back almost twenty years), parents and teachers organized a large demonstration on City Hall Plaza. Just in time, a local businessman stepped forward and organized a private fund-raising campaign to save Timilty's expanded schedule. Today, the school is part of the Massachusetts ELT Initiative and again publicly funded.

District Funding

How about additional underwriting from the school district? Until recently, this generally took the form of extra funding for an innovative experimental or lab school such as the University Park School in Worcester, Massachusetts, or the Timilty School in Boston. In both of these cases, the innovations (which went beyond the schedule change) proved valuable and the school posted impressive results, but had little or no effect on the system. All too often, even successful experiments in public education are more or less ignored rather than copied.

More recently, as the national movement for state standards and annual testing has grown, and has now been locked in by the provisions of NCLB, districts have been looking for strategies to address schools that chronically lag. As noted, a growing number of districts—Miami-Dade, New York City, Pittsburgh, Boston—have developed turnaround packages for targeted schools. In all of these, the districts have funded the increased costs by carving out sufficient funding to pay for teachers' extra time as negotiated in the overall contract or in a special attachment to the existing contract. Some schools have also made innovative use of Title I funds—the federal money that comes to schools based on the number of low-income students served, and which can be used flexibly to raise student achievement.

State Support: The Massachusetts Example

The third potential source of revenue is the state. Most states supplement local funding and direct the largest share to the poorest districts. In some states this choice is voluntary; in others it is considered part of a state constitutional obligation to provide a free, high-quality public education to all children, regardless of the size of their district tax base.

Increasingly, some states are pursuing initiatives that earmark some new funding for educational strategies that their governors and legislature deem especially promising—such as the ELT Initiative in Massachusetts. Because this program is the first of its kind in the country and appears to hold promise as a model for other states, it's worth looking at how it works in some detail.

Under this program, districts can apply for state funding for one or more of their schools to expand school time by at least 25 percent for all students in that school. Expansion can include longer days, longer school years, or both. The school is free to develop its own plan, but is strongly encouraged to redesign the entire day and not simply add some time to the end of the old schedule.

The school needs to explain how the added time will help it meet its academic and educational goals. While allowing design freedom, the program makes clear the expectation that ELT schools will add

- Enough time to make a real difference in student achievement in core academic subjects
- Time for enrichment in arts, music, drama, sports, and other facets of a well-rounded education that help students get more engaged
- Time for teachers to work together in common planning for their students and to receive professional development targeted to the new school schedule embedded into the daily routine

Schools and their districts can apply for a grant to support a planning process up to eighteen months long. During that planning period, a school redesign committee explores and refines options for the school. Not all redesign committees conclude that expanded learning time is right for their school.

Not all plans ultimately get sufficient buy-in from parents, teachers, the union, and the school board to take the next step. The state Department of Education operates a quality filter, providing detailed feedback on preliminary proposals and exercising the right of approval on all final plans.

The state tacitly acknowledges that local districts cannot generally afford ELT without state aid and that ELT can only continue with state funding. Plans that pass all hurdles receive state funding at the rate of $1,300 per student per year. The state regularly reviews progress at these schools and has commissioned Abt Associates, a firm nationally recognized for its work in assessing public policy outcomes, to provide a multiyear evaluation. Massachusetts currently plans to review the entire ELT program after four years to decide whether to make the new day schedule a permanent part of some or all schools' basic educational foundation, and how to properly cover the costs of such a permanent change.

In the initiative's first year, the 2006–2007 school year, ten pioneering schools in five districts across the state went ahead and changed to a new day schedule for 4,700 students. In the second year, all the first-year schools renewed (though one was merged with another in its district to form one larger school) and nine more schools were added, bringing participation up to eighteen schools and more than 9,000 students. As of October 2007, more than a hundred more schools from twenty-nine school districts with more than 50,000 students were in the planning process to potentially convert to a new school day in either fall 2008 or fall 2009.

While Massachusetts has developed the leading state-level effort to fund expanded learning time, several other states are considering their own initiatives. Following years of litigation that eventually established that New York State was not adequately funding education for poor children, the state adopted a four-year plan to increase school spending by billions of dollars. Under that plan, fifty-six districts with poorly performing schools must enter into a "Contract for Excellence" with the state, in which they specify how they will spend the significant new money, which can be spent on any of five strategies, including "Increased Time on Task." Many districts are advancing plans to expand learning time for at least some students, though few have yet to undertake whole school-schedule redesign to a new school day. In New Mexico, Governor Bill Richardson has been advancing a proposal to have the state support expanding learning time at some of its schools.

Pros and Cons

Each of the three revenue sources—private fundraising, special district funding, and new state support—has strengths and weaknesses. Private fundraising comes with few strings, doesn't depend on political currents, and allows a single school to get about the business of adopting the new school day. But very few schools have the ability to raise the amount of money needed to fund a major expansion in learning time, and it is hard to imagine a plan for broad use of the new day schedule based on large-scale private fundraising. Schools that depend on private money to support their added time must reach annual fundraising goals or be forced to scale back. And we agree with those who maintain that public education is meant to be publicly funded and should not depend on charitable support for core needs.

District funding has helped a significant number of schools expand their schedules. It is generally well-tailored to local circumstances since it arises locally and by definition reflects district priorities. It has two major flaws, however. First, since it usually represents a reallocation of existing funds rather than new money, it comes at the expense of other projects that have their own merits and proponents. Second, it has turned out to be unreliable over time. In New York City, Rudy Crew's successor disbanded the "Chancellor's District." In Worcester and Boston, high-performing schools (University Park and Timilty, respectively) that relied on the new school day saw their extra funding cut back when budget pressures on the district forced tough choices. While some argued for retaining such successful experiments, many more argued, successfully, that fairness required "extra money" to be cut first. In Miami-Dade, the School Improvement Zone was launched as a three-year commitment; despite good results, as of late 2007, there was a widespread expectation in Miami that the added time would be pared back or eliminated after the 2007–2008 school year in response to budget pressures.

State funding holds the greatest promise for permanent change. Many state constitutions are now understood as guaranteeing an adequate public education. If expanded-learning-time efforts come to be seen as fundamental to meeting that guarantee, state funding could become permanent. Moreover, states can choose, as Massachusetts and New York have, to direct some of their annual funding increases to district initiatives promoting conversion to a new school schedule—and tie such new funding strictly to successful efforts. Since this kind of funding cannot be used for other purposes and represents genuinely new money; it preempts any debate over whether the community can afford what opponents would otherwise call a "luxury" or whether the money could be better spent on something else. Finally, states generally have broad-based taxation authority, unlike most local school districts, which are limited to the property tax. As a result, they can guarantee that funding for conversion and maintenance of the new school day becomes permanent.

The federal government has a potential role to play as well. The current congressional chairs of the committees governing K–12 education—Senator Edward Kennedy of Massachusetts and Representative George Miller of California—have proposed incorporating a demonstration program under the next reauthorization of No Child Left Behind that would stimulate a number of other states and districts to try the new school day. This proposal, authored by Representative Donald Payne, would recognize the federal obligation to help states and districts figure out how to meet the lofty goals of No Child Left Behind. This funding would provide a critical catalytic role, and longer-term federal support may need to be part of the total funding enabling the expansion of the new school day.

GETTING CHANGE TO HAPPEN

In our experience, the most important single step in leading a change to the new school day is the first one: generating an open dialogue about the current schedule and how well it does or doesn't serve the needs of students, families, and communities. When we ask a room full of people whether the schools that children now attend have the same schedule they, their parents, and their grandparents followed, heads nod. When we ask them what other institutions—work, the family, transportation, entertainment—have changed so little in that time, people generally get the point—they quickly see that the current schedule is rooted in past traditions and needs, with little to do with modern life or their children's future. Polling data confirm our experience. A national 2006 Phi Delta Kappa/Gallup poll asked "How do you feel about extending the school day in the public schools in this community by one hour?" Respondents favored the idea by better than a 2:1 margin: 67 percent to 31 percent. Admittedly, it's much easier to get people to agree that the current schedule is antiquated and inadequate than it is to get agreement on the proper solution. But the greatest enemy of change to a new school schedule—or anything else, for that matter—is sheer inertia, so the willingness to consider change is an absolute prerequisite.

Once people are willing to consider the possibility that a different, expanded schedule may be needed for schools, the obvious question becomes, Time for what? The goal, after all, isn't more time: it's enough time to achieve some agreed-upon desired results. In our experience most people agree that schools should help all (or as nearly all as feasible) students obtain the foundation they will need to be productive workers and thoughtful citizens in the twenty-first century. We also find broad agreement that a good education is well-rounded; that it shouldn't be limited to basic math and literacy but should also include other subjects—such as science, history, foreign languages, geography—and other expressions of humanity: music, drama, arts, and physical development, including health, physical education, and sports.

Assume that many parents, teachers, and other residents can be drawn into a discussion about educational goals and the inability of the current school schedule to achieve them. The key to turning discussion into action is to target the people who are needed both to authorize and to execute change. In general, we believe that this requires two somewhat separate efforts—one from the grass roots up; the other from the policymakers down. Only when the people in charge of setting school policy and school financing agree with parents, teachers, and principals can a change this size come about.

Adopting Policies That Make Change Possible

For single schools, especially new ones and autonomous charter schools, connecting these two levels can be quite easy. Once the founders of the KIPP schools received the support of the Houston superintendent, they could shift from setting policy to executing it as the first two teachers at the first site. At least a third of all charter schools significantly expand learning time because their boards and leaders can just decide to do so; hire teachers based on the new schedule, and recruit students and families aware of and often attracted by it.

Large-scale change, however, will require transforming large numbers of existing public schools, and that takes separate but coordinated efforts to create support from the leaders as well as the people who will live with the change. Attracting the interest and eventual support of leadership turns out to be surprisingly doable.

The modern standards-based accountability movement has forged a broad consensus that education can no longer mean that students have "served their time" by showing up on enough days for enough years to be allowed to graduate. Instead, acceptable education is now being defined as students' attaining a measurable amount of academic skills and knowledge. While each state has different standards, and tests them differently as well, the convergence of the standards-based movement with the No Child Left Behind Act (which provides a federal mandate for this approach) has focused enormous scrutiny on how our schools are progressing toward the new vision. The results, as detailed here and in too many places to count, remain disturbing. Absolute results are disappointing, and the achievement gap between affluent and disadvantaged students remains large and troubling.

These results have created a widespread sense of urgency and appetite for reform among politicians and education public-policy leaders. Virtually every governor and mayor runs on a platform of "fixing the schools," but beyond the traditional rhetoric, there is a mounting sense that we are not on the path to success. Modest progress is visible, to be fair, but not at the rate needed to imagine victory is simply a matter of staying the course.

Some big-city mayors have wrested control of the city school system from elected school boards so they can try to drive faster change. Chicago, New York City, and Boston stand out in this regard and are role models for many other cities to follow. Whereas superintendents were once routinely hired from within the ranks, a movement to bring in outsiders as change agents has emerged. For example, Roy Romer, former governor of Colorado, served as superintendent of the Los Angeles Unified School District. The Eli and Edythe Broad Foundation funds a program allowing credible and visible leaders from other careers—graduates include a former governor, a Disney executive, a U.S. District Attorney, and a three-star Air Force general—to take a ten-month course preparing them to compete to be a big-city superintendent of schools.

The charter school movement, begun in Minnesota in the late 1980s and now supported by enabling laws in most states and embodied in several thousand schools across the country, arose out of a hunger to accelerate innovation and experimentation as well as to provide parents with more choices. While the schools cover an enormous gamut of strategies, philosophies, and quality, and the movement itself has engendered a great deal of political controversy, it has also transformed educational debates by infusing a spirit of innovation and an aura of competition, and by providing a breeding ground for start-up entrepreneurs, a brand new concept in public education.

Major philanthropists have zeroed in on public education and have pursued innovative strategies. The largest foundation in the world, the Bill and Melinda Gates Foundation, identified U.S. public education as one of its two prime funding areas and has played a central role in promoting the small-schools movement. The Broad Foundation has carved out a focus on management, leadership, and talent, and the Broad Prize for Urban Education has become coveted by mayors and superintendents across the land. Several foundations emphasizing competition, choice, and innovation have helped fund large-scale expansion of successful charter schools like the KIPP Academies. In this environment, elected and appointed officials are seeking out the best new ideas for change.

Transforming the public school schedule to expand learning time requires committed top-level leadership to put the idea on the agenda, to provide the tools schools need, and to secure the necessary funding. In Massachusetts, the first converts to the idea were the co-chairs of the education committees in the House and Senate. Senator Robert Antonioni had been chair for a number of years and saw the need for bigger changes. His willingness to sponsor legislation providing the initial funding for planning grants to districts to considering conversion was crucial. Though new to the post of House co-chair of education, Representative Patricia Haddad brought her experience as a former middle school teacher and became a staunch ally. Commissioner of Education David Driscoll had tried approaches to expanding learning time for some students in his home town of Melrose, where he was superintendent in the 1980s. He knew students needed more time, so he embraced the nascent program, staffed it with some of his best people, and made it a funding priority—both keys to the program's initial success. More recently, newly elected Governor Deval Patrick, who credits fine educational opportunity for his own remarkable personal achievements—from Chicago public housing to a legal career to a prominent appointed Federal office—has embraced ELT and made it both a cornerstone of his long-term vision for the state and a practical funding priority. He and the legislature agreed to double state budgetary support in his first year in office. The appointment of Harvard School of Education professor Paul Reville, chairman of the Commonwealth's Commission on Time and Learning (which called for expanding learning time) in the 1990s, as the new chairman of the Board of Education also bodes well.

BUILDING GRASSROOTS SUPPORT

While elected and appointed officials must provide the regulatory and financial wherewithal, schools, teachers, and parents (and sometimes students) must be ready to seize the opportunity. Redesigning the entire school schedule requires a good deal of work and a significant leap of faith—even though we think the results to date are genuinely compelling. The principal must believe that the change will unlock new energy, creativity, and demonstrable results, while teachers must embrace not only a new schedule but often a new way of approaching material and managing their classrooms. Parents must decide that the disruption and risk inherent in any major change will be more than offset by the greater learning opportunities afforded their children. And while, to be honest, students are rarely consulted in such matters, their cooperation is essential. For the new school day to work, they need to buy in or at least be willing to go along. Students can rebel in a variety of ways, but the evidence so far suggests that attendance is up, disciplinary problems are down, school climate is improved, and students are learning more in school.

In our view, the key to this grassroots enthusiasm lies in providing enough process and planning time for many people to become co-owners of the new plan, and allowing plans themselves to be flexible and varied enough so that participants can include their own interests and priorities. In Massachusetts, schools make it into the ELT Initiative only if they and their district complete a strong, persuasive application.

Principals who go down this path gain extraordinary tools to improve their schools, but they also have to invest time, energy, and skill to gently guide their schools and communities to consensus. Teachers who are included from the get-go on the redesign committee and encouraged to think through the priorities and methods for the school become fierce advocates and leaders of the conversion process. For example, a kindergarten teacher at one school considering conversion joined the redesign committee as an outspoken opponent of the new school day. By the end of the process, she had become a champion of the new schedule. Uninvolved teachers are often cooler and more skeptical—and sometimes move into opposition.

Similarly, parents have a variety of reactions—some born of specific responses to the new schedule and its contents, some born of their confidence, or lack thereof, in the public schools' ability to manage significant change. Inviting parents to serve on the redesign team—including skeptics—ensures both that the voices of parents are factored in and that built-in advocates emerge among the parent community. Our experience suggests that there can never be too much communication between the redesign committee and all the school's constituencies: teachers, parents, school board members, and students.

When the Request for Proposals for the first round of ELT planning grants came out in August 2005, new school day proponents held their collective breath—would anyone step up and apply?

This was, after all, an unprecedented program with no direct role models—almost all existing new day schools in Massachusetts were either charter schools or experimental schools, not converted standard district schools. Moreover, there was no certainty that it would be possible to move from support for planning grants—a mere $500,000 in the first year—to funding for a full-scale program costing millions of dollars a year. And the application deadline for planning money was just a few weeks away! The verdict came in quickly—sixteen districts applied for planning money right off the bat. And while some of those were not able to make it to the finish line, five districts with ten schools did. Since then, as we can't resist repeating, we have seen accelerating momentum with eighteen ELT schools now in operation and more than a hundred schools in the funding-planning process for launch in the fall of 2008 or 2009.

The evidence is in: A very significant number of frontline teachers and principals knew all along that they needed more time to get the job done and have been willing to work hard to bring the catalyst of an expanded schedule to their school. Thousands of parents have seized on the idea as well and have been willing to allow schools to disrupt their previous routines. Once they saw the new day schedule in action, they became strong advocates for the benefits. Even students, often initially at best lukewarm toward the prospect of yet more school, have been surprisingly supportive once they have experienced the new school day. They seem to really enjoy the elective enrichment opportunities, which they can choose from a wide variety of engaging activities, and regularly praise the pace of the new day, observing that teachers now have enough time to answer their questions.

When the top-down desire to innovate in search of higher academic achievement can connect with the bottom-up appetite for more time to teach and learn, a powerful dynamic is unleashed. We appear to be witnessing this very dynamic in Massachusetts, where the ELT Initiative shows signs of accelerating growth.

RESISTANCE TO CHANGE

We've found the main obstacle in the effort to create new day schools or convert existing schools to this new schedule to be inertia, a general resistance to changing course. As a well-known management consulting aphorism has it, "Change is great—when someone else is doing the changing!" Resistance to change is more of an issue for teachers, parents, and students, as they are the ones doing the changing. By contrast, elected and appointed education leaders are often more positively disposed toward innovation since many have become convinced that only significant change will allow them to reach the new national goals. However, even at the policy level, serious obstacles remain. One of the most difficult is the pressure on state officials to cede control to local authorities. A state education commissioner, say, or a legislative-committee chair who wishes to create a state program targeted to expanding learning time will surely run into resistance from local districts where at least some of the mayors, superintendents, and school board members resist any restrictions coming from federal or state programs. Local leaders always press for increases in unrestricted aid.

The best counterargument is simply to highlight how modest educational gains have been while state and federal funding have grown, in real dollars, for many years in a row. Put bluntly, there is no evidence that throwing more money at the problem without additional changes—remember Newark's $20,000 per student per year debacle—will make any difference at all, and leaders know this. Under these circumstances, providing support for promising new approaches that may break the logjam and accelerate gains is a thoughtful, even prudent, choice.

Another powerful argument for supporting change on school schedules is the role model of public charter schools. One of the main arguments for charter schools when they were introduced was that they could serve as laboratories for innovation for the rest of public education. With more than four thousand charter schools now serving more than a million children, there is a lot to look at. About one-third of these schools, including many of the highest achievers, use considerably more time than the traditional schedule. It's not as though we don't know what the new school day can actually produce.

The major remaining challenge we have encountered in some places is with parents, which often comes as a surprise. (See our discussion in Chapter Thirteen.) Polls do not consistently bring out this concern, since by a wide margin parents and all adults favor the idea of expanding school time to enable more

academic work and enrichment in arts, music, drama, and
sports. The great majority of parents who have experienced the
new school schedule—and we know this because we've surveyed
them—have been very enthusiastic.

However, a significant minority of parents react with alarm
when a principal or superintendent proposes expanded learning
time for their schools. The frequency of that reaction and the
vehemence of resistance from those concerned grow as the socioeconomic status of the parents rises. Few affluent communities
in Massachusetts have even considered applying for ELT planning grants; the handful that have done so have elected not to
proceed. And several communities that would generally be considered blue-collar or middle-income have had pitched battles
over whether to proceed with a new day schedule. Even though
healthy percentages, usually clear majorities, of parents in these
communities have favored expanding learning time in their children' schools, the vocal dissenters who come to meetings and
contact officials are the ones who make themselves heard.

In our experience, if the proportion of parents dissenting is
substantial, energetic, and vocal, the school community will end
up pulling back from proceeding. The process of institutional
change takes time, persistence, and delicacy. Loud, emphatic
opposition is far easier to mount and often carries the day. After
all, elected officials, including school board members, know that
support from people who think they did right is apt to be much
less ardent than opposition from voters who feel slighted. Since it
is always easier to embrace the status quo and to suggest studying
new ideas to death, the advantage goes to sufficiently inspired
and widespread opposition.

So far, the most effective solution to this varying level of support from parents has been to offer a new day schedule to parents who want it. Happily, these are the parents of students who
most clearly need it—those whose schools are furthest behind in
high-stakes testing and whose family incomes are not sufficient to
buy remedial and enriched education. Choice is a powerful tool
for ensuring support from parents. In almost every community
that has adopted expanded learning time, not only have the bulk
of the parents at the schools been supportive; the school board

has allowed parents to pick a different school in that community should they prefer to opt out.

In the longer term, the level of middle-class parent adoption of the new day schedule is likely to depend on two key variables. Most important will be the performance of the schools that do convert. The better they do academically and the more satisfied the parents at these schools, the more the word will spread that the new school day works, and parents will increasingly ask, "Why is my district *not* taking advantage of this opportunity?" Second, as America's discourse over education and opportunity continues, more middle-income parents may decide their children need a more challenging education to face the globally competitive twenty-first century with confidence.

TAKING THE FIRST STEP

We know that some of what you just read will seem intimidating: it not only seems like a lot of work—it *is* a lot of work. But the rewards we've seen and have tried to describe are downright inspiring, occasionally breathtaking. Making real change is also one of the great human experiences—and face it: if you've read this far, you're already far more interested in these issues, and in how to make educational change, than 90 percent of the population. We hope we've given you some ideas of what's worked, and why, and how your community might take advantage of the experiences we've seen so far. And remember, the National Center on Time and Learning (www.timeandlearning.org) has a ton of resources online, and a staff that's gaining more experience in these matters all the time. Drop us e-mail, or give us a call!

┌─────┐
│ 15 │
└─────┘

BLUEPRINT FOR SUCCESS

Lessons Learned and Open Questions About the New School Day

Simply extending the day is not necessarily going to create success. It is so important to be able to have a plan and to have support for your plan. . . . There needs to be buy-in—and it's not something that you can just pick up and do because you want to.
—ELT DIRECTOR AND TEACHER,
EDWARDS MIDDLE SCHOOL, BOSTON

My advice to administrators would be that you need to get as many people involved as possible, especially the teachers; parents, the students, what they want. Explain what your reason behind ELT is. It's [what] we need to move forward.
— TEACHER AND MATH AND SCIENCE DEPARTMENT HEAD,
KUSS MIDDLE SCHOOL, FALL RIVER, MASSACHUSETTS

IN THIS CHAPTER, WE HIGHLIGHT a dozen design principles we believe should be part of future new day schools. Our conclusions are based on our direct experience in helping create such schools, our visits to schools, our review of the available data, and our best judgment. They are certainly worthy of debate and are not meant to be comprehensive or exhaustive. We wrote this book both to encourage more people to seek change and to help those who want to make the new school day work. Here we share our perspectives on key issues.

We end the chapter with some thoughts on some of the key open issues that call for more experience and data and perhaps innovation. The new school day is still young as an educational strategy; we should learn a good deal over the next few years. We hope our candor about matters that need more thought and work will help stimulate a creative, productive dialogue as well as more research and experimentation.

LESSONS LEARNED

It is possible to go about spreading the new day schedule to schools and to put it in place at any given school in any of a number of ways. Experience is too new and the data is still too sparse for anyone to be certain about which approaches work best in what circumstances. However, in our view some emerging patterns allow us to recommend twelve features as key elements of strong designs for new day schools:

- Voluntary participation for schools
- Mandatory participation for students
- Whole school redesign
- Significantly expanded time
- Clear academic focus
- Well-rounded education
- Data-driven continuous quality improvement
- Time for teacher collaboration, planning, and professional development
- Individualization
- Time for up-front planning
- Partnerships with outside resources
- Starting with individual schools, building for scale

VOLUNTARY PARTICIPATION FOR SCHOOLS

Policymakers looking to enable or even drive the growth of new day schools need to decide between two basic choices: either *requiring* some or all schools to change to the new day schedule or *allowing and supporting* the adoption of expanded learning time by conventional schools that want to convert, or by newly created schools, or both. We favor voluntary participation, though we acknowledge the importance of being able to require it under certain circumstances.

The people who staff the most impressive new day schools in America believe passionately in the value of more time well spent and have built their schools around it. Charter schools such as the KIPP Academies and Roxbury Prep and experimental district schools such as Achievable Dream Academy and Timilty consider expanded learning time to be a core pillar of their academic design, and they use the time extensively, imaginatively, and holistically. They recruit teachers and administrators based on this schedule and students and families who sign up know what they are getting into. These schools often also pursue many other innovations, driven by their strong sense of mission and urgency.

An exciting addition to the new school day movement is the Massachusetts Expanded Learning Time Initiative, in which established public schools have opted to convert from their old schedule to the new day schedule. They are full of energy and determination to use the gift (a word they use a lot) of more time to help their students and schools flourish. While the process of converting is inherently more challenging than starting from scratch, they hold out a model for change and improvement that could be followed by literally thousands of other public schools serving millions of children. By contrast, most of the charter and experimental district schools are not obviously scaleable enough to change the overall course of American education. While the charter schools and experimental district schools serve well as pioneers and role models, the Massachusetts ELT schools provide a blueprint that can be adopted more or less as it stands.

The alternative to choice—that is, to allowing new schools to start up based on the new school day and helping existing schools that want to convert to the new schedule—is to *make* some or all schools adopt it. This strategy could come about in one of two ways. First, at least theoretically, a state or district could simply mandate a major change in the legal minimum number of instructional hours or days. None have done so, and we don't anticipate any soon because of the cost implications and the resistance to such one-size-fits-all change. We also don't think it would be wise to mandate the new day on such a uniform and broad basis. One day, policymakers may decide to consider such sweeping change—but that day is not here yet, and we are not at all sure such mandatory, top-down thinking will ever work very well.

The other category of mandated expansion of learning time is very real and rapidly growing—in turnaround schools. Under the No Child Left Behind Act as well as under many state standards–based reform laws, a growing number of schools are being identified as chronically underperforming. By 2010, experts estimate that this number will reach five thousand schools—up from today's two thousand. These are schools that have been posting dismally low results year after year. Under NCLB, they are labeled "Restructuring," meaning that they need deep change. States and districts are increasingly facing the question—what do we do about them? How do we act boldly enough to break through? How do we act constructively enough while pressing for real change?

Expertise on how to intervene and how to press a turnaround agenda is growing rapidly. A report issued in November 2007 by the Mass Insight Education & Research Institute and commissioned by the Bill and Melinda Gates Foundation, *The Turnaround Challenge: Why America's Opportunity to Dramatically Improve Student Achievement Lies in Our Worst-Performing Schools,* lays out recommendations based on a number of efforts by cities and states to date. In identifying what should be part of interventions (based on what they report "high-performing high-poverty schools" are doing) they cite an "extended school day and longer year." And in fact, intervention programs in New York City, Miami-Dade, Pittsburgh, Boston, and Chicago have all included, among a series of changes, adding about one hour per day to school in all intervention schools. In this book, we visit two of those schools, both in the Miami-Dade School Improvement Zone, one of the most visible efforts in America.

Schools that superintendents or chancellors have redesigned from above can show meaningful academic gains. We appreciate the sense of urgency in district offices when schools have been lagging far behind for years. And because we believe that more time helps, we appreciate why using an expanded school schedule as part of a turnaround plan for chronically underperforming schools can make sense. But we also have seen the qualitative difference in charter schools, experimental district schools, and

Massachusetts ELT schools when the principals and teachers and parents have worked together to bring about a new day school instead of having it forced upon them from above. These are schools with a shared sense of purpose, where the added time is seen as a blessing and an opportunity rather than something imposed from outside. In the best of the "turnaround schools," new leadership and teachers who want to be there do help create some of the same sense of shared excitement in the service of real student progress, but the difference remains perceptible.

Over the longer haul, policymakers will have to decide what to do about chronically underperforming schools; given all the evidence compiled in this book and elsewhere that more time helps, we expect the new school day to be part of that ongoing effort.

Outside that effort, we favor focusing energy and resources for creation of the new day on schools that want to change over and even compete for the opportunity to do so. The likeliest prospects for success are the schools where proponents of the new day are willing to have their plans scrutinized and reviewed by independent bodies, such as state departments of education, to ensure sound planning and sufficient capacity to effect the change.

It seems to us both fairer and more effective to target scarce resources to those schools where the desire for change is greatest. These have consistently proven to be schools where kids have the greatest need, so this approach meets the fairness test as well as the practical concern that, to work at its best, redesigning and expanding the school day needs all constituencies on board. Moreover, since a truly voluntary approach leaves the door open to all schools, it both answers the occasional criticism that the new resources are only there for the low-performing schools and allows some schools with more proficient students to demonstrate how more time can translate into reaching even higher standards.

MANDATORY PARTICIPATION FOR STUDENTS

Many schools find ways to provide more time to some students who need it most academically, in some cases through tutoring, in others through mandatory summer school. In New York City, nearly one-third of all students, chosen because of their lower academic performance, stay for two-and-a-half more hours each week and receive small-group instruction and tutoring. These efforts, certainly better than doing nothing, face two key limits. First, they address only academic needs and usually do so in a remedial fashion that can fall short of truly engaging students. Second, many students simply do not comply. Summer school attendance is always well short of complete. At Miami Edison Senior High, a Zone school where the standard schedule has been expanded by one hour per day, students who still have real academic difficulties are also referred to "mandatory tutoring." While compliance with the new schedule is essentially universal, we were amazed to hear that only about 10 percent of those told to come for so-called mandatory tutoring actually do so.

By expanding the schedule for all students, a school helps students get extra help without feeling the stigma of being selected for what amounts to academic detention. Students at new day schools often describe the reaction of their friends at traditional schools, especially at first, as making fun of them for having to stay longer, but they describe themselves as readily falling into the habit of the new schedule. Since everyone at their school has the same hours, it becomes the norm.

Redesigning the whole day—as opposed to adding an extra period at the end of the day—pretty much requires all students to be on the new schedule. Adding time to core courses such as English and math so that students can work in small groups and on their own at their own levels, so that students can pursue exploratory, project-based learning, so that science labs can be done in one day, and so that enrichment classes can be woven into the fabric of the day requires a thoroughgoing change. Changing the culture and pace of the school for all teachers and students involves establishing a truly new school day for everyone.

WHOLE SCHOOL REDESIGN

The easiest way to add learning time is to tack it on to the end of the schedule—follow last year's plan and figure out what to do with a couple more hours. But in this case easiest is far from best. Schools planning to convert to the new day schedule do better when they start from scratch and consider everything anew. In part that means adding time to existing features of the day.

Few teachers or principals would dispute the value of more time each day for math and for English. But should they be added as block scheduling, as at Achievable Dream Academy, or as a second math and English class each day, as at Roxbury Prep? We see evidence of both approaches working and think each school should carefully consider its preferences and capabilities, and then choose its own path.

Ideally, schools will consider how to make their students' education more well-rounded, not just stronger in the core academic subjects. But what constitutes adding breadth? At the Dr. Martin Luther King, Jr. School in Cambridge, added time has allowed every student in every grade, from junior Kindergarten on, to gain first exposure and then knowledge of Mandarin Chinese. At the KIPP Academy in the Bronx, New York, every student learns an instrument and plays in the school orchestra. And how do you add both more time for students to learn and more time for teachers to work together? Should all sports take place at the end of the day or does KIPP Houston get it right with elementary students playing soccer in the gym in the middle of the day, before returning to classes? All of these good questions can only be answered by taking a whole school redesign approach— and the answers will show tremendous variety, at least until the education community has had years of experience to study and reflect on the results, and perhaps even then.

SIGNIFICANTLY EXPANDED TIME

To make a real difference in the depth and breadth of education, schools need to add hundreds of hours per year—not just a few minutes a day. While adding ten minutes a day or an hour a week could help a little bit, it will not allow for whole school redesign; it will not resolve the unnecessary tension in today's schedule between math and music, between sports and reading. We see some real impact in schools that add one hour per day but see even more results when the new schedule adds closer to two hours per day or even more. Adding this much new time not only allows the school to make vital additions to core subjects and leaven academic time with enrichment time, it also makes for a more sensible pace to the day for all involved. It allows adding time to such so-called frills as lunch and recess—both of which humanize a school day currently in danger of becoming a treadmill for far too many kids and teachers.

CLEAR ACADEMIC FOCUS

A significant risk in expanding the school day is the temptation to think of the day as a palette from which to take a little bit of time for this and a little bit for that, and a few new things—and not enough clear focus. For schools that want to really change their kids' academic performance, whether to help far more students reach basic proficiency in core subjects or to add the sort of science, technology, and engineering content that will open doors for their students in the twenty-first-century economy, teachers and principals must set priorities and make choices. At the Jacob Hiatt Magnet School in Worcester, Massachusetts, the top priority was improving literacy skills, so the redesign team rebuilt the whole day around a core two-hour, sacrosanct literacy block the first two hours every day. At the Edwards Middle School in Boston, math was a top priority, so the team both expanded class time and added competitive Math Leagues to the day.

WELL-ROUNDED EDUCATION

Many schools considering the new school day do so to counteract disappointing academic results. That's a compelling motivation; by now it should be obvious that we believe more time, well spent, can make an enormous difference in how well students learn the core academic subjects: reading, writing, and math. But we also believe that students would benefit from a more expansive definition of a well-rounded education. Setting academic standards, and testing whether students are reaching them, has forced the public schools to narrow their focus on core academic time. We think the evidence shows that the pursuit of academic proficiency and even excellence need not come at the expense of exposure to a broad array of subjects and fields; nor need it be pursued to the exclusion of children's social, emotional, or physical development. Restoring balance to children's education can be one of the more compelling reasons to bring an expanded schedule to any school. Redesign teams do best by their students when they make sure the added time is used both to strengthen academics and to add breadth and variety to their students' education. The Hiatt School's alignment of outside enrichment activities with the in-school curriculum is a sterling example of this balanced redesign—since it coexists with a new two-hour literacy block every day.

Data-Driven Continuous Quality Improvement

The process of converting to a new school schedule affords schools the opportunity to use data to inform decision making and to adopt a data-driven continuous quality improvement (CQI) approach. CQI is a method, arising from the manufacturing world, that focuses on a cycle of taking action for improvement, measuring results, and then taking informed further action for improvement. Adding time to the day creates options for schools and teachers about how to use that time to improve what students learn. It is a perfect opportunity for teachers and principals to engage in a constructive, ongoing dialogue about what kids are learning, how that learning can be measured, and how it can be improved. Then, as the school collects new results, these results become the subject of additional conversations, and school leaders can decide whether the choices they've made for how to use the added time are meeting their objectives or whether they need to be adjusted.

It is also important to focus on measuring things beyond just academic test scores. Schools need to look at attendance, behavior, engagement, and measures of physical health and social-emotional development, as well as reading and math scores. Parent satisfaction and school climate matter; so does teacher satisfaction. There is a management saying: "You can only manage what you can measure." The corollary is also true: Those who value dimensions beyond academic skills must find ways to measure them reliably and use them to guide their strategy.

We've seen several excellent examples of continuous assessment. At Roxbury Prep, the math teachers analyze their students' performance—in great detail—on a variety of standardized tests each year to see how well their students are using what they've been learning and where the curriculum needs reworking for the coming year.

Even more ambitious, because it involves thirty-nine schools, is the data collection effort of Miami's School Improvement Zone. "Before Dr. Crew came to Miami, *data* was just a word that was out there," says District Supervisor Diana Taub, "but we need to know what works and the quality of instruction. We're now data-driven for teaching and learning, first in the Zone and now throughout Dade County. We have short mini-assessments and weekly assessments to see where do students need the help, to change the instructional focus. We're looking at the learning gains of particular teachers. All of our teachers have our data binders."

Her boss, Dr. Geneva Woodard, associate superintendent for the Zone, picks up this ball. "We needed to know: How could we improve teaching styles? What could we do to increase student performance? Now it's a way of life for us. We required the binders in the Zone, and it's caught up to the district—not as intensely as we do it, but there's a conversation."

"All of you have these big binders?" we ask, a little skeptically.

"We can't take a chance without the data," she answers with conviction. "It's like poking around in the dark. That principle is key in terms of how data is used to drive instruction. Miami Edison High was a six-time "F" school—finally they came off the list!"

"They got within eight points of a C," said Assistant Superintendent Blanca Valle kindly. "It was such a hurt in their hearts to get so close and not make the grade."

"Our whole district was affected by the science scores," explained Woodard, discussing the first year the Florida test, the FCAT, had tested science. "In spite of that Miami Edison was able to pull out; they made greater gains in reading and math and writing that overcompensated for what they didn't get in science, and made other schools in the Zone see how important it is to do their best."

Halfway across the country the next day we asked Sam Lopez, testing coordinator and former principal at KIPP Academy Houston, if the binders were overkill. "No, when you've got a really low-performing school, you need them. Especially when you have to do major overhaul. Then you have to let teachers know, 'I'm holding you accountable.' If that's what you need to do, you can do it by the unit, or monthly, whatever's going to work. Mr. Whitney [the principal] doesn't ask that of us." His face broke into a big smile and his eyes twinkled. "He'll do that with the beginning teachers."

TIME FOR TEACHER COLLABORATION, PLANNING, AND PROFESSIONAL DEVELOPMENT

Under the current school schedule, teachers have surprisingly little time to meet with each other regarding their teaching goals, techniques, or even lesson plans. One of the real hallmarks of charter public schools with new school day schedules, like the KIPP Academies and Roxbury Prep, is the amount of planning and collaboration teachers are expected to engage in: grade-level planning, subject-level planning. And beyond planning time, teachers need enough time for targeted professional development to learn more effective teaching strategies.

At Achievable Dream Academy, principal Catina Bullard-Clark talked about planning the way Geneva Woodard talked about data: "Planning is a huge part of the whole school. Until a few years ago, just the middle and high school got planning periods, and the elementary school didn't. 'We teach all the subjects—we need time to plan,' they said. So we went to a shortened Wednesday schedule, and now teachers are involved in rigorous planning. Without planning, the extra time would be wasted." Teachers "get some time in the morning [when the kids are in a pep session] for a quick grade-level meeting. They don't eat with the kids so they have time to get together to do additional planning." Resource teachers and instructional assistants cover activities when the kids just need monitoring to keep the peace, and the teachers make good use of that time.

All the Massachusetts ELT schools develop plans to add substantial time for teacher planning and professional development, so they can make better use of the expanded schedule. They have learned what other new day schools know—one of the most important and challenging aspects of developing a new day schedule is to balance the focus on student learning time with the focus on teacher planning and learning time. Both are important and neither can be allowed to overwhelm the other.

INDIVIDUALIZATION

Perhaps the greatest blessing of the new school day is the opportunity to individualize education for children—to match it to their needs, skills, and preferences. Too often the conventional school day makes a one-size-fits-all approach necessary, with little time for genuinely individual instruction. But children are all different, and the new day offers the chance to break the mold.

In academic classrooms, individualization means leaving plenty of time every day for students to work in small groups and on their own at their proper level and pace. For the most advanced, that means more challenge. For the struggling it means more help, and for the rest it means a sensible pace and more depth. It definitely means tutoring. Time and again as we visited new day schools and looked for the magic curricular bullet, what we found instead was an approach that allowed so much time for teachers to work with students individually that everyone got what they needed.

Beyond core academics, individualization means a generous breadth of enrichment offerings and plenty of choice left to students, even young ones. Kids really appreciate that opportunity to select, and it gives them a chance to discover and then pursue their own interests. It also means plenty of time for socialization and for socioemotional learning, since how children learn to deal with others ends up being a big part of their lives at work and at home long after they leave school.

TIME FOR UP-FRONT PLANNING

As noted in Chapter Fourteen, converting a school from a standard schedule to the new school day takes a lot of planning before the fact. So whenever schools consider conversion, we cannot emphasize enough how important it is for them to have a significant block of time—eight months to a year, at minimum, to consider how to change the day, how to reorganize the curriculum, how to adjust teacher schedules, how to build support for the change, and the myriad other considerations from the logistical—buses and snacks—to the profound—what should education at our school include? Without the planning-grant stage of the Massachusetts ELT Initiative, we doubt that the program would have been nearly as successful or effective. For a change of this magnitude, preliminary planning time is vital for everyone concerned. It allows for a deliberate process, one in which doubts can be raised and answered, proponents can get more educated on the subject, skeptics can be gradually brought on board, and communities can get informed. Without building in substantial planning time before a school makes the decision to take the plunge, conversion efforts set themselves up for likely failure.

Time alone is not sufficient to ensure a strong planning process. Strong leadership, broad participation, and sufficient resources to do the work are all critical as well. Efforts must include both considerable attention inside the school from the principal and the teachers, and well-executed communications outside the school with the parents, potential community partners, policy-makers, and the teachers' union.

PARTNERSHIPS WITH OUTSIDE RESOURCES

The new school day offers a tremendous opportunity to bring more outside partners and resources to bear on the goal of help-ing fully educate the students at the school. While the expan-sion of core academic time should almost always be delivered by existing teachers, the addition of other subjects, the inclusion of enrichment in arts, music, drama, and sports, and even the injec-tion of more project-based and experiential learning into core subjects, all offer opportunities to bring outside organizations and individuals into the school. The instinct of most schools con-sidering a new school day is to focus chiefly on how to deploy more of the existing resources. That is a mistake if it is at the expense of dismissing the potential for specialized, enthusiastic, and cost-effective partnerships.

Whether it is the Hiatt School's creative use of cultural and other organizations' capabilities right in the curriculum, or the Edwards School's partnership with Citizen Schools to offer apprenticeships with citizen volunteers for every sixth grader, or Mario Umana's partnership with the YMCA which provides swimming lessons for the students, or any of the dozens of other working partnerships we have observed at new day schools, expanded learning time can mean expanded learning partnerships. Many potential partners have invested considerably in developing outstanding approaches to their subject of interest, and many have the ability to bring in people, ranging from college students to community members to professionals to retirees, who would not otherwise necessarily cross paths with students. Besides taking advantage of their ability to provide the enrichment itself, bringing in these other people creates many positive opportunities for exposure and relationships, and broadens the civic investment in local educational success.

This type of partnership needs to be a two-way street that benefits both the school and the outside organization. It takes somewhat more time and certainly more communication to pull this off, but the benefits can be powerful and long-lasting.

Schools should look to—but also beyond—traditional youth-serving organizations when considering such partnership opportunities. While the experienced players bring many advantages, many communities with too few experienced choices have other good opportunities to use outside resources to strengthen the school. Nearby colleges and universities can offer a variety of ways to help, both on the school's campus and the college's campus. Organizations that don't normally offer such programs can sometimes help—Hiatt has formed a strong working relationship with the Paul Revere House in Boston, for example. Finally, the community may include individuals such as retired teachers, or others willing to help flexibly on a part-time basis. In Miami-Dade's Improvement Zone, schools have learned that retired teachers make terrific teachers for their remediation classes in literacy and math.

Starting with Individual Schools, Building for Scale

We advocate rolling out the new school day by starting with individual schools that want to put it to work, have a good plan to do so, and have the capacity to execute a plan. But we also believe it's crucial that the new day strategy move beyond the one-of-a-kind, pioneering, experimental-school world into large-scale use. Already, more than a thousand such schools are in operation.

Many are truly singular like Roxbury Prep and Achievable Dream. Some have begun to spread out, like the KIPP Academies. But we believe that far more students, families, and communities could benefit from the new day and that we need approaches that hold out the potential for reaching them in large numbers.

The Massachusetts ELT approach can be scaled fairly widely, and more than a hundred additional schools have entered the planning process to consider converting. The same approach could be used by other states; as we write, Senator Edward Kennedy and Representative George Miller have proposed that a national demonstration program be funded by the federal government as part of the next version of the Elementary and Secondary Education Act (currently called the No Child Left Behind Act).

Under the Massachusetts law, districts must apply with their schools and must highlight how converting one or a few schools can lead to district-wide gains. Some of the initial districts are now considering changing all their schools, or at least all the elementary and middle schools, to the new day schedule. This would greatly simplify many things, ranging from contracts with employees and bus companies to the expectations of children and parents, and would eliminate the risk of conflict between those that have more time and those that don't. It would also address issues such as what time extracurricular activities and town sports should start. We encourage policymakers to think about the long-term goal even while beginning the new school day on a more limited scale.

SOME KEY QUESTIONS YET TO BE ANSWERED

While we believe that the more than one thousand public schools currently employing some version of the new school day offer ample evidence of its effectiveness and potential, we recognize that several important issues need further analysis, discussion, data, and experimentation. We raise them here in the spirit of full disclosure and in the hope of provoking further work in this emerging field of time and learning.

HIGH SCHOOL MODELS

The schools profiled in this book are predominantly elementary, K–8, or middle schools. KIPP does operate some high schools now and Achievable Dream has begun adding grades to become a K–12 school. And the Miami-Dade School Improvement Zone has some high schools, including the one we profile in this book. Quite a few charter high schools use the new school day to achieve their missions. In Massachusetts, the first high school to join the Expanded Learning Time initiative did so in the fall of 2007 and two more high schools were in the late stages of planning for potential conversion in 2008.

Nonetheless, we find that in considering conversion to the new day, two major concerns unique to high school students have not been answered as fully as we would like. Those two issues are student jobs and extracurricular activities (including sports). About one-third of sixteen- and seventeen-year-olds hold part-time jobs, and the rate is much higher in some schools. Many work to earn money for personal expenditures, some to help meet their family's basic needs. In any case, the hours of that work may overlap with time targeted for expanded learning, and that creates several hurdles and questions for the new day effort.

Meanwhile, almost half of all high school senior boys and a third of high school senior girls report spending considerable time on athletic teams, while a quarter report significant time commitments to music or performing arts, 15 percent to academic clubs, and 10 percent each to a newspaper or yearbook and to student government. These are clearly worthy activities and should be incorporated into any new day schedule. But they are also time-consuming and not immediately easy to integrate.

Lastly, high schools need to prepare their students for college or work. They need to offer students an ever-wider variety of specialized courses. These considerations, not relevant to elementary or middle schools, must factor into a new day design for high schools.

We are convinced from both a needs point of view and from the success of the few existing models that high schools can and should adopt the new day. But we also believe that it will take more creativity to address and incorporate the work and extracurricular activity considerations and to customize the new day structures to the academic and social developmental stage of older teens. We think that the day for these students could be quite a bit more flexible and could allow, especially for those students doing adequately or well academically, the opportunity to work, to pursue extracurricular activities, and to pursue advanced courses, including college courses, all as part of their new day schedules.

COST AND FUNDING

We have cost data from many existing new day schools and we know that in Massachusetts an annual state contribution of $1,300 per student has been adequate to enable multiple districts and schools to proceed. But we do not fully know what the new school day should cost. Partly that is because of the number of different versions, and partly it is because the cost of the largest item—personnel time—is inextricably entwined with the overall agreements with employees—mostly teachers—on compensation and hours. Also, schools are notoriously weak on cost accounting systems, so allocating costs accurately to the traditional day versus the new day is not always easy.

We do believe that it is possible to consider different models that would have different cost implications. The creativity and flexibility of the staffing plan, the degree of use of technology and partners, and the level of professional experience and compensation of the local teachers may all significantly affect the actual cost per student, one way or the other.

We discuss funding extensively in Chapter Fourteen. What long-term mix of local funding (especially in more affluent districts), state funding, and federal funding is appropriate remains to be determined. We believe and argue here that the case is compelling for the new day to far better serve the pressing needs of the most at-risk children from the lowest-income families in the lowest-achieving schools. These are the top-priority targets for state government and the federal government, and we believe that they should see the new school day as an opportunity to drive improvement where it is needed most—and where it will have the largest initial effect.

SUMMER

We have argued throughout this book for the new school day—by which we mean the expanded school schedule. We address the importance of summer in Chapter Twelve. We feel that extending the school year into the summer is important, but it is also in need of new models. Most summer experts argue persuasively that summer ought to have an academic component—but one that is more limited than the school year and perhaps one that feels quite different. KIPP schools, for example, use their summer expansion to start students into their next grade *before* they have their vacation and return to that grade in the fall. And during those three weeks there is less homework and more exploration. Achievable Dream runs thirty days a year longer but breaks up school periods with intersessions that include more academic work for those who need it and more enrichment for others. We believe summer should surely have a greater enrichment and social component. We suspect that many school systems will never want to fully run a summer term; many teachers may prefer vacation, and the costs and complexities may outweigh the benefits. There may be an even greater role for outside organizations to lead such a summer term.

MOST EFFECTIVE TEACHING AND LEARNING STRATEGIES FOR EACH SUBJECT

While more time on task is worthwhile, we believe that the added time is even more valuable when it's used to do things differently as well. There needs to be considerably more formal research on what works well. We know of one recent carefully designed experiment that asked the kind of question we think needs to be investigated extensively. In this case, the researchers compared six different strategies for adding twenty minutes per day (less than we see in most new day schools) to literacy and carefully measured the difference in impact. Not all interventions were equally valuable. That is the kind of research we need for reading, writing, and math, and also for other subjects. We also need to understand the best ways to design the overall day. For example, does breaking up learning with engaging enrichment and sports help keep minds fresh?

EFFECTIVENESS IN DIFFERENT CIRCUMSTANCES

Most experience with new day schools has come in urban schools with predominantly at-risk children from lower-income families. We argue here that the best proof of success comes from the schools that have voluntarily pursued the new school day; both the charter and experimental district schools and the Massachusetts ELT schools. We know far less about how well it works in several other settings. As discussed earlier, it is a pressing matter to determine how well expanding learning time, especially about an hour per day of chiefly academic time (which is at the moment the main strategy being tried) works in turnaround schools. The results in New York City's Chancellor's District and now in Miami-Dade's School Improvement Zone show some promise. Less direct evidence has emerged from middle-income, suburban, and rural districts, and there is almost no evidence from vocational education schools. In many of these cases, the goals will be different, the time will be used differently, and the outcomes may be different. We need to know.

HOW MUCH TIME?

This is perhaps the biggest unresolved question. We chose to focus this book on one model—about two hours per day of additional time. Some of our example schools use more—KIPP schools, for instance—and some less, such as those in the Miami-Dade Zone. Educators and policymakers need to know the minimum amount required to make any significant difference. We argue here that it has to be enough to cause redesign and real change. It's also necessary to know whether the benefits continue to increase as time expands further.

At some point, one must assume diminishing returns will cut in, and much above two hours per day seems both too expensive and too invasive for most schools and families. But we know that boarding schools—the ultimate expanded-learning-time schools!—work very well for many private-school families and have begun (as in the SEED school in Washington, D.C.) to show promise for children at the highest risk. As with the others, it is unlikely that this question will have one best answer for all circumstances—but it is a question of crucial importance to every district and individual school contemplating the new day.

CONCLUSION
Time for Change, Time to Learn

Expanded learning time is the
future—it has to be.
—PATRICIA GAUDETTE, PRINCIPAL, JACOB HIATT
MAGNET SCHOOL, WORCESTER, MASSACHUSETTS

IN THE LAST GENERATION, AMERICAN education has stagnated, and too many of us have resigned ourselves to mediocre
public schools. Those of us who want more for children—academics
as well as enrichment, solid skills as well as well-roundedness, arts
and sports as well as reading and math—have felt stymied by the size
of the system, the entrenched interests, the recent history. Those
who can afford it (and some who can't) move to suburbs reputed
to have strong schools, send kids to private schools, or purchase
the additional instruction and activities the schools fail to provide.
When, as authors, we have broached the subject of this book with
friends and colleagues, we hear a good deal of interest, but also a
deep pessimism about even the possibility of genuine change.

As parents and as citizens, we worry for the future of our country when our public schools don't come close to preparing so many
of our children for life, for responsible citizenship, for higher education, or even for earning a living. We cannot forget the man in
Rochester, Massachusetts, who stood up at a public meeting and
explained how few high school graduates could meet the standards
of his truck-leasing company in reading, writing, and math. We also
worry about the growing tendency to focus children's education

increasingly narrowly on core instruction in reading and math, when the truth is that children need a genuinely well-rounded education, one that includes the arts, history, science, and knowledge of other cultures, as well as of their own bodies and emotions. We are troubled by a complacency that equates minimum passing scores with the skills needed to thrive in the twenty-first century. And we remain alarmed by a persistent achievement gap—as well as an opportunity gap—that inevitably translates into an employment, income, cultural, and social chasm between economic classes and between races, the consequences of which threaten the foundation of American democracy.

But these dreary thoughts evaporate when we walk into schools that have adopted the new day. In Miami and Worcester and Fall River and Newport News and Houston and Boston, in schools in struggling, low-income neighborhoods, we see open faces, energy, lights in the eyes of the children and the teachers, and perhaps most thrilling of all, genuine joy in the acts of teaching and learning. We've taken you into new day classrooms where we've seen teachers teaching and students learning—in small groups and large, independently and with their peers, concentrating and laughing, using computers and networked calculators, all guided by their teachers at a pace designed for instruction that works. We've also seen first-graders learning soccer and eighth graders performing Shakespeare, second and sixth graders reading to each other on the playground, and seventh graders intently playing chess. This is the education parents want for their kids, where everyone knows their kids' names, and the kids feel special and noticed, fussed over and praised, invited and pushed and helped to meet the highest standards.

For too long, principals and teachers have seen the clock as their enemy. Everyone knows there's simply not enough time in the current school schedule to teach kids the skills and knowledge they need to succeed now, or will need to thrive in this globalized century. Everyone in education knows that it takes time, lots of it, to help children learn—and that the harried pace of most public schools means that too many of their students will gain only a surface knowledge of the subjects they're exposed to. And in some schools—Expanded Learning Time Initiative schools all over Massachusetts, KIPP schools throughout the country, turnaround

Improvement Zone schools in Miami, Achievable Dream Academy in Newport News, Virginia, Boston's Roxbury Prep, and scattered others—teachers and principals have decided to do something about a problem they've all known about for decades.

Every one of them has chosen to expand the amount of time devoted to student learning as fundamental to their ambitious educational goals. In most of these schools at least two-thirds of the children qualify for free or reduced-price lunches. Principals and teachers know that children from low-income communities often need some extra help getting ready to focus and ready to learn, as well as extra time to practice what they've learned in a supportive environment before they return home.

We've discovered that once the school day is expanded and redesigned to add the kind of enrichment activities traditional schools are now cutting, kids get so engaged that they want to stay *later* at school. Not every child, of course, and at the beginning many students resist the idea of "more school." But once they experience the new school day, *no one* wants to go back to the old 2:30 dismissal time. That's right. Instead of rushing out the door, they like staying later, sometimes to play chess or music or sports, other times to do artwork, or play music, sometimes to do their homework with teachers who will help them willingly, and sometimes so they can get the one-to-one tutoring they need. "Can I have tutoring?" kids routinely ask their teachers at Roxbury Prep in Boston, where Saturday classes are proving so popular that the directors have to raise more money to pay more teachers to come in Saturdays too! That's right: there are kids across the country enjoying coming to school on Saturdays, where their minds and spirits and (often) bodies are fully engaged, rather than staying at home to watch television or play video games.

In Newport News, many of the kids prefer school to their home neighborhoods: school is safer, more secure, and more reliable. We said in the title to this book that the new school schedule was already making "smarter kids." That's shorthand for the fact that they do learn a lot more, learn better, and are able to demonstrate what they've learned a whole lot better. They get hooked on learning and school, and show that in their speech, in their behavior, and in their test scores.

When kids do well in school, they learn the skills that both make them want higher education and prepare them to do well in college. Wouldn't we rather have schools that got students ready to begin college work when they arrive on campus, instead of having to attend the remedial classes that about a third need today? Nowadays too many students attend college simply because they need a credential, not because they want to learn. New day schools help kids get enough of an education in the arts so they can take advantage of the rich cultural offerings of the collegiate curriculum and community. If schoolchildren get engaged by learning early and master the skills they need to learn successfully and enjoyably, they get a thirst for learning that lasts a lifetime, and truly helps them to thrive in the most rapidly changing society of all time.

We also said the new schedule was making parents happier, and it is. Wherever the new school day has been adopted, parents prefer it. Some love it. The polls in Massachusetts show overwhelming support among parents. The fact that *all* the initial ELT schools remained in the program the second year speaks volumes. Parents see changes in their children—and changes in their family lives. They love seeing their children engaged by school; they love seeing their kids getting core academic instruction as well as enrichment. And when their kids look forward to school, they think they've won the lottery.

But parents worry about far more than their children's academic progress. They start by being concerned about their children's safety, and the current school day puts their safety at risk more than any other single social policy in the country. If you think about it for even a minute, it's utterly obvious that no families with two working parents and no single-parent families were ever consulted on the six-and-a-half-hour day, which only meshes with the lives of families in which a parent or grandparent can be home to meet the school bus. While only 30 percent of women were in the workforce a generation ago, 70 percent are now—and the school day hasn't changed! Single-parent families are a fact of life now, and in these families the parent almost always works outside the home. A public school system that paid attention to the real needs of children and families would never have allowed this state of affairs to come about. Instead we have, in effect, abandoned far too many of our children.

As a result they spend huge amounts of unstructured time, unsupervised, in front of televisions and computer screens, watching programs or playing games ranging from the useless to the appalling. Like most of us they succumb to slick advertising, and their snack choices feed an epidemic of childhood obesity. Far too often, understandably searching for something interesting to do, they hang out on the street or with their equally unsupervised friends, ready prey for trouble of all kinds. America's children deserve better; so do their parents. Parents worry about their children every day, all afternoon, and turn themselves inside out trying to provide supervision and structure for their kids—and still often fail. Of course the new school schedule makes parents happier—the wonder is they haven't *demanded* a new school day long before now.

Since the plain fact is that juvenile crime triples between three and six in the afternoon, we don't know how it could be any clearer that the new school day would, in one simple stroke, eliminate much juvenile crime, reduce teen pregnancy and the incidence of sexually-transmitted diseases, keep kids safer themselves, and make all of our streets and neighborhoods much safer places to be in the afternoons. Senior citizens wouldn't have to rush home in the afternoons "before the kids get out of school." Local malls and businesses wouldn't complain about crowds of loitering young people. Kids' tobacco, alcohol, and drug use would decrease, and decreasing demand is one of the few ways to really successfully fight our currently laughable "war on drugs." Fewer children would die in car accidents, and there would be fewer victims of reckless teenage drivers. Who knows? Auto insurance rates might even decrease. As it was for parents, the real question is why our law-enforcement and political leaders didn't demand the new school day decades ago.

Without question, the greatest educational need in this country exists among students and schools in low-income neighborhoods, which is one reason many parents have been suing states to enforce genuine equity in education funding—far too much of which is tied to neighborhood-sensitive property taxes. These are the schools in which the lowest performance on statewide tests has been concentrated. We think the evidence is overwhelming that the new school day can make an immediate difference in what the children in these schools can achieve. That's why we think it's a moral imperative to bring the new school day to these schools—as rapidly as possible.

But as we have argued throughout *Time to Learn,* we think that the standard school day is short-changing students and parents in middle-income and affluent communities as well. Few schools in these neighborhoods are acing the statewide tests, and far too few of their graduates have obtained anything near the genuine proficiency they need to take real advantage of higher education or lifelong learning. Despite what they may say about their neighborhood schools, the most affluent parents are spending enormous amounts of money and time supplementing the limited offerings of the conventional school schedule, purchasing a custom version of the new school day and hoping it will be enough. With good reason they too worry about the temptations and pressures besetting their teenaged children. So we have little doubt that while parents in affluent suburban communities currently appear the least eager to adopt the new school day in their public schools, they too will eventually see the advantages of a school day that truly meets the needs of their children and aligns better with their own work schedules.

All of us know, deep down, that the world has changed. It has become tougher, more competitive, and less forgiving in our new global age. Why, then, would we remain satisfied with a school day that became widespread when computers existed only in science fiction? No one really knows exactly when the six-and-a-half-hour day became standard in American education; it seems to be one of those practices that slowly solidified over the course of the twentieth century. But no one has ever mounted an educational case on its behalf, either. And no one does now.

Kids shouldn't have to win a charter school lottery (or the demographic lottery, for that matter) to get a great education in the United States of America. We've written this book because, as parents and as Americans, we believe all our country's children deserve an education that is right for the times they are growing up in, right for the world they will work, live, and raise families in. It's time for us to learn what they need—and act on the knowledge. You're reading this book because you care about education and are looking for a way to make it better. We're happy to help out (see Chapter Fourteen), but the next step is up to you, and the conversations you have with your neighbors, fellow parents, teachers, principals, school board members, and public officials. Together we can make the new school day a reality, and give all our children the time they need to learn.

FURTHER READINGS

Alexander, K. L., Entwisle, D. R., and Olson, L. S. "Schools, Achievement, and Inequality: A Seasonal Perspective." *Educational Evaluation and Policy Analysis,* 2001, *23*(2), 171–191.

Aronson, J., Zimmerman, J., and Carlos, L. *Improving Student Achievement by Extending School: Is It Just a Matter of Time?* San Francisco: WestEd, 1999.

Austin, W., Dais, R., Forgues, J., and Harris, L. *Calculated Success: A Step-by-Step Guide to Math Instruction That Works.* Boston: Project for School Innovation, 2003.

Bennett S., and Kalish, N. *The Case Against Homework: How Homework Is Hurting Our Children and What We Can Do About It.* New York: Crown, 2006.

Berliner, D. "What's All the Fuss About Instructional Time?" In M. Ben-Peretz and R. Bromme, Eds., *The Nature of Time in Schools Theoretical Concepts, Practitioner Perceptions.* New York: Teachers College Press, 1990.

Block, C. C., Cleveland, M. D., and Reed, K. M. "When Twenty Minutes of Literacy Instruction Is Added to the Day: Which Learning Environments Increase Students' Overall Achievement, Vocabulary, Comprehension, Fluency, and Affective Development?" 2004. Available online: http://teacher.scholastic.com/products/research/pdfs/ER_Using_books.pdf. Access date: December 18, 2007.

Bransford, J. D., Brown, A. L., and Cocking, R. R., Eds. *How People Learn: Brain, Mind, Experience and School.* Washington, D.C.: National Academy Press, 2000.

Carpenter, S. "Sleep Deprivation May Be Undermining Teen Health." *Monitor on Psychology,* October 2001, *32*(9).

Centers for Disease Control and Prevention. "Overweight and Obesity." November 17, 2007. Available online: www.cdc.gov/nccdphp/dnpa/obesity/index.htm. Access date: December 19, 2007.

Chenoweth, K. *It's Being Done: Academic Success in Unexpected Schools.* Cambridge, Mass.: Harvard Education Publishing, 2007.

Christeson, W., Kass, D., and Pelleran, K. P. "Detroit's After-School Choice: The Prime Time for Juvenile Crime or Youth Enrichment and Achievement." Fight Crime: Invest in Kids Michigan, 2006. Available online: www.fightcrime.org/reports/detroitasbrief.pdf. Access date: December 18, 2007.

Coleman, R., Spencer, T., Perkins, H., and Hodge, J. *Standing in the Gap: A Guide to Using the SAME Framework to Create Excellent Schools.* Newport News, Va.: Union Learning and Leadership Center, 10858 Warwick Blvd., Newport News, VA 23601.

Cooper, H., Nye, B., Charlton, K., Lindsay, J., and Greathouse, S. The Effects of Summer Vacation on Achievement Test Scores: A Narrative and Meta-Analytic Review. *Review of Educational Research,* 1996, *66*(3), 227–268.

Cosden, M., Morrison, G., Gutierrez, L., and Brown, M. "The Effects of Homework Programs and After-School Activities on School Success." *Theory Into Practice,* Aug. 2004, *43*(3), 220–226.

DeGregory, L. "Out of Play." *St. Petersburg Times,* March 29, 2005. Available online: www.sptimes.com/2005/03/29/Floridian/Out_of_play.shtml. Access date: December 18, 2007.

Driscoll, D. P. "Tough Choices in Education." *Boston Globe,* op-ed, February 28, 2007.

Duffrin, E. "Survey: Recess, Gym Class Shortchanged." Catalyst Chicago, October, 2005. Available online: www.catalyst-chicago.org/print/index.php?item=1775&cat=30. Access date: December 18, 2007.

Farbman, D. *The Forgotten Eighty Percent: The Case for Making the Most of Children's Time Out of School.* Boston: Mass 2020, 2003.

Farbman, D., and Kaplan, C. *Time for a Change: The Promise of Extended-Time Schools for Promoting Student Achievement.* Boston: Massachusetts 2020, 2005.

Fox, J. A., Flynn, E. A., Newman, S., and Christeson, W. "America's After-School Choice: Juvenile Crime or Safe Learning Time." Fight Crime: Invest in Kids, 2003. Available online: www.fightcrime.org/reports/asTwoPager.pdf. Access date: December 18, 2007.

Gardner, H. *Frames of Mind: Theory of Multiple Intelligences.* New York: Basic Books, 1997.

Gardner, H. *Multiple Intelligences: New Horizon.* New York: Perseus Books, 2006.

Gill, B. P., and Schlossman, S. "Villain or Savior? The American Discourse on Homework, 1850–2003." *Theory Into Practice,* 2004, *43*(3), 174–181.

Goleman, D. *Emotional Intelligence: Why It Can Matter More Than IQ.* New York: Bantam, 1997.

Hannaford, C. *Smart Moves: Why Learning Is Not All In Your Head.* Arlington, Va.: Great River Books, 2005.

Hoxby, C. M., and Murarka, S. "New York City's Charter Schools Overall Report." Cambridge, Mass.: New York City Charter Schools Evaluation Project, July 2007. Available online: www.nber. org/~schools/charterschooleval/nyc_charter_schools_report_ july2007.pdf. Access date: December 18, 2007.

Jarrett, O. S., Maxwell, D. M., Dickerson, C., Hoge, P., Davies, G., and Yetley, A. "The Impact of Recess on Classroom Behavior: Group Effects and Individual Differences." *Journal of Educational Research,* 1998, *92*(2), 121–126.

Jensen, E. P. *Learning with the Body in Mind.* San Diego, Calif.: Brain Store, 2000.

Johnson, D. "Many Schools Putting an End to Child's Play." *New York Times,* April 7, 1998. Available online: http://query.nytimes.com/ gst/fullpage.html?res=9506E0DB1E3AF934A35757C0A96E95826 0. Access date: December 18, 2007.

Khadaroo, S. T. "Do Longer Hours Equal More Learning?" *Christian Science Monitor,* June 14, 2007.

"Killing PE Is Killing Our Kids the Slow Way." *American School Board Journal,* August 2005.

Koppich, J. E. "Using Well-Qualified Teachers Well." *American Educator,* Winter 2002. Available online: aft.org/pubs-reports/american_ educator/winter2002/UsingTeachers.html. Access date: December 19, 2007.

Kralovec, E., and Buell, J. *The End of Homework: How Homework Disrupts Families, Overburdens Children, and Limits Learning.* Boston: Beacon Press, 2000.

Learned-Miller, C. "March Message from the Principal." Dr. Martin Luther King, Jr. School, 2007. Available online: www.cpsd.us/ MLK/principal.cfm. Access date: December 18, 2007.

Learning Point Associates. "Critical Issue: Science Education in the Era of No Child Left Behind—History, Benchmarks, and Standards." 2005. Available online: www.ncrel.org/sdrs/areas/issues/content/ cntareas/science/sc600.htm. Access date: December 18, 2007.

Manzo, K. K. "Older Students Play Catch-Up on Uncovered, Vital Lessons." *Education Week,* June 14, 2006.

Massachusetts Commission on Time and Learning. "Unlocking the Power of Time: The Massachusetts Commission on Time and Learning Final Report." November 1995. Available online: www.doe. mass.edu/edreform/timelearn/tlrep.html. Access date: December 20, 2007.

McMurrer, J. "Choices, Changes and Challenges: Curriculum and Instruction in the NCLB Era." Washington DC: Center on Education Policy, 2007.

Mason-Dixon Polling & Research, "Chiefs of Police, Sheriffs and Prosecutors: Attitudes Towards Youth Crime And Violence Prevention Strategies." Fight Crime: Invest in Kids poll, August 2002. Available online: www.fightcrime.org/reports/nationalkids-poll2002.pdf. Access date: December 18, 2007.

Mulhall, P. F., Stone, B., and Stone, D. "Home Alone: Is It a Risk Factor for Middle School Youth and Drug Use?" *Journal of Drug Education,* 1996, *26*(1).

Murnane, R., and Levy, F. *Teaching the New Basic Skills: Principles for Educating Children to Thrive in a Changing Economy.* New York: Free Press, 1996.

National Association for Sport and Physical Education & American Heart Association. "2006 Shape of the Nation Report: Status of Physical Education in the USA." Reston, Va.: National Association for Sport and Physical Education, 2006. Available online: www.aahperd.org/naspe/ShapeOfTheNation/. Access date: December 20, 2007.

National Center for Education Statistics (2005). "NAEP 2004 Trends in Academic Progress: Three Decades of Student Performance in Reading and Mathematics: Findings in Brief (NCES 2005 -463)." U.S. Department of Education, Institute of Education Sciences, National Center for Education Statistics. Washington, DC: Government Printing Office.

National Education Commission on Time and Learning. "Prisoners of Time: Report of the National Education Commission of Time and Learning." Washington, D.C.: U.S. Government Printing Office, April 1994. Available online: www.eric.ed.gov/ERICDocs/data/ericdocs2sql/content_storage_01/0000019b/80/16/0c/2f.pdf. Access date: December 20, 2007.

National Education Commission on Time and Learning. "Prisoners of Time: Schools and Programs Making Time Work for Students and Teachers." Washington, D.C.: U.S. Government Printing Office, September 1994. Available online: www.eric.ed.gov/ERICDocs/data/ericdocs2sql/content_storage_01/0000019b/80/13/98/04.pdf. Access date: December 20, 2007.

National Science Teachers Association. "NSTA Position Statement: The Integral Role of Laboratory Investigations in Science Instruction." 2007. Available online: www.nsta.org/about/positions/laboratory.aspx. Access date: December 18, 2007.

National Sleep Foundation. "2006 Sleep in America Poll: Highlights and Key Findings." 2006. Available online: www.sleepfoundation.org/atf/cf/%7BF6BF2668-A1B4-4FE8-8D1A-A5D39340D9CB%7D/Highlights_facts_06.pdf. Access date: December 18, 2007.

National Sleep Foundation. "2006 Sleep in America Poll: Summary Findings." 2006. Available online: www.sleepfoundation.org/atf/cf/%7BF6BF2668-A1B4-4FE8-8D1A-A5D39340D9CB%7D/2006_summary_of_findings.pdf. Access date: December 18, 2007.

Nierenberg, S., Fong, S., and Deitch, A. "After-School Worries: Tough on Parents, Bad for Business." Catalyst Report, 2006. Available online: www.catalyst.org/files/qa/PCAST%20QA.pdf. Access date: December 18, 2007.

Pardo, N. "All Work, Less Play in Chicago Public Schools." *Chicago Reporter* Survey, June 1999. Available online: www.chicagoreporter.com/index.php/c/Cover_Stories/d/All_Work,_Less_Play_in_Public_Schools. Access date: December 18, 2007.

Pennington, H. C. "Expanding Learning Time in High Schools." Washington, D.C.: Center for American Progress, 2006. Available online: www.americanprogress.org/issues/2006/10/pdf/extended_learning_report.pdf. Access date: December 20, 2007.

Pennington, H. C. "The Massachusetts Expanding Learning Time to Support Student Success Initiative." Washington, D.C.: Center for American Progress, 2007. Available online: www.americanprogress.org/issues/2007/01/pdf/MALearningTimeReport.pdf. Access date: December 20, 2007.

Prevost, L. "Saved by the (Later) Bell." *Boston Globe Magazine*, April 29, 2007.

Rideout, V., Roberts, D. F., and Foehr, U. G. "Generation M: Media in the Lives of 8-18 Year-Olds." Kaiser Family Foundation Study, March 2005. Available online: www.kff.org/entmedia/upload/Executive-Summary-Generation-M-Media-in-the-Lives-of-8-18-Year-olds.pdf. Access date: December 18, 2007.

Rocha, E. "Choosing More Time for Students: The What, Why and How of Expanded Learning." Washington D.C.: Center for American Progress, 2007. Available online: www.americanprogress.org/issues/2007/08/pdf/expanded_learning.pdf. Access date: December 20, 2007.

Rone, D. "The Issue Is Education." *Newark Star-Ledger,* July 25, 2005.

Rose, L. C., and Gallup, A. M. "Thirty-Seventh Annual Phi Delta Kappa/Gallup Poll of the Public's Attitudes Toward the Public Schools." 2005. Available online: www.pdkintl.org/kappan/k0509pol.htm#2. Access date: December 18, 2007.

Roxbury Preparatory Charter School. "2005–2006 Annual Report." August 1, 2006. Available online: www.roxburyprep.org/pdf%20files/Annual%20Report%202005-2006.pdf. Access date: December 20, 2007.

Rubin, B. M. "Many Schools Pull Plug on Recess." *Chicago Tribune,* September 27, 2001.

Schemo, D. J. "Failing Schools See a Solution in Longer Day," *New York Times,* March 26, 2007.

Silva, E. "On the Clock: Rethinking the Way Schools Use Time." Washington, D.C.: Education Sector, January 2007. Available online: www.educationsector.org/usr_doc/OntheClock.pdf. Access date: December 20, 2007.

Silver, L. "How Recess Promotes Focus for ADHD Children." Attitude, n.d. Available online: http://additudemag.com/additude/article/807.html. Access date: December 18, 2007.

Silverman, F. "Tutoring Services See Business Boom." *District Administration,* September 2005.

Time, Learning and Afterschool Task Force. "A New Day for Learning." Flint, Mich.: C.S. Mott Foundation, 2007. Available online: www.edutopia.org/pdfs/ANewDayforLearning.pdf. Access date: December 21, 2007.

Trickey, H. "No Child Left Out of the Dodgeball Game?" CNN broadcast, Thursday, August 24, 2006.

Tyre, P. "Learning Takes Time." *Newsweek,* January 22, 2007.

Wahlstrom, K. L., Davison, M. L., Choi, J., and Ross, J. N. "School Start Time Study: Final Report Summary." Center for Applied Research and Educational Improvement, Aug. 2001. Available online: http://cehd.umn.edu/CAREI/Reports/docs/SST-2001ES.pdf. Access date: December 18, 2007.

Willingham, D. T. "Practice Makes Perfect—But Only If You Practice Beyond the Point of Perfection." *American Educator,* Spring 2004.

INDEX